£6

SPORTING TERRIERS

Their Form,
Their Function
and Their
Future

THE WARRENER'S DOG.

SPORTING TERRIERS

THEIR FORM,
THEIR FUNCTION
AND THEIR
FUTURE

David Hancock

The Crowood Press

Previous Books by the Author

Dogs As Companions – 1981
Old Working Dogs – 1984 (reprinted 1998 and 2011)
The Heritage of the Dog – 1990
The Bullmastiff–A Breeder's Guide Vol 1 – 1996
The Bullmastiff–A Breeder's Guide Vol 2 – 1997
Old Farm Dogs – 1999
The Mastiffs – The Big Game Hunters – 2000
The Bullmastiff–A Breeder's Guide – 2006 (one volume hardback edition)
The World of the Lurcher – 2010

First published in 2011 by The Crowood Press Ltd,
Ramsbury, Marlborough, Wiltshire, SN8 2HR

www.crowood.com

© David Hancock 2011

British Library Cataloguing-in-Publication Data
A catalogue record for this book is available from the British Library.

ISBN 978 1 84797 303 0

Page 1: Group of Terriers of early 19th century – from left Skye, Scotch, English Smooth,
Crossed Scotch, Dandie Dinmont and Bull Terrier
Page 2: The Warrener's Dog
Page 3: Terriers of 1843, from Compton's *The Twentieth Century Dog* of 1904
Page 5: Terrier with rabbit, depicted in 1854

Typeset and designed by D & N Publishing, Baydon, Wiltshire

Printed and bound in India by Replika Press Pvt Ltd

CONTENTS

TERRIER AND RABBIT.

ACKNOWLEDGEMENTS

The author is grateful to the staff at Sotheby's, Christie's, Bonhams, Arthur Ackermann Ltd, David Messum Galleries, Richard Green & Co., The Bridgeman Art Library, the Wallace Collection, R. Cox & Co., Lane Fine Art, The Kennel Club, The American Kennel Club, The National Trust and private collectors, (especially the late Mevr A.H. (Ploon) de Raad of Zijderveld, Holland, who gave free use of her extensive photographic archive of sporting paintings) for their gracious and generous permissions to reproduce some of the illustrations used in this book.

AUTHOR'S NOTE

Some of the illustrations in this book lack pictorial quality but are included because they either contribute uniquely historically to or best exemplify the meaning of the text. Old depictions do not always lend themselves to reproduction in today's higher quality print and publishing format. Those that are included have significance beyond their graphic limitations and I ask for the reader's understanding over this.

Where quotes are used, they are used verbatim, despite any vagaries in spelling, irregular use of capital letters or departures from contemporary grammar. For me, it is important that their exact form, as presented by the author originally, is displayed, as this can help to capture the mood of those times. Readers should however keep in mind that, with the passage of time, some words change meaning: Victorian writers, for example, often used the word 'awful' in the sense that we today would use the word 'awesome'; a 'boney hound' in their parlance meant not a gaunt, underfed dog but a strongly boned one.

Finally I have used capital letters to denote breeds of dog, so that for example Irish Terrier refers to the breed of that name, but Irish terrier means a terrier from Ireland, not necessarily from the breed of that name. Similarly a Fox Terrier refers to that breed of dog; fox terrier refers to a terrier used on fox, not necessarily of the breed of that name. Such a format allows the reader to discern the difference between the two descriptive meanings. In quotes, however, I have still kept rigidly to the exact construction and case of the original, despite the looser and often inconsistent use of capital letters this may bring.

Terrier and fox, from Daniel's Rural Sports, *1805.*

DEDICATION

This book is dedicated to terrier-men everywhere, the countrymen who, down the centuries, have produced *real* sporting terriers, then passed them on for the next generation to enjoy. Their rewards were not rosettes but respect. Their commitment was not wallet-led but inspired by the pursuit of performance. They took pride in what their dogs could do, not what they looked like. We owe so much to their devoted, selfless, purposeful desire to breed an honest, determined, steadfast small sporting dog, and should honour their memory by perpetuating their work in producing genuine earth-dogs, not mere ornaments.

Sporting terriers – our servants, our companions and, so often, our pride and joy.

PREFACE

Terriers are essentially country dogs that adapt to city life. They are hunters that can be trained to behave to suit our modern styles of living, as well as conforming to the pressures of contemporary thinking in an increasingly urban society. Their great enemy, the rat, is still a serious threat to our health and the economy but is also widely kept nowadays as a pet. We bred terriers to be highly proficient killers of ground vermin and now we expect them to ignore every cat and squirrel that crosses their path. We bred them to possess stamina, spirit and tenacity, yet some breeders keep them in small cages for much of their lives. Their purpose never demanded exaggeration of any kind, but now we breed them with excessive overcoats, needlessly short legs and elongated backs. We overlook the fact that the working anatomy is nearly always the healthiest one. In respecting their heritage we must also respect their simple needs; terriers need stimulation, they need an outlet for their energy and they need to be perpetuated not to suit some show ring fad, but in a sound form, in an empathetic environment and with acknowledgement of their famed 'terrier spirit'. Terriers are a very special group of dogs and long may they be here to gladden our hearts with their modest needs, irrepressible energy, sheer pluckiness and very straightforward attitude to life.

Books devoted to terriers are a relatively recent addition to our sporting bookshelves. In 1896, in his preface to the first edition of his *A History and Description of the Modern Dogs of Great Britain and Ireland: The Terriers*, Rawdon Lee wrote: 'This, I believe, is the first occasion upon which a volume has been published dealing entirely with the Terriers.' He wrote this at a time when the bookshelves were stacked with books on gundogs and hounds, and when the show ring was inspiring a new range of books on companion, or toy, dogs. He went on to write:

> In describing the Terriers in all their varieties, I have endeavoured to give particulars as to their working qualifications and their general character, as well as their so-called 'show points'; and my desire to prevent, if possible, a useful race of dog from degenerating into

a ladies' pet and a pampered creature, only able to earn his owner gold on the show bench, is my reason for treating so fully of him as he is concerned in that sphere which Nature intended him to occupy.

In compiling this volume, I wish to continue that ethos; terriers often make good 'ladies' pets' and the show bench has saved some terrier breeds from oblivion, but whatever their role, terriers deserve to be perpetuated in their authentic functional form. That truly is, as Rawdon Lee so picturesquely put it, 'that sphere which Nature intended him to occupy'.

This book is not a manual, it does not cover animal husbandry, breeding, training or endless anecdotal accounts of hunting experiences, with subjective advice on how to instil working skills in either the handler or the terrier. It is a celebration of earth-dogs, wherever they are found, whether they are from a Kennel Club-recognised breed, an ancient type never formally recognized or a newly emergent type. It establishes their true form, relates that to their classic function, which decided that form, and discusses their future. Terriers are the perfect companions for a young teenager; they too never really fancy adulthood, are slow to show respect, can be temperamental and have decided views of their own. They have 'attitude' without an attitude problem and we should respect them for the individuality they demonstrate in a world where conforming is all.

Two dogs at a fox earth (after Pautrot).

A UNIQUELY BRITISH DOG

The terrier has a most acute smell, is generally an attendant on every pack of Hounds, and is very expert in forcing Foxes or other game out of their coverts. It is the determined enemy of all the vermin kind; such as Weasels, Foumarts, Badgers, Rats, Mice, &c. It is fierce, keen, and hardy…

A General History of Quadrupeds
by Thomas Bewick (1790)

Terriers were very commonly used to accompany packs of foxhounds for the purpose of unearthing the fox, and, when in vogue, were in colour either black and tan, or pied with white and yellow. They were usually of a medium size; if too large, they were unfitted for penetrating the sinuousities of an earth, or

The Earth Stopper.

creeping up a confined drain; if, on the contrary, they are too diminutive, they cannot keep pace with the hounds of the present day…

An Encyclopaedia of Rural Sports
by Delabere Blaine (Longman, 1870)

Those rather quaint words from the past, and nearly a century apart, tell you a great deal about the collection of sporting dogs grouped together as terriers, not just their purpose but their size, character and role in the hunting field too. In this book I express my admiration for the group of dogs known as terriers: their impudent appeal, their perpetual optimism, their renowned tenacity and their sheer vivacity. I also argue for a return, especially in show dogs, to their functional form: a build which would allow them to perform in the field, even if they are not required to; traditional head shapes rather than fad-induced ones; good forward extension rather than restricted reach; weatherproof coats rather than fluffy woolly ones. In particular, I feel the terriers' sporting instincts should be encouraged.

There is something uniquely British about terriers, our Territorial Army once being proud to have the soubriquet of The Terriers used to denote its character. There are of course terrier breeds in other countries, for example the Russian Black, the Australian, the Brazilian, the Cesky and the German Hunt Terrier. But I suspect that in most cases the inspiration, type and breeding stock came from here. If you fancy the lesser-known terrier types, there is a wide range to choose from. You could try a Capheaton, a Balla, a Patterdale, a Fell, a Plummer or a Lucas from here, or even a Rat Terrier or a Toy Fox Terrier from America. If you want a really big one, try the Russian Black Terrier, which can be 30in at the shoulder or mastiff size. The American hunters have developed a 90lb Airedale, half again as big as ours, of interest if you are seeking a big hunting dog. You will have problems getting a Balla terrier,

Terriers going to ground, from The Sportsman's Cabinet, *1803.*

with perhaps only fifteen pure Ballas in England. They come from Ballanantey in Ireland and are red prick-eared, foot-high dogs with strong sporting instincts.

Breed Expansion

> Old pictures of terriers dating back 300 years illustrate cross-bred looking creatures, some of them bearing more or less the distinctive characteristic of the turn-spit. Others indicate a considerable trace of hound blood, but not one, so far as the writer has come across, is hound marked, or bears any more white than is usually found on the chest or feet of any dog.

Those words, from Rawdon Lee's 1896 *Modern Dogs: The Terriers*, may well surprise fanciers of West Highland White, Fox and Soft-coated Wheaten Terriers. White terriers feature prominently in our breed lists today.

If you look at the Kennel Club's list of terrier breeds in 1908, you will notice that it contains just sixteen breeds, a far cry from the twenty-six listed today. The ten more recent additions include the Australian, Glen of Imaal, Lakeland, Norfolk, Norwich, Parson Russell, Cesky, Staffordshire Bull Terrier, who no doubt will one day be joined by the German Hunt, Brazilian, Patterdale, Plummer and Sporting Lucas Terriers. We could so easily have had Cowley, Rose-neath, Clydesdale, Paisley, Cheshire, Shropshire, Devon and Otter Terriers too – recognition of breeds of dog so often relies on determined promotion just as much as ancient type.

The terriers as a functional group are essentially British, with the distinguished breeds from Scotland, Ireland and Wales combining with those of England to give the canine world the much-loved terrier breeds valued everywhere. A long history is often claimed for breeds of terrier, but I doubt if terrier men in past centuries ever bothered much about pure breeding. In his *The Book of all Terriers* of 1971, John Marvin writes:

> Despite claims made by writers who champion the antiquity of several of today's Terrier breeds, years of careful research have failed to disclose a single reference to any reproducible breed prior to 1800. In fact, the only deviations from the earliest descriptions are variations noted as to coat, size and legs.

In his *Field Sports* (1760), terriers are described by William Daniel as being one of two sorts: one is rough, short-legged, long backed and very strong, usually black or light tan colour, mixed with white; the other smooth-haired and more pleasingly formed, with a shorter body and a more athletic appearance, usually reddish-brown or black with tan legs. Prototypes of subsequent breeds are hinted at here. French and German writers of previous centuries have made reference to dogs functioning as terriers, not just Dachshund types but Pinschers and Schnauzers too. In Britain we may have captured most of the terrier breed market if not the terrier function, but we have long had distinguished terrier-men.

Famous Terrier-Men

A quarter of a century ago, I used to have long conversations with that fascinating old terrier-man Bert Gripton. Bert could give the word 'curmudgeonly' a bad name. He was once so outrageously rude to a fellow terrier fancier that those of us present just laughed out loud. But he was still worth listening to, and was rightly famous throughout the international terrier world. The son of a gamekeeper, he had been a groom at Badminton, a trumpeter in the Royal Horse Artillery, a pest controller for the Ministry of Agriculture and finally worked for a footwear firm, which allowed him to keep his big van on retirement for his terrier-transport. Bert said that his terrier knowledge came from an old gypsy, a Mr Baker, terrier-man to the Albrighton.

Bert believed that no two terriers worked the same. He claimed that a real terrier-man should be able to identify his underground quarry from the baying of his dogs, as it differs when faced with rabbit, fox or badger. He had a long connection with otter-hunting, beginning with the Hawkstone and then moving to the Border counties. He once said that irresponsible and boastful terrier owners did more harm than any opponent of field sports. I believe he was once a member of the Jack Russell Club early on in its life but gave up out of his dislike of its heavy commitment to showing. He spoke to me of producing a book one day; it would have been worth reading.

How I wish I had had the chance to meet other revered terrier-men: Ralph Hodgson of Durham, Lewsyn Blucher of the Bwllfa pack, Arthur Heinemann of Devon and O.T. Price. Ralph Hodgson began to follow the Braes of Derwent at the age of ten in

1909, purchasing his first terrier, a Sealyham/Wirehaired Fox terrier cross in 1916. In time his unique skills at terrier rescue paved the way for some memorable terrier rescues in the Durham area. Lewsyn Blucher, as W. Lewis Williams was better known, died in 1940, after a life spent hunting and fox catching by way of hound, terrier, trap, gun and snare. He was expert in the use of the 'Gist' trap. He favoured his own brand of short-legged rough-coated terriers, presumably now lost to us.

Whatever the origin, the nomenclature, the literature or the characters behind the terrier type, this group of dogs deserves our admiration, not just for their valuable work in vermin control but for their effect on our spirit; it is difficult to be depressed, idle or bored when terriers are about. Their sheer joie de vivre lightens our day, their renowned tenacity can inspire us and their sustained curiosity can shame us into comparable activity. May we have terriers with us for a very long time.

A common rough-haired terrier with a gamekeeper in Shropshire 1870.

There are terriers of sorts which through long usage as house-dogs and pets have lost most of their essential qualities as outdoor working companions for the man with a gun. But in spite of this decline in their native gifts – no fault of their own – they still preserve the gallant spirit of less urbanized ancestors, and most of them, with a little training and opportunity, can easily be turned into first-rate rabbiters, ratters and fox-bolters.

From *The Dog in Sport* by James Wentworth Day
(Harrap, 1938)

Ay, see the hounds with frantic zeal
The roots and earth uptear;
But the earth is strong, and the roots are long,
They cannot enter there.
Outspeaks the Squire, 'Give room, I pray,
And hie the terriers in;

The warriors of the fight are they,
And every fight they win.'

Ring-Ouzel

The Terrier Group: The common physical features are a robust and tightly-knit frame, well-muscled, small-to-medium in size, with the head rather long, without any dome, the ears small, triangular and usually folded over to the fore. Coat is mainly rough with a dense soft undercoat, protective eyebrows and no featherings. The tail is usually docked but when of natural length is fairly short. Such breeds as are still sent to earth are usually short-legged. The cubist effect of square bodies and rectangular heads is due to a temporary modern phase of fashion and does not represent a true family characteristic.

From *Dogs in Britain* by Clifford L.B. Hubbard
(Macmillan, 1948)

Old English broken-coated terrier of the early nineteenth century (Richard Ansdell, 1837).

CHAPTER 1

ORIGINS AND BREED DEVELOPMENT IN ENGLAND

The Emergence of the Earth-Dog

The Terrier is querulous, fretful and irascible, high-spirited and alert when brought into action; if he has not unsubdued perseverance like the bulldog, he has rapidity of attack, managed with art, and sustained with spirit; it is not what he will bear, but what he will inflict …as his courage is great, so is his extensive genius: he will trace with the Foxhound, hunt with the Beagle, find for the Greyhound, or beat with the Spaniel.

Those epic words by Sydenham Edwards, in his *Cynographia Britannica* of 1800, tell you more about the terrier tribe than some books with 100 pages on them. He has succinctly captured their role, their nature, their value and their soul. Just over two centuries

The Harvesters' Companions *by Philip Stretton (1892).*

Terriers 'other than Skye, Dandie and Fox' of 1868–72, depicted in 'Stonehenge's' books of that period.

A Feast for Five *by Arthur Wardle (c1900), depicting two Irish, a Fox Terrier dam with pup and farm collie.*

Bobbery pack on rat by J.F. Herring Junior (1820–1907).

Terriers rabbiting by J. Langlois, depicting sporting terriers in Scotland in the nineteenth century.

before him, the Cambridge scholar Dr Caius had listed them as part of the hound family and suggested their name came about 'because they (after the manner and custom of ferrets, in searching for conies) creep into the ground, and by that means make afraid, nip, and bite the fox and the badger.' He didn't consider, though, whether the word 'terrier' could come from the French word *terre* (earth) or the Latin *terrere* (to frighten), from which our word 'terror' derives. 'Terrors' would provide a much more suitable word

Terriers waiting by a rabbit hole by G. Armfield (1850).

origin for such a feisty group of canines – and they certainly do frighten underground prey.

Thirty years earlier still, in 1543, Dr Still had composed a poem, which read:

> Body and limb go cold,
> Both foot and hand go bare;
> God send teroures so bold, so bold,
> Heart will harbour no care,

and stressed that terriers' boldness was a feature even then. A century later, Nicholas Cox, in *The Gentleman's Recreation* (1667), described them as of two sorts, one with legs more or less crooked with short coats and another straighter in the leg and with long jackets. Another century passes, and we find William Daniel, writing in *Field Sports*:

> There are two sorts of terriers, the one short-legged, long-backed, very strong, and most commonly of a black or yellowish colour, mixed with white; the other is smooth-haired and beautifully formed, having a shorter body and a more sprightly appearance, is generally of a reddish-brown colour, or black with tanned legs.

Both were relying on French descriptions of Basset Hounds, as did Turberville, Blome and their followers. The authentic voice of the British terrier-men was not being heard, mainly because they did not come from the educated or monied classes.

Breeding a Vermin Killer

In *The Dog* (1880), 'Idstone' records, when recounting Dr Caius's description of terriers:

> These, doubtless, were the stout sort of Terriers for which, as fox killers, James I. wrote to his friend the Laird of Caldwell, naming the Earl of Monteith as having good ones of the kind; and which sort were generally accepted as good from 1677 downwards, bred without much attempt at refinement, and they remained simply crook-legged, hairy, vermin-dogs, until it was deemed requisite to establish something neater and more pleasing to the eye in connection with the handsome and high-mettled Foxhound.

There is more than a hint here of terrier-men going entirely for performance rather than beauty of form, perhaps lacking the means to indulge in handsomeness for its own sake.

The first reliable description of variety in our terriers is provided by Taplin in *The Sportsman's Cabinet* (1803):

> Terriers of the best blood, and most determined ferocity, are now, by the prevalence of fashion, bred of all colours: red, black (with tanned faces, flanks, feet, and legs) and brindled sandy; some few brown pied, white pied and pure white; as well as one sort rough and wire-haired, the other soft, smooth, and delicate, the latter not much inferior in courage to the former, but the rough wire-haired breed is the most severe biter of the two.

It is significant that no description of a terrier, down the ages, has been deemed complete without mention of the terrier-spirit, the combative attitude of this group of dogs.

Hound Influence

It is of interest that the same factors that apply to the inheritance of scenthounds apply to wire and smooth-haired Fox Terriers. A narrow head is dominant over the broader hound-like head. The sharp nose is dominant over the blunt nose; wire hair is dominant over

---

> ### Terrier Sub-Groups
>
> **Basset/dachshund type**: for example the Dandie Dinmont, the Skye and indeed some so-called Jack Russells
> **Beagle or small scenthound type**: for example the Fox Terrier, Manchester or the Pinscher breeds
> **'Griffon' or coarse-haired type**: for example the Border, Lakeland, the terriers of Scotland (except the Dandie and Skye), the Irish, Sealyham, Airedale, the Schnauzer varieties, Kerry Blue, Wheaten and perhaps the Smoushond of Holland
> **Hybrids**: for example the Bedlington, the English White (that was) and the Bull Terriers

short hair; and the short legs of the Dachshund, Basset Hound and Scottish Terrier are (incompletely) dominant over the normal longer legs of the Fox Terrier. The colour of the Dachshund, whether wire, long-haired or smooth, is determined by the same determiners that affect scenthounds. In 1916, Wellman wrote of experimental crosses between Fox Terriers and Basset Hounds in which the vast majority of the progeny were black and tan and short-legged. From these facts it can be seen that in time it would not be difficult to produce a narrower-headed, sharper-muzzled, shorter-legged, wire-coated earth-dog from a hound origin.

The terrier breeds are, however, likely to have more than just a hound background. As Darwin himself once wrote:

Terriers in an Interior *by G. Armfield (1855).*

Terriers depicted in 1800 – types not breeds.

A breed, like a dialect of language, can hardly be said to have a distinct origin. A man preserves and breeds from an individual with some slight deviation of structure, or takes more care than usual in mating his best animals and thus improves them… When further improved by the same slow and gradual process, they will spread more widely and will be recognized as something distinct and valuable, and will then probably first receive a provincial name.

In such a way did we develop our Rothbury, Manchester, Aberdeen, Reedwater, Glen of Imaal, Patterdale, Norfolk, Poltalloch, Clydesdale and Yorkshire terriers. The root stock of many was the old rough-coated black and tan common terrier of Britain, used by many hunts before hound-marked dogs became fashionable.

It is not wise to regard the many nineteenth-century writers on dogs as authorities on terriers. Firstly, they copied from each other, sometimes consolidating falsehoods that are still today regarded as facts. Secondly, as so many did before them, they often wittingly or unwittingly plagiarized the masterly work of Jacques du Fouilloux (*La Venerie*, 1560), a few even passing off his words as their own. He was writing, not surprisingly, of French dogs, as was De Foix in his *Livre de Chasse* (1401), brought to us as *The Master of Game* by Edward, Duke of York. Youatt, 'Idstone', 'Stonehenge' and Dalziel, for all their valuable words on dogs in Victorian times, are not so well informed on terriers. Vero Shaw gives much more detail;

Robert Leighton, into Edwardian times, provides even more information on the developing show breeds of terrier. But it is not until quite late in the twentieth century that we get coverage of working terriers. At last, it is not educated men writing second-hand about dogs of which they have little knowledge, but informed writers: Sir Jocelyn Lucas, Pierce O'Conor, Rosslyn Bruce, Geoffrey Sparrow, Dan Russell, Brian Plummer and their like all cover a subject they are well acquainted with, giving working terriers long overdue attention.

Emerging Breeds

Robert Leighton, writing early in the twentieth century, had a wide knowledge of terriers. In *Dogs and All About Them* (Cassell, 1914), he gave an admirable summary of the emerging and non-emerging breeds:

> A wire-haired black and tan terrier was once common in Suffolk and Norfolk, where it was much used for rabbiting, but it may now be extinct, or, if not extinct, probably identified with the Welsh Terrier, which it closely resembled in size and colouring. There was also in Shropshire a well-known breed of wire-haired terriers, black and tan, on very short legs, and weighing about 10lb or 12lb, with long punishing heads and extraordinary working powers. So too, in Lancashire and Cheshire one used to meet with sandy-coloured terriers of no very well authenticated strain, but closely resembling the present breed of Irish Terrier; and Squire Thornton, at his place near Pickering in Yorkshire, had a breed of wire-hairs, tan in colour with a black stripe down the back…Possibly the Elterwater Terrier is no longer to be found…

He knew of the terriers of Scotland, writing of the Border Terrier in Galloway, Ayrshire and the Lothians, going on to state:

> There are many more local varieties of the working terrier, as, for example, the Roseneath, which is often confused with the Poltalloch, or West Highlander, to whom it is possibly related. And the Pittenweem, with which the Poltalloch Terriers are now being crossed; while Mrs Alastair Campbell, of Ardiscraig, has a pack of Cairn Terriers which seem to represent the original type of the improved Scottie.

Rabbit shooting with terriers, an engraving by Godby & Merke, 1807.

It was Leighton who initiated the breed title of Cairn Terrier for that breed. He accepted that whether a distinct type was recognized as a breed or not was a rather hit and miss affair.

The showing of dogs, launched in the 1870s, mushroomed at the end of the nineteenth century and this expansion continued into the twentieth century despite two world wars. Individual breeds of terrier, once recognized by the Kennel Club as such, became

The Earth Stopper, *early nineteenth-century coloured print.*

isolated genetically, with some breeds originating in a relatively tiny gene pool. Small red tan terrier: ears down, it's a Norfolk, ears up, it's a Norwich; is this the essential criterion for one breed to be identified from another, or just loosely controlled breed identification? Here are two admirable breeds separated, visually at any rate, solely by ear carriage. Is that enough, or, one day when numbers are low or inheritable diseases encountered, will they merge? Horrifying for their devotees, perhaps, but does the general public appreciate such niceties? Does the man in the street know a Welsh Terrier from a Lakeland? Does the dog-owning community, all six million members of it, really care about breed differences? Those concerned with sporting terriers care less about breeds and much more about performance.

The emergence of the terriers and their subsequent evolution into breeds has left us with a dilemma. Do you breed them to fit the accepted show-ring phenotype or to respect their working function? If you stop for a moment thinking about the type of dog that goes underground and consider other small mammals that do, you obtain a different mental image. Rabbits, badgers, foxes, prairie dogs and especially moles, operate very successfully underground. Does coat colour matter for them? Do they need to be well-boned, have very long muzzles, excessively long coats, a 'cobby' build, or resemble in any way the type of horse called a hunter? What do those that operate above and below ground have in common? Three particular features come to mind: appreciable elasticity of torso, an eel-like construction for the neck and back (which is comparatively long) and a short thick coat. But what physical features do the Kennel Club-approved standards for registered terrier breeds demand? It is worth a glance at them.

Airedales, both varieties of Fox Terrier, Norfolk and Norwich Terriers and the Welsh Terrier are required to have short backs. The West Highland White, Norfolk and Norwich Terriers are expected to have compact bodies. The Welsh Terrier has to have straight front legs, as does the Parson Russell. The Australian and Irish Terriers have to have front legs that are perfectly straight. The Sealyham has to have its point of shoulder in line with its point of elbow. The Airedale has to show little space between its ribs and its hips. The Bedlington has to have front legs that are wider apart at the chest than at the feet (the strangely desired 'horseshoe front'). The Wire-Haired Fox Terrier has to have its tail set high; the Smooth is expected to have its tail set rather high, and, in its forequarters, little or no appearance of ankle in front. These stipulations are not wise. They are so easily misapplied by those who have never seen a canine miner at work.

Breed Development

In the following chapters, I describe how the breeds developed, or, in some cases, did not survive despite their clear identity. In most registered breeds, fashion has prevailed over function and, in later chapters, I illustrate how show-ring criteria or breeder whim threatens soundness in so many terrier breeds. The Kennel Club is now, commendably, insisting on the recognition of function in terrier breeds registered with them, and not before time. It will be timely and important for the survival of these breeds as sporting dogs; we all need to keep in mind where they came from.

Foundation stock in the sporting terrier breeds often came from hunt kennels or working sources and so the breeding basis was sound. Gradually and remorselessly, however, both the anatomies and the coefficients of inbreeding have in some of these breeds reached unacceptable levels and a rethink is now urgently required. Away from the show ring, unrecognized breeds, like the Fell, Sporting Lucas and Patterdale have thrived, not in large numbers, but in true terrier form. Newly created breeds like the Cesky and Plummer Terriers are more popular than some age-old breeds, with the ubiquitous Jack Russells replacing the once heavily fancied Fox Terrier. If the twentieth century was the one in which the terrier breeds 'arrived', then the twenty-first century could be the one in which the terrier varieties 'came and went'.

Boys Ferreting with Terriers *by W.W. Morris (c.1900).*

Scottish Terrier was only beginning to be recognized as a distinct breed. The Welsh Terrier is quite a new introduction that a generation ago was seldom seen outside the Principality; and so recently as 1881 the Airedale was merely a local dog known in Yorkshire as the Waterside or the Bingley Terrier. Yet the breeds just mentioned are all of unimpeachable ancestry, and the circumstance that they were formerly bred within limited neighbourhoods is in itself an argument in favour of their purity. We have seen the process of a sudden leap into recognition enacted during the past few years in connexion with the white terrier of the Western Highlands, with the Cairn Terrier and with the Sealyham; and at the moment the hitherto ignored terrier of the Borders is receiving tardy recognition. Yet the West Highland Terrier was known in Argyllshire three hundred years ago, while the Sealyham Terrier was hunting the otter in Pembrokeshire when Wales was inaccessible to all but the most adventurous of travellers.

The Complete Book of the Dog by Robert Leighton (Cassell, 1922)

What really must continue is the unquenchable spirit in this type of dog; breeds may in time just lose favour, but any breed bearing the description of terrier has to have that very special 'get-up-and-go', the never-say-die attitude of the true earth-dog. May that spirit never be lost; it is a precious feature of the canine world and the terrier is very much Britain's contribution to the sporting dogs of the world.

The terrier, among the higher order of sportsmen, is preserved in its greatest purity, and with the most assiduous attention; and it seems of the utmost importance not to increase its size, which would render him unsuitable for the purpose in which he is employed, that of entering the earth to drive out other animals from their burrows, for which his make, strength, and invincible ardour, peculiarly fit him. On this account, he is the universal attendant upon a pack of fox hounds, and though last in the pursuit he is not the least in value.

Biographical Sketches and Authentic Anecdotes of Dogs by Thomas Brown (1829)

Some of the breeds of terriers seen nowadays in every dog show were equally obscure and unknown a few years back. Fifty years ago the now popular Irish Terrier was practically unknown in England, and the

The Lost National Breed

The English White

For a country that has produced more breeds of terrier than any other and for a country in a group of islands that did more than any other to establish terriers as a canine type, it is quite extraordinary that England does not have a national terrier, as such, by

English White Terrier, a sporting dog with elegant charm.

This nineteenth-century depiction was entitled A Manchester Terrier *by artist I. Robertson.*

English Terriers *(1881), depicting an English White, a Manchester and miniature Black and Tan Terriers.*

name. The terrier breeds of Welsh, Irish and Scottish terriers have each long been recognized as such, if never used – unlike the Bulldog – as national symbols. Claims have been made for the Manchester Terrier to be the terrier of England, and it has also been claimed that the Welsh hijacked the old broken-coated black and tan terrier of the British mainland and made that type their own. Toy dog owners can point to the English Toy Terrier, but purists might see this tiny breed as a Toy Manchester and better named as such.

For the Australians, the Germans, the Czechs and now the Japanese and the Brazilians to have a national terrier and not the English could be seen as absurd and unacceptable. Even the Tibetans have one – at least by name! So did the Maltese, for a while. There may well be more so-called Jack Russells gracing (or disgracing!) the terrier scene of England than any other breed type, but as yet no one has tried to give it a national tag even though hound-marked terriers have featured in many parts of England (and Wales) for at least a century. Yet we did once have an English terrier, not a toy, by name: the English White Terrier.

White Bull Terrier fanciers may claim that the blood of the English White lives on in their breed. But the English White Terrier was once so well known and bred so true to type that a renaissance would be justified and

English Whites depicted by Arthur Wardle, 1890.

Cropped-eared English White Terrier of 1900.

an absurd gap in the list of terrier breeds thereby filled. Breeders of all-white dogs know of the problems of pigmentation, deafness and even sterility associated with this colour, but skilful dog breeders, determined to breed out such faults, will normally triumph, as so many all-white breeds demonstrate today.

In his book *All About the Bull Terrier* (1973), the late Tom Horner wrote: 'When Hinks set out to breed a strain of whites (i.e. bull terriers) he was perhaps inspired by the White English terrier, which at that time had attained a far higher standard and had much more grace of form and quality than anything he could find among the old style Bull-and-Terrier.' How pleasing it would be to have that 'grace of form' once more restored to us in a breed of dog.

In his *Terriers* (1922) Darley Matheson recorded: 'The writer would like to see really serious attempts made to revive the English white terrier, because it is a type, or rather variety, of dog which makes an excellent companion…'. I agree and was interested to read of his recommended blend to resurrect the breed: a cloddy type of Bull Terrier bitch to a Whippet dog, with a further outcross to the Manchester Terrier. He envisaged a 15–18lb dog and outlined a rough likely breed standard. He favoured a Fox Terrier ear for such a recreated breed, knowing full well that the ban on cropping, together with sterility, led to the demise of the original breed.

Some might like to argue that nowadays the ubiquitous Jack Russell has a claim to be the national terrier of England by virtue of sheer popularity. In *Show Dogs* (1925) Theo Marples wrote, on the English White, that 'there is little doubt that the breed is a Lancashire production, where it has for the most part abounded, particularly in its palmier days of nearly half a century ago.' The breed was not classified separately by the KC until the early 1890s. Three of the most prominent early fanciers all came from Bolton in Lancashire.

In *The Kennel Gazette* of January 1889, a contributor using the nom de plume 'Union Jack' wrote:

> I am glad to see that efforts are being made to make white English terriers more popular. This beautiful breed has had a great many ups and downs and many of them quite in a wrong direction. We shall never see better stamp of terriers than old Tim and Godfree's

Prince, the winners at Birmingham in 1865 and at Islington in 1869…

This hints at a show career for the breed of around half a century. The disappearance altogether of this much-admired breed from the KC's lists is a sharp reminder for the worthy people, including those at the KC, now giving attention to the list of vulnerable native breeds, twelve of them in the Terrier group.

In *Dogs and All About Them*, Robert Leighton wrote on the breed:

> At the Kennel Club show of 1909 there was not a single specimen of the breed on view, nor was one to be found at Edinburgh, Birmingham, Manchester, or Islington, nor at the National Terrier Show at Westminster. It is a pity that so smart and beautiful a dog should be suffered to fall into such absolute neglect. One wonders what the reason of it can be.

The English Terrier in Art

What did the original breed actually look like? What is the evidence from photographs and paintings? Dealing with the latter first: one of the difficulties of researching such a breed is that sporting dogs, favoured by the nobility, such as pointers, setters, spaniels, hounds of the chase and especially coursing dogs have been portrayed exhaustively (if often inaccurately) down the centuries. Dogs of the working classes, however, such as sheepdogs and ratting terriers, have been seriously neglected.

If you look at English naive painting, from say 1750 to 1900, and in particular the work of artists such as Clark, Sturr, Whitehead, Balls and Roebuck, you begin to get a much better appreciation of the street dogs of their time. Scholars and art historians are verbose on the subject of classical art and mainly silent on the subject of folk art or naive painting. Seventeenth-century Flemish painters may be revered, but ordinary English people had their art too. For a dog historian or breed researcher, naive art is a largely untapped source. Look at Thomas Roebuck's *Crib* (1860), *The Royal Rat Catcher* by J. Clark even earlier and the work of unknown artists of the same period, such as *Bear Baiting* and *The West Bromwich Sweep*. There you see the all-white terrier very valuably depicted.

English Whites portrayed in folk art, English School, late nineteenth century.

Going back even further, the painting in St Mark's Library in Venice, entitled *The Grimani Breviary* (1515), shows the distinctive white terrier type quite clearly. Of course before the days of pedigree dog breeding, white hound-like and white terrier-type dogs abounded, but this particular portrayal is of significance. It shows a distinct type rather than just a passing resemblance to an emerging breed of those times. Today we lack not only a genuine terrier with English in its name but this time-honoured type of dog too.

'Crib', a Sporting Dog *(Thomas Roebuck, 1860), a fine portrayal of this now sadly extinct breed.*

The timeless white 'terrier'– detail from The Brevarium Grimani, *1510–20.*

Victorian and Edwardian Interest

Victorian and Edwardian writers such as Hugh Dalziel and Robert Leighton had firm views on the English White. Vero Shaw complained about the introduction of Italian greyhound blood, leading to a loss of terrier characteristics. He quotes James Roocroft of Bolton, a prominent breeder of English Whites, as making adverse comments about some specimens showing 'in a marked manner a cross of the snap-dog breed'. He described the breed as 18in at the shoulder and weighing 19lb.

W.D. Drury, in *British Dogs* (1903), states that 'the White English Terrier has undergone considerable modification since public dog shows came into being'. He also commented on a loss of terrier character in the breed. But he writes admiringly of the breed: 'A good specimen of the White English Terrier is quite an aristocrat amongst Terriers – a high class, superior type of dog, fit company for anyone.'

Dalziel, in *his* book *British Dogs* (1888), shows where Drury obtained the first of the above quotes from – verbatim! (Such blatant copying is so dangerous when the facts are wrong, as lazy researchers tend to see repetition as corroboration.) Dalziel felt that 'the wheel back and hooped tail, inherited from no very remote ancestor, are very objectionable, and are generally accompanied by a soft "unvarminty" look'. Just over thirty years later, Robert Leighton was recording that he had not discovered a single specimen of the true type in the last ten years (that is, from 1912 to 1922), but went on to write in *The Complete Book of the Dog* that: 'It is apparent that the Whippet was largely used as a cross with the English terrier, which may account to a great extent for the decline of terrier character in the breed. Wiser breeders had recourse to the more closely allied Bull-terrier.'

Leighton writes that 'Mr Shirley's prize-winning Purity was by Tim out of a Bull-terrier bitch' – a founder member of the Kennel Club winning with a cross-bred dog was surely a sign of the times! Ash describes the first white terrier as appearing in an illustration in the illuminated manuscript depicting the Ordinance of Charles the Bold of 1473. Meanwhile Rawdon Lee, strong on the breed histories during his lifetime but weak on ancestry, describes the English White as a modern breed.

Vero Shaw, writing in 1897, stated that 'where twenty years ago a dozen good White English Terriers could be found, it would today be a very difficult matter to find one, and the breed may now be regarded as extinct … The breed has played a great part in the production of many breeds which are now enjoying great popularity'. The rightly popular white Bull Terrier certainly owes a lot to the English White. Fifty years ago, the forthright Brian Vesey-Fitzgerald had no doubt as to why this breed disappeared, writing: 'In the case of the English White Terrier, "improvement" was responsible: the breed was "perfected" to death.' Vero Shaw gave the view, however, that 'in the white English Terrier the correct shape and action are very hard to obtain', adding that 'so little encouragement is, however, shown to breeders in their efforts to improve the variety, that the classes which appear at our shows are naturally meagre…'. I would like to think that today's Kennel Club would provide encouragement in such a case.

Shaw clearly admired the breed, pointing out that 'the intense brilliancy of their jackets contrasts so beautifully with surrounding objects, and their temperaments are so vivacious and affectionate, that they deserve to be more fully known and appreciated; and this, we trust, will some day be the case'. Those words sum up what many people are seeking in a pet dog: the close companionship of a loyal, handsome animal. Yet if this type is not easy to breed, the more wallet-conscious ones will look elsewhere. Dr Lees Bell, over a century ago, summarized these breeding difficulties:

> All breeders have, I daresay, experienced the same difficulty of breeding pure white puppies with level heads and fine skulls, together with proper English terrier lines of body. The puppies are either foul-marked, or have domed skulls and whippet bodies, or they have level heads, with the thick skull and wide chest and general stoutness of body of the bull terrier.

I wonder if the pursuit of an entirely white dog, without any other markings at all, was perhaps the cause of some of these breeding problems.

I suspect that the English White Terrier was, until the late nineteenth century, a distinct breed type favoured by the working classes, especially by sweeps, pugilists and rat-catchers. The advent of dog shows brought about the pursuit of a daintier-looking dog and this tendency, allied to the ban on ear-cropping, led to the disappearance of the breed – a sad loss.

The Issue of Colour

The renowned 'Idstone' took the view that the coloured specimens rejected in favour of pure white were decidedly the better dogs. In *The Dog* (1880), he wrote, 'since the exhibition of dogs has been a prominent feature in the fashionable amusements of large cities, the dog [that is, the smooth-coated terrier] has been so cultivated that white dogs only are admissible'. He suggested that the wholly white dogs were being favoured because of the colour of their coats ahead of other more important physical features. This, when linked to the distaste in Boxer and German Shepherd Dog breeders for white coats in their breed, shows how limiting and sometimes irrational human taste can be. It could well be that the English White Terrier was lost to us precisely because its fanciers favoured all-white dogs despite their lack of soundness and virility. Successful breeding is always about the wise selection of stock.

Patriotic Challenge

For many members of the public, a medium-sized, short-coated dog, without the instinct to hunt game or herd sheep, which is a lively companion without demanding huge amounts of exercise, would make an ideal house pet. If the English White Terrier could be re-created, then bred true, be of stable temperament and free of the many inheritable defects currently plaguing so many pedigree breeds, then the British public would surely respond. The Russians have created their Black Terrier as a scientific project. A Czech enthusiast has created the Cesky Terrier using British stock. We ourselves certainly have the genetic material and the breeding expertise to restore a national terrier to our currently incomplete, however distinguished, list of native terrier breeds. What a challenge for a skilled breeder! And what an accomplishment for a bunch of patriotic dog fanciers wishing to leave something worthwhile behind them as their life's work. I cannot think that they would be out of pocket either in these days of resurgent patriotism.

The terrier is very British: the Welsh, the Scots and the Irish have their own national terrier by name, so

A Study of Three Terriers *by Edwin Loder (1867), showing two English Whites and a Manchester Terrier.*

where is the English Terrier to complete the full house? Any talented breeder able to restore our white terrier would certainly have a permanent place in the breed's history. A re-created English White Terrier would reintroduce an old-fashioned, once much-admired national breed of terrier. I much prefer the old-fashioned Sealyham and Bull Terriers to the contemporary specimens; but then, I don't consider the term 'old-fashioned' to be in any way derogatory. Can we please have our terrier back? And, unlike our Mastiff, Bulldog and Pointer, with English in its title? Come on terrier-loving patriots, get to work! What a gentle but effective way to demonstrate national pride!

A Proposed Breed Standard for the English White Terrier

The English White Terrier is an ancient British breed, registered by the Kennel Club over a century ago and featuring at dog shows at the end of the nineteenth and the beginning of the twentieth century. Before that the breed was a popular companion dog, ratting terrier and useful all-round sporting terrier. There are records both photographic and artistic of the breed a century or so ago. The first breed club and breed standard predate most of those of the other terrier breeds

Head study of English White by E. Mondy, 1875.

recognized by the Kennel Club. This distinctive breed lost its place in the terrier list partly due to the outlawing of ear-cropping but mainly due to the insistence of its fanciers on entirely white specimens. This led to cases of albinism, a loss of virility and too delicate and fragile a dog. The breed was subsequently disenfranchised by the KC in 1903. Now the breed is based on mainly white dogs, with an ear, eye or root of tail marking, but embracing all-white specimens too, so that past problems in the breed do not recur.

Historic role: All-round companion terrier, able to assist with terrier tasks.

Working role: Ratting and rabbiting terrier, not an earth-dog.

General appearance: Compact, balanced, elegant, lithe and strong; cleanly made; workmanlike and alert; wholly without exaggeration; a smooth-coated medium-sized tailed mainly white terrier with drop-ears and a symmetrical build, with no sign of coarseness. Neat, graceful, more racy than stocky.

Type: The breed resembles a white version of the Manchester Terrier; it must not have prominent eyes, a Whippet-like bone structure or any sign of albinism.

Characteristics: Alert, watchful, keen, inquisitive, calm and friendly; sprightly, extremely agile with quick reactions, a curious nature and an eager, interested expression.

Temperament: Companionable, equable, self-confident, stable and tolerant of other dogs; outgoing, with no sign of shyness.

Aptitude: Willing, eager for exercise, biddable, enthusiastic when put to work.

Construction: Symmetrical, balanced, strong but never thickset, lithe and lightly built but never Whippet-like.

Forefront: Wedge-shaped skull, with more length than width and the cheeks never full, with no visible cheek muscles; cleanly chiselled; the muzzle tapers towards the nose, with no trace of snipeyness; the stop is slight but discernible, with fair breadth between the ears; the skull is balanced, with equal length both forward and aft of the stop. The eyes are almond-shaped but never prominent, small, dark and full of life, with darker rims. The ears are small and V-shaped, set in the topline of the head, dropping forward with the fold of the ear above the level of the skull, hanging close to the head, above the eyes, raised when alert but never prick; the leathers are fine. The bite is a scissors (upper teeth closely overlapping the lower), with the teeth strong and regular. The mouth is tight-lipped with dark pigmentation; the nose is well-formed, black, with clear nostrils. The neck is graceful, gradually tapering from the withers to behind the ears, slightly arched at the crest, displaying no throatiness.

Forehand: The shoulders are clean, sloping, with definite spacing between the blades, the distance from withers to elbow equalling the length of the front leg below the elbow; the shoulder blades and the upper arm should be the same length, with good angulation at the point of shoulder; elbows tucked well in and an adequate spread, but no sign of barrel chest. The forelegs are straight, with the dog noticeably up on its pasterns.

Torso: The body is compact but not short; the chest is deep but not broad, the ribs are well-sprung and carried well back; there is noticeable tuck-up in the underside of the loins, that is, the belly; the topline is slightly dipped but nearly level. The bone structure is not too fine, strong and flat, not sturdy.

Hindhand: Strong and muscular, with good angulation at the stifle but without a placement of the hindfeet beyond the rear end of the dog, that is, the feet should be placed below the croup when the dog is standing normally. The feet must be compact, with strong pads and well-arched toes. The hindlegs should be straight (when viewed from behind), well muscled and strongly constructed. The hocks are well let down. The tail is undocked, of whiptail type, carried low, between the hocks, low set-on, thick at the root, tapering along its length.

Movement: Springy, harmonious, free-striding, effortless and smooth, with good extension fore and aft and plenty of drive from the rear.

Coat: Colour: wholly white, with no sign of albinism; or mainly white, with tan, red or brindle ear or eye markings or marking near the tail, displaying the classic 'extreme white piebald' gene, which produces this coloration. Texture: close, smooth, dense and glossy, not too fine, firm to the touch, hand-resistant when back-brushed. The underline and inside of thighs must not be bare.

Size: Height: dogs 16–18in; bitches 15–17in. Weight: dogs 19–21lb; bitches 17–20lb. Sample dimensions based on Alfred Benjamin's Silvio, which was considered a typical dog (Dalziel, *British Dogs*, 1888): age 3; weight 22lb; height at shoulder 16½in; length from nose to set-on of tail 25in; length of tail 8½in; girth of chest 19½in; girth of loin 16in; girth of head 12in; girth of arm 1in above elbow 7in; girth of leg 1in below elbow 4½in; girth of muzzle 6in; colour white.

Faults: Disqualifying: deafness; albinism; luxating patella. Serious: cow-hocks; out at elbow; Hackney action; prick ears or incorrectly set or poorly carried ears; thick skull; any sign of cloddiness or coarseness. Others: too heavily marked, with body patches; pinning in or plaiting on the move in the front action; coarse coat; exceeding 22lb weight and 19in at the shoulder.

The establishment of breed type will take time; any look of the Whippet or Italian Greyhound or a 'Toy' appearance is not wanted. The nearest model at this stage of the breed's development is a 'white Manchester Terrier', but with a livelier nature and stronger hindquarters. The above notes are intended to be a discussion document, not the finished article, but offers a comprehensive text for future draftees.

Terriers from the North of England

For many centuries the northern counties of England have been famous for the gameness and the working ability of the terriers bred there by hard-bitten breeders who cared not at all for appearance and whose estimation of a dog was based solely upon its prowess in the field. These terriers were known by a number of names, usually associated with the district in which they were bred – a custom which led to almost identical strains being known by different names. This tended to baffle the stranger visiting the north until, within comparatively recent times, clubs were formed and a common name for the breed chosen.

The Book of Terriers by C.G.E. Wimhurst
(Muller, 1968)

Cumberland Hunt: Hounds and Lakeland Terrier *by Vernon Stokes.*

If you look at the annual registrations of some pedigree terrier breeds from the north of England, you could be forgiven for thinking that terriers from that part of Britain are not popular. Each year only around 300 Lakelands, 500 Bedlingtons and 130 Manchesters are newly registered to swell the ranks of those breeds. But away from the show ring breeds from the north, unknown to the general public, yet valued as working terriers, are less well-known, less-publicized types like the Fell and the Patterdale. Some might claim that the latter are only offshoots of the Lakeland or the

perennially and deservedly popular Border Terrier, which boasts around 9,000 annual registrations with the Kennel Club. But, despite its lack of separate recognition, the Fell Terrier especially is gaining respect as a working terrier type. The Airedale I do not consider here; it came from a hound background, was never intended to be, and never could be an earth-dog and is, in French terms, a hunting griffon. But the old black and tan rough-haired terrier may have contributed to its development and is worth a glance.

The terriers of the north worked in the most testing terrain.

Border Terriers by Arthur Wardle (1890).

Mixed Ancestry

At the time the Reverend John Russell was hunting on Exmoor, there were Cheshire Terriers, Shropshire Terriers, Suffolk Terriers, Elterwater and Reedwater Terriers. John Benson had some really hard terriers running with the West Cumberland Otterhounds, as did the renowned Tommy Dobson in the Cumberland lakes, Tom Andrews the Cleveland huntsman, the Earl of Macclesfield in Warwickshire and Squire Danville Poole at Maybury Hall in Shropshire. Some of these are perpetuated in today's pedigree terrier breeds but behind many of them is the old black and tan rough-haired terrier, never recognized in England as a distinct breed and snapped up by enterprising Welsh terrier fanciers and given their nation's name.

Sporting terriers, some of them black and tan, were firmly linked to Yorkshire, even called Halifax Terriers and Blue and Tan Terriers. They threw the long

Otter Terrier owned by the Earl of Cadogan, 1846.

Wire-haired sporting terrier out ratting, by Landseer.

Lakeland Terriers, a working strain first shown in 1931.

Anthony Chapman, huntsman of the Coniston, with some of his hounds and terriers.

coat, as well as the smooth and wiry varieties. The long-coats became favoured as companion dogs, their size being 'bred down' and their coats 'bred up' to leave us with today's Toy Yorkshire Terrier, bred like a tiny pinscher. The casually dubbed 'King of the Terriers', the big terrier from the Vale of Aire or Airedale Terrier, probably has common ancestors with the little Yorkie.

Today's Lakeland Terrier represents the old rough-coated black and tan dog, while the undervalued Manchester Terrier represents the smooth variety. If you look at books devoted to terriers of a century ago, you could be forgiven for missing any reference to the Lakeland Terrier. Darley Matheson's *Terriers* (1922) does not list it, while Pierce O'Conor's *Sporting Terriers* a few years later only contains an illustration of 'a working terrier from Lakeland', which resembles a Border Terrier. He gives no words on this breed but finds space for two paragraphs on the Otter Terrier, whilst admitting that it was probably extinct. But Hutchinson's *Dog Encyclopaedia* of 1934 has ten full pages on the Lakeland, including eighteen photographs. A dozen years earlier, from the names of Patterdale, Fell, Coloured Terrier and Elterwater Terriers, the breed title of Lakeland became accepted in the show ring, a breed club having been formed in 1912, with KC recognition being achieved in 1921, a year after the Border Terrier. Less than half a century later,

a Lakeland Terrier went Best in Show at Crufts then Best in Show at the prestigious Westminster show in America the following year – some achievement.

The Bedlington Terrier

The breed title of Bedlington Terrier does scant justice to such a capable all-round hunting dog; if anything the Bedlington is a pedigree lurcher, whose blood is much valued by lurcher men. As a breed, the ancestry of the Bedlington is, relative to most breeds, well documented and free from myths. From the celebrated hunt terriers, Peacham and Pincher of Edward Donkin of Rothbury to the nailors' terriers in the Northumbrian village of Bedlington itself, from Joseph Ainsley's dog and

Working-type Bedlington Terrier.

Christopher Dixon's bitch and their offspring, the prototype Piper and Coate's Phoebe, came the foundation of the breed. The breed changed from a 15lb dog in 1830 to a 30lb dog by 1870. This breed is often dubbed a rabbiting dog, but it uses its nose too much to make just a gifted sighthound; it excels at putting up rabbits for waiting lurchers or Whippets, its nose working ahead of its eyes. It is a great ratting breed and renowned for its work on otter.

In an interesting letter to *Field Sports* magazine in 1949, a writer signing himself 'A.S.' contributed:

> At one time otters were exceedingly abundant on the Northumberland streams, especially the Coquet, Aln, and Till. They had one particular enemy – a man named Will Allan, who regularly hunted the waters for otters in the eighteenth century. He owned three famous ottering dogs, renowned for their prowess, named Charlie, Phoebe and Peacham. Will was so proud of them that he set a high value on them. It is recorded that Will used to visit Eslington from Hepple, where he lived, with these grand helpers, and killed otters for Lord Ravensworth at Eslington, on the river Aln. Will used to assert that 'When my Peacham gies mouth, I durst always sell the otter's skin.' It is also said that Lord Ravensworth once desired to buy Charlie from Will, and told his agent to inform that worthy to state his price – he could have a good sum for the dog. But Will's reply was: 'His hale estate cann' buy Charlie!'

That is some tribute both to the man and his dog.

In the quaintly titled *Dogs: Their Points, Whims, Instincts and Peculiarities*, edited by Henry Webb (Dean & Son, 1883), it is stated:

> The Bedlington is essentially a vermin terrier, on land or in water, as many who have owned him will testify. He will do, and has done, what it is possible for a dog of his description to perform. The Reedwater foxhounds (Northumberland) are attended by some four or five of the breed, descended from Donkin's strain, as good as are to be procured, and the subscribers to the Carlisle otter hounds can tell many a tale of his usefulness. Instances of his courage could be supplied without number…

It is significant that the breed was prized as a vermin terrier on land or in water and valued by those hunting the otter.

Bedlington Terrier, 1904.

A Unique Coat

Mention is sometimes made of the use of blood from small Otterhounds, Bull Terriers and an infusion of Whippet too, in the development of the breed. But little reference is made to the origin of the distinctive topknot, the highly individual linty coat and the range of self-colours in the breed. Much is made of the unique use of the word 'linty' to describe the breed's coat-texture. The word 'lint' comes from the late Middle English 'lynnet', a word describing flax prepared for spinning; it could be that the word linty describes the *colour* of the flax, and the dog's coat – a very pale sandy-liver colour – rather than its *texture*. The true Bedlington coat is never like lint, but twisty, not curly, crisp rather than hard or soft, dense and weatherproof. In Vero Shaw's authoritative *The Illustrated Book of the Dog* (1881), there is a breed standard for the Bedlington, in which the colour portion reads: 'Blue, liver, linty or sandy, in the different shades of each.' The required texture of the breed's coat doesn't use the word linty in this very early breed description.

There was a dog with a topknot and a tight linty-twisty coat in light liver on the Berwick coast and up into the Cheviot Hills at the time the early types of Rothbury Forest Dog were emerging. It was known locally as the Tweed Water Spaniel, but Tweed Water Dog would have been more accurate. Water Spaniels have the marcelled coat texture, as the American Water Spaniel illustrates. Water Dogs have the 'poodle-coat' as the Italian, the Spanish and the Portuguese Water Dogs demonstrate. Water dogs have long been favoured by the gypsy community, with gypsy families like the Jeffersons, the Andersons and the Faas, living in the Rothbury Forest at the start of the nineteenth century. They were famous for their terriers, long-dogs and water dogs. I believe that the distinctive coat of the Bedlington comes from a water dog origin.

In *The Live Stock Journal* of November 1875, there is a letter, which reads:

> About thirty or forty years ago I remember well people crossing these Terriers with the Bull-terrier, in order that they might stand more wear and tear for fighting purposes, which were then so extensively sought. A few years after that they again crossed them with our Poodle dogs, so as to get linty-haired Terriers…but as soon as they come into contact with

'Broc', they are generally seen to come faster backwards than they went in, which was not the case with our real Bedlingtons…

In the same edition of this journal, the breed is described as a northern counties Fox Terrier. So many of our native terrier breeds could have ended up with very different breed titles.

Terriers from the Borders

This is a unique terrier breed, a silent worker, but one with a low-set ear, a pronounced occiput, a domed skull and a hare-foot for speed not digging. In his book on working terriers (1948), Dan Russell wrote:

> I know that I am standing up to be shot at when I say that I believe that the qualities I have detailed are more often found in the Border Terrier than in any other breed. To me, these little northerners are the ideal terriers. They are dead game, they have stamina, nose and endurance, and their little heads seem to be packed full of commonsense. There is in the expression of a Border Terrier an implacable determination which is seen in no other breed.

From that source that is praise indeed. However, some claim that the Border, and indeed the Lakeland, is too hard a terrier, just too tenacious, often being

Rock, a Coniston Hunt terrier of the Lakeland type.

A famous brace of Mr Dodd's Border Terriers; note the length of these terriers' backs.

unavailable for work because of injuries sustained in needless combat.

In *Hunt and Working Terriers* (1931), Lucas writes of the Border Terrier:

> Many Masters of hounds think that they are too hard, or apt to become so, killing their fox instead of bolting him. That this is sometimes the case is not unlikely, for it must be remembered that in the Fell and Border countries it is often necessary to kill foxes by any means possible.

That explanation also shows how the country and its special challenges lead to the need for a responding capability from sporting dogs. Lucas appends in this book a list of the terrier breeds employed by the various hunts at the end of the 1929 season, and the Border Terrier is the choice of many. But even as assiduous a researcher as the late Brian Plummer admitted:

> As with all northern breeds of working terrier, the origin of the Border Terrier is obscure though there has been much speculation as to how the breed was first developed out of the heterogeneous mish-mash of types that spawned not only the Border, but also the Dandie, the Bedlington and possibly the Lakeland terrier.

In the breed standard of the Border Terrier, under the characteristics description, there is the phrase 'capable of following a horse', which is often interpreted as a requirement for the breed to run with the hounds. But the breed was often employed with foot-hounds, not the mounted field. The physical needs of an earth-dog and a running dog are in conflict. I wonder if originally a phrase like 'able to follow the hunt' – that is, to support the hounds once the quarry had been located as being underground – was used. The country over which the hunting took place and this breed was used

David Stevens of the Crawley & Horsham, with his five generations of Lakelands (photo: Ian Tolputt).

Gyp, a famous Lakeland Terrier in 1930.

was not always suitable for mounted huntsmen. In similar country, the Scots and the Cumbrians never sought a leggy terrier, able to run with the moving hunt. In his book on terriers of 1896, Rawdon Lee writes: 'Some of the terriers follow hounds regularly, and are continually brought into use, not only amongst the rocks and in rough ground of that kind, but in equally or in more dangerous places – wet drains or moss holes, or "waterfalls", as they are called in Northumberland.' Not much scope for mounted huntsmen here! In his informative book on the breed, Walter J.F. Gardner queries: 'How many of the world's top athletes are short-legged or short-backed or both? How many animals which go to ground or can gallop and stay long distances have a short back?' This is discussed in Chapter 3.

Widespread Cross-Breeding

Nowadays we relate to *breeds* far more than our sporting ancestors; breed purity was never a requirement for a working terrier, performance was all. The types favoured by terrier-men were proven workers, judged not on coat colour or texture, height at shoulder or shape of skull, and often from mixed ancestry. As Richard Clapham wrote in *Foxes, Foxhounds and Fox-Hunting* (Heath Cranton, 1932):

> Some of the best all-round working terriers today are to be found with the fell foxhound packs in the Lake District. They are practically all cross-bred, with Bedlington, Border, etc., blood in them … in the land

of the dales and the mountains the only criterion of a terrier is working ability, first, last and all the time.

In similar vein, no claim was made on names for types favoured in different areas. As terrier expert Mossop Nelson wrote in W.C. Skelton's *Reminiscences of Joe Bowman and the Ullswater Foxhounds* (Atkinson and Pollitt, 1921):

> I have a great feeling about keeping to the old breed of what has sometimes been called the Patterdale terrier: brown or blue in colour with a hard wiry coat, a narrow front, a strong jaw, not snipey like the present show fox terrier, but at the same time not too bullet-like to show a suspicion of bulldog cross – a short strong back, and legs which will help him over rough ground and enable him to work his way underground.

It is worth noting that Mossop Nelson was stating what the terrier required to do his job best, rather than what cosmetic points the breeder or owner wished to bestow on it. Concern has been recently expressed over the KC's willingness to register blacks and brindles as Border Terriers, but for sportsmen coat colour is never a problem. I have heard terrier-men using this breed declare that the red-nosed ones were the keenest scented. In the United States, Border Terriers earn around 114 earth-dog titles every year, more than any other terrier breed.

A correspondent to *The Field* magazine in 1886 wrote:

> The dormant spirit of an old fell hunter has recently been keenly awakened at the mention of the Elterwater terriers, which breed, I am informed, is nearly extinct… The Elterwater terriers had plenty of go in them, and no shaking or trembling at your heels, in frost and snow, like so many of the terriers of the present day.

Elterwater is near Rydal, just north of Lake Windermere, while Patterdale is some 10 miles south of Rydal, at the southern end of Ullswater. Eighty years ago, the Eskdale and Ennerdale Hunt was using six couples of working Fox Terriers, whilst the Coniston Hunt was using the Fell type. The Border Terrier, also called the Reedwater Terrier, the Cheviot Terrier, the

Manchester Terriers of the 1890s by Arthur Wardle.

Ullswater Terrier (even Joe Bowman's terrier) and the Robson Terrier (after the Master of the Border Hunt) was favoured by the North Tyne Foxhounds. Always with terriers, their devotees have the firmest of views about the best type for the job in their hunt country. It is of interest that unlike their Scottish counterparts, the terrier-men of Cumberland favoured the drop ear on their dogs, or what they called 'latch-lug't' ears; prick-eared dogs were rarely preferred.

In his book on the Fell Terrier, Brian Plummer makes a point for me. Whilst discussing a visit to terrier-men in the Lake District, he comments that on

The Manchester Terrier

The ban on ear-cropping may well have been the kiss of death to the smooth-coated black and tan Manchester Terrier, for it has never been popular since that time, despite its many virtues. More famous in the rat-pits than as an earth-dog, this handy-sized, easily managed, companionable little breed is strangely undervalued, both by sportsmen and pet-owners. Accused of lacking 'gameness' and handicapped by weak hindquarters and straight stifles, it is making a slight comeback despite its small numbers. In 1909 only 83 were registered with the Kennel Club. A hundred years later that annual figure has risen to 135, still less than half that of the Lakeland Terrier. I attended the annual show for this breed a couple of years ago and, whilst noting great variation in the quality of movement between exhibits, found much to admire in their temperament and companionable qualities. With a trouble-free coat, a total lack of overt aggression, yet plenty of spirit, they have much to offer as a canine companion.

the journey back one of his travelling companions states quietly, 'They're a different breed of person'. All of them agreed. The terriers of the north are different breeds too, but each one has its own special appeal.

The northern terrier of today, workmanlike and hard-jacketed.

They were developed in the hardest of hard schools and we owe it to remarkable breeders such as Joe Bowman, Tommy Coulson, Cyril Breay, Frank Buck, Gary Middleton and Brian Nuttall to perpetuate their years of devoted attention to their outstanding terriers. William Hazlitt, writing in 1821, in his *Table Talk*, could have been describing terriers from the north, when he wrote: 'A rough terrier dog, with the hair bristled and matted together, is picturesque. As we say, there is a decided character in it, a marked determination to an extreme point.' Terriers from the north of England certainly possess and display 'decided character' as well as 'a marked determination to an extreme point'; that is what makes them the sporting dogs they are.

> When speaking of fell hunting, mention must be made of the terriers, which are indispensable for bolting foxes from the rock-earths. Without them many a fox would have to be left that richly deserved killing. The terrier most suitable for work on the fell should weigh from 15lb. to 16lb.; coat thick and wet-resisting; chest narrow, but not so much so as to impede the free action of heart and lungs; legs sufficiently long to enable the dog to travel above ground with ease to himself; teeth level, jaw strong but not too long; ears small and dropped close to the head, so that they are less likely to be torn by foxes. Most Lakeland terriers are of the so-called 'Patterdale' breed, with more or less Bedlington blood in them… Fell terriers have to follow the huntsman all day over rough going, perhaps in snow; thus they are better for being a bit on the leg.
>
> Richard Clapham, writing on fox hunting in Lakeland, in *Fox Hunting* (The Lonsdale Library, Volume VII, 1930)

Although the Bedlington Terrier is only a newcomer, I think he has a great future before him with regard to popularity and esteem. The breed can well afford to depend upon its merits to push its way to the front, and the more well-bred specimens get spread about, in the greater demand will the dog most assuredly be. The Bedlington I look upon as a farmer's friend and country gentleman's companion. No breed of Terrier can compare with him for stamina, fire, courage and resolution. He will knock about all day with his master, busy as a bee at foxes, rabbits, or otters; and at night, when sort of dog would be stiff, sore, and utterly jaded, he will turn up bright as a new shilling, and ready for any game going. He takes to the water readily, has a capital nose, is most intelligent and lively, and, as I have said, as a rough and ready friend about the fields and woods he has no equal.

> *British Dogs* by W.D. Drury (Upcott Gill, 1903)

THE LESSON OF THE FOX TERRIER

Changing Popularity

When I was a boy Fox Terriers were everywhere, especially at harvest time. Once the first choice of some hunts as hunt terriers, they became a favourite companion dog, yet, unlike, say, the Cocker Spaniel, gradually faded from the scene. In some ways they reflect the changes in our society: a preference for exotic dogs and exotic holidays, a desire for flashier canines and cars and a failure to acknowledge the merits of home-grown products, whether they are from dog-breeders, dairies or dockyards. In 1910, the Kennel Club registered more than 1,500 smooth Fox Terriers and more than 1,300 wire-haired Fox Terriers, against nearly 700 Cockers. Seventeen years later, more than 10,000 Fox Terriers of both coats were registered against well over 4,000 Cockers; both breeds had arrived.

In 2009, more than 22,000 Cockers were registered with the KC, against just 133 smooth and 604 wire-haired Fox Terriers. The Cockers had arrived and

Fox Terriers of 1904, Jock and Blizzard of Argenteau.

Three famous early Fox terriers, from left: Old Jock, Grove Nettle and Tartar.

Today's Smooth Fox Terrier, a winning puppy from Cumbria: Leconridge Adversary.

stayed, the Fox Terrier as a breed is under threat. For such an honest, companionable and fussless breed to falter is a pity, for their working use to all but disappear is simply tragic. Fox Terriers were first listed as a distinct type in 1862 and both wires and smooths were interbred for many years after their show ring debut. By 1890, however, some clearly defined bloodlines began to predominate in each coated variety.

CHAMPION GO BANG   CHAMPION THORNFIELD KNOCKOUT
Two good terriers formerly owned by Major G. M. Carnochan

Photo by Reveley, Wantage.
SMOOTH FOX TERRIER DOG, DARLEY DALE (Property of Mr REDMOND).

Smooth Fox Terrier of 1905, showing stronger shorter muzzle and greater breadth of chest.

Photo by Watson
THE GREAT MEERSBROOK BRISTLES
The most famous of all terrier sires. Imported and exhibited in America by Mr. C. W. Keyes, East Pepperell, Mass.

Top: Two good terriers: Ch Go Bang (left) and Ch Thornfield Knockout (right); below: the great Meersbrook Bristles, the most famous of all early Fox Terrier sires.

Names such as Ch Barkley Ben and Ch Meersbrook Bristles appear at the beginning of all Wire Fox Terrier pedigrees. This breed was founded upon several strains that were derived from packs of Fox Hounds' hunt terriers with the main sources being dogs like Old Jock, Old Trap, Old Foiler, Old Buffer and Belvoir Joe, who had perhaps the greatest influence on the modern breed. The latter's son Belgrave Joe is found way back in most pedigrees. Old Trap was sired by a black and tan dog; Old Foiler's dam, Judy, came from the Rev John Russell's strain.

Working Background

In *British Dogs* (1903), Drury writes: 'I think few will differ from me when I say that the Grove and Belvoir have taken more pride in their breed of Terriers than any other pack, and have crossed them as carefully as they did their Hounds.' That is some praise. The Belvoir preferred the 'old black and tan' sort, getting stock from a noted breeder William Singleton of Grantham, who, Drury states, 'kept them free from Bull for over forty years'. The Belvoir pack has long been famous for its tricolour or parti-coloured hounds. There is an inference here too that regular infusions of bull-and-terrier blood were practised by working terrier breeders. Drury also observes that 'even to the present day, or at least till very recently, the Duke of Beaufort has kept up a breed of black-and-tan Fox-terriers, and excellent dogs they are too'. Most Fox Terriers nowadays in both coated varieties appear to be mainly white and favoured as such.

I wonder how wise it was to seek separate recognition for terriers carrying a different coat but coming from the same root stock. Recognition of more than one breed from the same root really does make a difference. Once the different breeds have become established with their separate stud-books, each gene pool becomes sealed and genetic isolation results. This is artificial and not how nature works. Just as crucial is the work of fanciers who develop breed points to the degree where the two breeds, from the same origin, are bred and judged differently. I would question the wisdom of this. Some breeds bearing the same basic breed name but featuring different coat textures have developed from separate roots, as with German Pointers, for example, and I can understand separate breed status for the Wire-haired and Long-haired from the Short-haired breed. This is not the case in the Fox

Smooth Fox Terrier Ch Sampler Maymorn by Reuben Ward Binks (1924–48).

Wire Fox Terrier Ch Newmarket Cackler by A.G. Haigh, 1908.

Terrier. One MFH is on record as stating that 'as all terrier-men know, a good way to get a real, hard, wiry, weather-resisting coat is to cross a wire with a smooth.'

In his *Modern Dogs: The Terriers* (1896), Rawdon Lee writes on the Fox Terrier that 'the two varieties ought to be identical, though one has a smooth, close coat, the other a hard close coat and somewhat rough.'

In *The Popular Fox Terrier* (1950), Rosslyn Bruce writes: 'The two varieties, the Smooth-coated and Wire-haired, are fundamentally the same breed.' Both these writers were experts on the breed and worthy of note. Both record in detail a common origin for what is now two distinct breeds. So many pedigree dog breeders are obsessed with breed purity when they

Two terriers and a Rat in a Trap by Charles Towne, 1823; these terriers show distinct Bull Terrier influence.

The Badger Bait by Lambert Marshall (1810–70), showing the stiffer-coated Fox Terrier type.

should, if they truly care about their breed, be obsessed with sound functional dogs.

Major Harding Cox, a leading figure in the canine world of this time, wrote, in *Dogs and I* (1928):

> For the manufacture of a smooth Fox-terrier the following recipe is to be commended. Take an old-fashioned ratting terrier and mate it with a White English Terrier of quality, cross the produce with a small-sized Bull-terrier, and then, in succeeding generations, breed to eliminate the Bulldog characteristics as introduced by the said Bull-terrier.

He ridiculed the whole concept of breeding leggy terriers capable of running with the hounds (*see* Chapter 3), writing that 'the theory anent [archaic, meaning 'concerning'] Fox-terriers running with Fox-hounds is a fatuous one.' He considered that such misguided thinking resulted in long-legged, badly constructed terriers no longer capable of being earth-dogs. It is significant to note the type of sporting terriers that have survived the quest for terriers that can 'follow the hunt'.

Terrier Construction

Harding Cox was also responsible for the famous letter to *The Field* magazine of April 1897, in which he expressed equally strong views about terrier construction:

> In the early seventies there was a reaction against the cloddy or cob-built Terrier – the 'brick with the four corners knocked off', as it was facetiously called…We now have dogs so narrow in front, so oblique in shoulder, that as a natural result they have flat sides, weak back ribs, long couplings, wedge-like and feeble quarters, with enough daylight under them to absorb a Norwegian summer. This is not the first time I have fallen foul of those misguided enthusiasts whose ambition it is to breed Terriers to live with hounds. I have no hesitation in positively stating that no Fox-terrier that ever was bred could live with any decent pack of Foxhounds when really carrying a head… I claim that for purposes of going to ground, and staying there as long as required, I would back a well-balanced, sturdy Terrier with good chest and ribs against

Head study of Fox Terrier by D.G. Steel (1856–1930) showing the original head in the breed.

Head study of Fox Terrier from the 1950s, showing the much longer, narrower head.

any of the leggy, narrow, and 'spiry' dogs of the show-bench today.

This aspect is discussed later on in the book, in Chapter 3.

The Fox Terrier is a breed I admire (and for me it is one breed), yet I have visited their rings at shows over fifty years and rarely been pleased with the entry. Upright shoulders, open coats in the wires, snipey muzzles and too short a back seem to be acceptable features. The breed standard, on the other hand, demands sloping shoulders, well laid back and, in the wires, a dense, very wiry coat. Both are required to have short backs – how short is not stipulated. This is no feature for an earth-dog breed; cobbiness may look smart 'on the flags' but it's a considerable handicap underground.

Rosslyn Bruce objects to the craze for elongated muzzles and the obliterated 'stop' that accompanies this feature. Most of the show Fox Terriers I see have over-long heads and hardly any 'stop' at all. He also wrote that 'an erroneous impression is prevalent that a Fox Terrier must be squarely built, and that by standing the Terrier sideways on, if of the ideal build and shape, he should fit into all the sides of a square'. He then makes a convincing argument against too square a dog. Yet, time and time again, down the years, I have seen square Fox Terriers win prizes at prestigious shows. Perhaps, as in so many breeds, the dogs are being bred to win prizes and not to improve the breed. To be fair to today's breeders, many of the faults I see are hardly new.

In *The Kennel Gazette* of 1884, there is a critique which reads: 'Diadem, the once-sensational, and the only remaining entry in the class, being third. She is far too short in body for my taste, has upright shoulders, and is not enough of a working terrier.' For a Smooth-Haired Fox Terrier to come third and be 'once-sensational' with these shortcomings is depressing. In a critique of 1933, Major Hayward, reporting on a Wire-Haired entry, wrote: 'With few exceptions looseness at elbows, weak fronts and bad feet and unsoundness prevailed, while hocks were too far away from the body.' He would not have liked the contemporary fetish for the hocks to be too far away from the body in far too many 'flashy' breeds. In the 1950s, Colonel Phipps was writing on the entry of the same breed: 'I only hope for the sake of the breed that it was

not a representative one as otherwise the outlook is not good... I am still of the opinion that breeders are losing or have lost sight of the fact that a Fox-terrier is primarily a working dog.' Time and time again, show fanciers admire a breed so much that they can't wait to move it away from its original blueprint and a word picture related to the function that shaped the breed.

In an article in *The Countryman's Weekly* in 2004, Jeremy Hobson posed the question: 'Why does the Fox Terrier have a greater following in France than in its country of origin?' He had been visiting the great French game fair, or Fete de la Chasse, in the Loire valley, watching the fine parade of clubs devoted to '*la venerie sous terre*', showing off their earth-dogs, mainly old-fashioned type wire and smooth Fox Terriers, but ones with deep chests, powerful shoulders and waterproof coats. Such packs were prized by British sportsmen from Kenya to the garrisons of India. It would be educational for show ring breeders of Fox Terriers to attend such a fair and see the crucial difference between their rosette-winning specimens and the much more functional terriers so highly rated by experienced French hunters. Our pedigree Fox Terriers do seem to be valued more for their silhouette than their skill as a terrier.

Half a century ago, in *The Domestic Dog* (1957), Brian Vesey-Fitzgerald wrote, when discussing the impact of fashion on the show ring dogs:

Wire Fox Terrier Ch Rowsely Courtly by G Muss-Arnolt (1858–1927), showing a dog without any exaggeration.

Smooth Fox Terrier by R. Morley, 1897; note the alertness and power captured by the artist.

It would be true to say that no show champion of twenty years ago – certainly in the terriers, and in most other breeds as well – would stand a chance today. In the terriers, at least, their heads would be described as

'coarse'; and none of the old champions, so highly regarded so short a while ago, would, of course, be standing up on his toes on stiff and useless pasterns.

Fifty years later we see the same faults in show terriers, faults which are now inbred and accepted by conformation judges in KC show rings as not just acceptable but typical, and therefore somehow desirable. As discussed in later chapters, 'Fox Terrier thinking', developed at the end of the nineteenth century, especially over front assemblies in terriers, has had far-reaching and long-lasting influences in far too many pedigree terrier breeds.

Working terrier breeders understand why certain anatomical features are important; without wishing to sound too cynical, far too many show breeders rate physical features solely by their ability to appeal to a judge. Functional terriers need a front assembly that supports their work and contributes to their success. Working dogs do not deserve the handicap of an unsuitable coat. In the last few years I have judged terriers, from unregistered terrier breeds, at their annual breed club shows and found really good shoulders and hard, crisp, weatherproof coats in the coated varieties. These were bred by men who used their dogs in the field but they were not KC-registered breeds. The Fox Terrier is very much part of the sporting heritage

Ratting with Ferrets and a Terrier *by John Emms (1897).*

Ratting *by John Emms (1897); note the substance of the terrier depicted.*

of England; it would be good to see them favoured by terrier-men once again, just as the Rufford and Grove packs did over a century ago.

It is often said that the show fox terrier is no workman. This is of course the case when they are not entered. So many terriers hardly leave their kennels except for the show bench, and are not able to look out for themselves like those running about all day. One of my prize terriers … was very game; she ran all last season with the Pytchley, and bolted many foxes.
Lady Edith Villiers, in *The Twentieth Century Dog* by Herbert Compton (1904)

The majority of even our best dogs are too big and leggy, and many are weak in hindquarters. The desire to obtain long-headed dogs, and the exaggerated importance so many judges appear to attach to the heads would seem to be responsible for this state of things. Coats also require more attention; a short, hard, close jacket is what is wanted. The keen, restless, dare-devil expression of a true terrier is too seldom seen.
Capt C.J. Wilkie, in *The Twentieth Century Dog* by Herbert Compton (1904)

In my opinion the present-day dog is much too large, and losing all terrier character; and, as a rule, the wires are very weak in their hindquarters, which is one of the most essential points of the working terrier…The type that some judges favour is totally at variance with the working terrier… To my mind there are not so many genuine, good, all-round terriers at the present time as there were fifteen years ago, when I started breeding. I consider the reason for this is that there are too many crazes, such as getting absurdly long, narrow heads and fronts to suit the present-day judge.
T.M. Fogg, in *The Twentieth Century Dog* by Herbert Compton (1904)

That the fox terrier of today is a great improvement, in so far as looks go, on his predecessors of forty or fifty years ago is beyond question, though whether he is better suited physically or morally for work underground is a matter of opinion.
From *Sporting Terriers* by Pierce O'Conor (1926)

The Launch of the Parson Russell Terrier

Here's Devon and Somerset's Terrier Pack!
Every one bred from 'Lynton Jack'.
Narrow and straight, with natural coats,
Possessing pluck worth many groats.
From *English Life* by Arthur Heinemann (1925)

Replacing the Fox Terrier

Before the Great War, the Fox Terrier, in its two coats, could muster over 3,000 registrations; nowadays the wire-hairs total less than 800 a year, the smooths less than 200. But nearly twenty years ago into the annual Kennel Club terrier list came the Parson Jack Russell Terrier (the Jack was later dropped), with just under 700. Before 1990 there were no Russells registered with the KC, the 'breed' was not even recognized by them. But Jack Russells have been with us a very long time, in the field if not in the show rings, and in some numbers. The Parson Jack Russell Club was formed in

Fox Terrier of Russell type by S. Fulton (1855).

Russell-type terrier by W.H.H. Trood (1899); the smaller Fox Terrier had long been favoured by some hunts.

1983, to prevent a lower-height dog becoming the norm. Outside the show ring there are probably more Jack Russells being born than Fox Terrier registrations before the Great War. The Reverend John Russell was a Fox Terrier man. He did not dock his terriers' tails. He did not strive to create a breed of terrier. But at a dog show in the 1870s, which attracted an entry of 150, he remarked: 'I seldom or never see a real Fox Terrier nowadays.'

Parson Russell favoured a terrier with length of leg, a narrow chest, a well-boned skull and a thick, hard, dense, close-lying coat. He modelled his terriers on Rubie's and Tom French's Dartmoor Terrier, and his first terrier, Trump, was the size of a full-grown vixen, with legs as straight as arrows and a coat that was thick, close and wiry. He selectively bred from good working dogs to produce more good working dogs – not to establish a physically identifiable type as a distinct breed. Many foxhound kennels favoured his type of hunt terrier, but it was essentially a working wire-haired Fox Terrier, never a separate breed. Truly, a real Jack Russell is a smaller wire-haired Fox Terrier and many a smaller wire-haired Fox Terrier could be called a Jack Russell. The Reverend John Russell, a founder member of the Kennel Club, judged Fox Terriers at the Crystal Palace show of 1874. In the breeding of his working terriers, Russell used a show bench Fox Terrier sire, Old Jock, though at that time much of the show bench stock came from hunt kennels.

Smooth Fox Terrier of Russell type by J. Bray (1909).

Trinity Jim, 1890–1901, one of Arthur Heinemann's terriers.

Contested Status

Sixty years or so ago, the famous Fox Terrier breeder, Dr Rosslyn Bruce, wrote these words to the publication *Dog World*:

> I firmly believe that if someone were to choose as apple-headed, crooked-fronted, broad-chested, flat-sided, short-necked, bulgy-eyed terrier as he could find in all the progeny, say, of our best Terriers, and call it a Parson Jack terrier, which it certainly would be, for they all are, that he would find enough admirers of it to form a new Parson Jack Russell Club, and make a small fortune in stud fees and pups. It has been done before. It is curious how a once great name is used to bolster up a modern fad…

The doctor was a prophet – as well as being the most knowledgeable terrier breeder of his time. To be fair,

the show version does not feature the Dachshund construction, and the KC-recognized breed has an ideal height of 14in at the withers, as well as a detailed standard designed to produce a working anatomy.

Renowned Breeders

Arthur Heinemann, who was born in 1871 and spent most of his sporting life on Exmoor, continued Russell's work, producing the famous Spider for use with the local Otterhounds. Heinemann, who judged the 'Working Fox Terrier' class at Crufts in 1909, introduced the Bull Terrier outcross, favouring a harder dog than the Parson. Heinemann was seeking a fox killer, Russell a fox bayer. The country they hunted was renowned for its terriers. The smaller Fox Terriers could so easily have been named Devon Terriers; Miss Alys Serrell had an excellent kennel of respected workers there, all smooths. In later life she went out with the Blackmore Vale and the Cattistock. She also kept a line of old black and tan terriers, considering them the original fox terriers. Her father had been a sporting parson and a friend of Russell's, who gave him terriers. Shorter-legged, hound-marked hunt terriers could have gone to the show ring as Cowley Terriers, for J.H.B. Cowley of Callipers, King's Langley, developed a magnificent strain of this type, originally based on a sire from the old Surrey Foxhounds and a dam from Cornwall. He maintained his own stud book and strove to breed to a set phenotype, something Parson Russell never did. But in the

A Rabbit Fancier, *Victorian engraving depicting the casually bred working terrier of the early nineteenth century.*

Heinemann's terriers, c.1910.

latter's time, the Rev. Peyton of Doddington in Cambridgeshire had such working terriers too, and they were the envy of every terrier-man who saw them, breeding true to type.

Round about 1890, an 'Old English Terrier Club' was formed seeking to draw attention to the hardy, hard-bitten varieties of ultra-game terriers from the various country districts. The worthy people behind this club were well-intentioned and genuine enough in their zeal, but so often the best dogs brought forward in this way won their class at shows bearing the names of the pedigree terrier breeds emerging at that time. The superb sporting terriers bred by the two sporting parsons Peyton and Russell live on in the wire-haired Fox Terriers of today; Alys Serrell's, and then Augusta Guest's, in the smooths; none of them sought a different breed. You could argue that if that situation was acceptable to Russell, then it should be good enough for us today. Augusta Guest died in 1960; her terriers could be traced back through Alys Serrell's to 1880. Arthur Heinemann died in 1930; in terrier-development terms, these are relatively recent events.

In *Jack Russell and his Terriers* (Allen, 1979), Dan Russell wrote: 'The standard for a real Jack Russell terrier is that laid down by "Otter" Davies, and one should not budge from it.' It was the description, in fact, of Trump, the parson's first dog, a terrier the size of a full-grown vixen, with straight legs and a thick, close, protective coat but not one with the profusion of the Scottie's. Dan Russell was adamant that the Jack Russell terrier 'is not a breed, it is a type', mourning

their ownership by townspeople, never given a chance to work. He added, 'By and large I think it would be a bad thing for the Russell type if it were recognised by the Kennel Club. We have seen what happens to other working breeds when the show people get hold of them'.

Registration Opposed

Ten years later, Greg Mousley from the hunting world was writing to *Hounds* magazine but really addressing the Kennel Club:

> Your Parson Jack Russell Terrier will not be allowed the benefit of a regular injection of working blood to keep it on the right track, because there are no true working terriers in your registry, simply because the true working terrier-man will shun your shows and very soon you will have another Fox Terrier. Even now, members of the Parson Jack Russell Club are first crossing K.C. Fox Terriers to their Jack Russells with disastrous results.

An experienced huntsman, he wrote a second letter later that year, 1989, saying: 'Let this pretender, The Parson Jack Russell, have its little boom and perhaps win Crufts on novelty value… it won't last, not a chance of it standing the test of time.'

Against that background, it is of interest to read some of the show critiques on the newly recognized breed of Parson Russell Terrier, which has seen registrations of more than 600 in each of the past nine

A working Jack Russell Terrier of today.

Crufts 1991: the newly recognized Parson Jack Russell breed appears for the first time.

years. The Crufts judge of 2010 reported, 'I found some exhibits with stilted and high short stepping movement.' The Crufts judge of 2009 noted that poor movement was still very much in evidence, with plaiting, paddling and a lack of coordination when moving away and advancing towards the judge. A 2009 championship show judge reported a lack of muscle tone and straight stifles, whilst another was tempted to withhold awards in some classes. The 2005 Crufts judge complained about cheeks resembling a squirrel with a mouthful of nuts and the loss of 'raciness'. A 2004 championship show judge commented on incorrect feet, a lack of depth in the brisket and 'disgusting' teeth! No doubt these dogs were bred from. But I know of show dogs that regularly work, both here and abroad, in this breed. One day an underground earth-dog test might be introduced, as it has in North America and on mainland Europe, which would provide a far better examination for a breed of sporting terrier.

Working Interest
It is good to learn that terrier fanciers from the hunting world are active in this newly recognized breed. Norman Handy worked and whipped in for the Warwickshire Beagles in the 1950s and later hunted with the West Warwickshire Farmers Foxhounds. He started showing the breed in the 1960s and has three bitches that are champions in the KC-recognized breed. Recently two experienced terrier-men's wives were in

the Parson Russell Terrier Club with champion dogs that have won at Crufts.

Fanciers of Jack Russells, whatever the precise title of their breed, face a dilemma. Those solely interested in the working dog fear alteration to their type carried out for cosmetic reasons only, and have good cause for concern. The shortened legs, lengthened coat and heavier head inflicted on the show Sealyham, the profusion of coat and near absence of leg-length in the Skye and the abbreviated stride, fore and aft, bestowed on the show Fox Terrier, are all sound reasons to be suspicious of KC-recognition and the triumphing of show ring criteria. On the other hand, for those anxious to establish an officially decreed breed description, a standardized appearance and the perpetuation of their breed, registration with a kennel club makes sense, despite the regrettable loss of the English White Terrier from the KC's terrier list. There are many Parson Russell Terrier fanciers who strive hard to retain the working anatomy in their breed and they deserve admiration. Of all our native terrier breeds, this one merits being perpetuated as a working dog.

An admirable strain of Russells (which also appear in the KC show rings) has been developed by Roger Bigland, once professional terrier-man to the Cotswold, then the Heythrop. He favoured a rough-coated dog, saying, 'I like them twelve to fourteen inches and they have to be narrow...I tend to use bitches as the dog side of my strain is inclined to be a bit aggressive… I've tried Borders, but I haven't got the patience, they enter so slowly, and the Lakeland is too hard for what I want'. He kept at least five couples of entered terriers, expecting to get seven seasons from them. His terriers were widely respected by MFHs.

Deep in Dorset, Eddie Chapman, a founder member of the Jack Russell Club of Great Britain in 1974, maintained a large kennel of the breed. He has been quoted as saying:

> When it was first put at a meeting of the Jack Russell Club of Great Britain that we should consider applying for Kennel Club registration, many of us predicted that the Kennel Club would ruin the terrier within ten to fifteen years. Well, how wrong can you get; they have ruined it from day one and in the worst possible way: by allowing pure Lakeland terriers to be recognized as so-called Parson Jack Russells. The Lakeland/Jack Russell cross produces a white terrier with a much bigger, stronger head than the pure Jack Russell and a thick coat which – from the showing point of view – is seen as a great improvement.

The Jack Russell is now more popular than the Fox Terrier.

The Importance of Anatomy

Eddie Chapman has stressed the importance of chest dimensions in his dogs, stating:

> A Jack Russell must be able to get where a fox goes, so the chest of a working Jack Russell must be in comparison to that of the fox. Many of the best old Jack Russell strains have a sort of collapsible rib cage, like a cat or a fox, which gives the terrier a tremendous advantage over a solid-chested terrier when trying to manoeuvre in a tight hole.

When the Jack Russell Club of Great Britain was founded, the standard height was set at between and 9 and 15in to cover as large a gene pool as possible. Some years later, it was found that this range had drawbacks, so the minimum height was increased to 10in. Eddie Chapman observed, 'We should have dropped it [the maximum height] back down to 14in; there are very few terriers over 14in that can get to a fox in a tight place.' The Kennel Club's guidance on the Parson Russell Terrier's height now reads: 'Ideal

Hunt terriers waiting for work.

Ferreting rabbits with a Russell-type terrier; early nineteenth-century coloured print.

height at withers: dogs 14in, bitches 13in… lower heights are acceptable, however.'

In Australia, a few years back, there was a proposal that the short-legged Jack Russells there should be separately named as 'Australian Jack Russells'. In the USA such dogs are called 'stable terriers'. In the UK there was disquiet when the KC wanted to allow the two Jack Russell clubs to register their stock with them, presumably to widen the gene pool. For those who work their terriers the main criterion will always be: can it work? Worries about opening registers, a loss of raciness, squirrel-mouths and the like matter less. Enormous importance too is often placed in the show ring, both KC and country show ones, on 'spannability', that is, whether the exhibit's rib cage can be enclosed in the combined span of the judge's hands. For me, the flexibility of the torso, the set of shoulder, the strength of loin, the hind angulation and, most of all, the *spirit* of the dog is much more vital. As a veteran sportsman recorded, on sporting terriers, in 1802: 'Size is not so indispensable as strength, but invincible fortitude must be equal to both.'

Where sporting people gather they also take their dogs. In recent years the dogs have differed. A decade ago Kennel Club breeds were the general choice at point-to-points, gymkhanas, hunter trials, and other occasions at which the country set meet. Nowadays at those same functions, attended by those same people, the working terriers known as Jack Russells generally outnumber all the long-established varieties added together. They have become a cult of people who know their stuff about the countryside.

Wilson Stephens, editor of *The Field*, in
his foreword to *The Jack Russell Terrier*
by Betty Smith (Witherby, 1970)

The fact that Russell, like other sportsmen who valued gameness rather than looks, refused to adhere strictly to standards already laid down paved the way for some of his less scrupulous successors to claim that their dogs were 'Jack Russell' terriers when in fact they bore little resemblance to the parson's original strain.

*Hunting Parson: The Life and Times of the Reverend
John Russell* by Eleanor Kerr (Herbert Jenkins, 1963)

The English Griffon: the Airedale

'The Airedale terrier cannot claim much in the way of ancient origin, as it was not until about 1853 that Wilfred Holmes crossed the local terriers ... with the otterhounds, in order to produce a larger and gamer type...'. So wrote Frank Townend Barton, in *The Kennel Encyclopaedia* (1930). This has long been the perceived wisdom on the origin of this distinguished breed, but I am not convinced. Barton, who did not conduct his own research but relied on other writers' work, was repeating the words of Leighton and others from the early twentieth century. I suspect that Yorkshire sportsmen blended the blood of the old broken-coated black and tan working terrier with that of the northern breed of black and tan wire-haired hound, sometimes called the Lancashire Otterhound. The Otterhound, as we know it, did not emerge as a breed until after 1880. The classic Otterhound coat colours did not appear in the emergent breed of Airedale, and its coat texture does not feature in the breed, although early specimens were often goat-haired.

A Terrier in a Landscape *by A. Duke; the old broken-coated black and tan terrier was once very much the terrier of England.*

For me, it is an enormous pity that this breed of Airedale ever became dubbed a terrier. That word should be reserved for earth-dogs, dogs that go to ground. In France the Airedale would have been called a griffon, a rough-coated hunting dog, a hound if anything. This breed should not be regarded as a terrier

A Terrier and a Spaniel *by J. Grimson (1870); such a rough-coated terrier was commonplace then.*

'Turk' by L. Waller (1891); typical Airedale foundation breeding material.

Black and tan wire-coated terrier of 1858.

and should not be judged by those more familiar with the breeds developed to go to ground. But above all, it should be regarded as a sporting dog, with the anatomy to allow it to function in the field. It is of course a remarkably versatile breed, able to undertake manifold tasks. My interest in them came from Colonel Richardson's use of them as service-dogs nearly a hundred years ago. This interest was increased when, as a young teenager working for my local vet, I went with him to visit Molly Harbut's world-famous 'Bengal' kennel of superlative Airedales, at Bathampton, near Bath.

A Versatile Working Dog

Airedales were used extensively in the Russo-Japanese War and First World War as sentry dogs, messengers and ambulance dogs, emerging as the best all-round war dog breed. Police forces from as far afield as American cities and Paris elected to use them too. Colonel Richardson, who was Commandant of the British War Dog School in 1916, recorded:

> I have owned and trained at one time or other, nearly every kind of dog suitable for guarding work ... but, as a result of all my work of years, it is my considered judgement, that for all-round watching and guarding work, the most reliable dog in size and character is the Airedale Terrier.

In 1920 the Airedale was the most popular breed in the USA. Over 5,000 were registered here in each of the years 1924, 1925 and 1926. Nowadays only a fifth

of that number is registered each year, against 14,000 GSDs and 5,000 Rottweilers. In 1949, John Watson MacInnes FZS wrote a book entitled *Guard Dogs*, which referred to Richardson's work, but made no mention at all of the Airedale, mainly recommending German breeds.

More honestly, in *Hounds and Dogs* (1932), a volume of the Lonsdale Library, Captain Banes Condy wrote: 'No book dealing with Sporting Dogs would be complete without mention of the Airedale Terrier', going on to state he had exported them to India to hunt jackal in pack 'where his good nose, hardihood, lasting capabilities and strength make him invaluable'. Banes Condy emphasized one point: 'People, both breeders and novices, have somehow or another got it into their heads that an Airedale must be a rich black and tan in colour. This is erroneous'. In the world of kennel clubs all over the world today black and tan is the favoured breed colour; in the United States some breeders favour all-black and all-red Airedales, no doubt shocking the breed-purists or coat-colour devotees.

An early fancier, E. Bairstow of Bradford, wrote, around 1890:

> In all my experience, I never came across any person who ever had an Airedale terrier over twelve months who would utter one word of disparagement against him... This breed owes its origin to the working or middle class inhabitants of Airedale and surrounding districts; take Bradford as the centre, and say about a 15 mile radius...

Do the good people who live in that catchment area now realize what their ancestors bequeathed to the sporting dog fraternity all over the world? Our precious sporting heritage slips away from us every year. Should not our Yorkshire-based breed devotees strive to celebrate such a local achievement? The towns of Rottweil and Leonberg would not miss such a chance! We promote their dogs with enthusiasm.

The Airedale in America

As a sporting dog, the Airedale has long been valued, mainly overseas. In *Hunting Dogs* (1909), the American sportsman-writer Oliver Hartley recorded: 'I have found out that the pure Airedale Terrier and the hound make the very best dogs for coon, lynx, mink, etc. Get a good Airedale and a good hound and you will have a pair of hounds hard to beat.' He went on to state that

American Airedales of 1905: Clonmel Royal Ruler and Colne Lucky Miss displaying the pin-wire coat.

Airedales were 'great water dogs and very hard workers and easily trained to hunt any kind of game. They are full of grit and fear nothing.' He further sang the breed's praises 'in hunting and dispatching coyotes, coons, badger and bay-lynx [reddish-brown lynx], any one of which is capable of putting up a good fight. Also he is a hunter, retriever, trailer of coon, 'possum, bear, wildcat, mink, coyote, deer, lynx, fox or small game.' That is some tribute from a highly experienced hunter, operating in difficult terrain.

In *The Coon Hunter's Handbook* (1952), another American sportsman, Leon Whitney, recommended the Airedale-hound cross, especially if a 'still-trailer' or

Airedale 'Colonel Warlock' of 1905; harsh-coated.

Described as 'The Airdale Terrier' in 'Stonehenge's' book The Dog *(1887).*

The Airedale champion Clonmel Terror of 1910; the closer coat and shorter broader head is apparent.

silent tracker was required. A third American sporting dog expert, Carl P. Wood, notes, in *The Gun Digest Book of Sporting Dogs*, the value of the Airedale-hound cross in hunting the black bear, a dangerous occupation for any dog. For Airedale blood to be so highly rated by three such experienced hunters is noteworthy. Meanwhile, all over Britain today there are under-exercised, unemployed but willing Airedales wasting away.

Field Testing
The all-round capability of the Airedale reminds me of the versatility of other comparable breeds, like the Schnauzers, the Smoushond, the Irish Wheaten and Kerry Blue Terriers and the Bouviers. A dog that can drive livestock, kill vermin, guard the farmstead and perhaps pick up in the shooting field too has enormous value to a cash-strapped farmer who isn't able to keep several breeds. Sadly, in Britain, the Airedale is largely ornamental. The experience of a man like Colonel Richardson is completely ignored as we rush to import more and more foreign breeds. It is comforting to learn of the work of the Airedale Club of America in promoting the field use of the breed.

This club, twenty years ago, formed a hunting/working committee to help promote and maintain the Airedale's innate hunting ability. In 1994, hunting tests and titles were conceived to test the breed in three areas. Firstly, the upland bird test requires the dog to find and flush two planted birds, retrieve a shot bird on land and complete one short water retrieve. Qualifying dogs receive the junior hunter-flushing certificate. In time, dogs can go on to earn senior titles by displaying greater proficiency in retrieving work. Secondly, the hunting dog retrieving test involves the retrieve of two chukars on land and two ducks on water, to earn in turn the junior, senior and master hunter-retriever certificate. Thirdly, the hunting dog fur test requires a dog to follow a pre-laid track of raccoon scent and to bark or bay its quarry when found, again to earn titles in order.

An Airedale qualifying in all three basic tests earns the title of junior hunter versatile or JHV, with senior and master titles also on offer. A few years ago, Moraine Prime Minister became the first show champion Airedale to earn the master hunter title in all three areas of expertise. It is so pleasing to learn of such a feat, as the Airedale is a sporting breed. I bet that Moraine Prime Minister does not have lifeless eyes! All dogs love to be useful. Every sporting breed needs a spiritual outlet and it is a shame that the British breed clubs are not giving their Airedales such stimulating activities. The 'English Griffon' would look very different if it had to prove itself in the field. I suspect too that the owner-dog bond would be enhanced as well. This is a sporting breed being neglected, an English breed not used by the English, who seem to regard showing the breed as the only worthwhile activity.

The North American Working Airedale Terrier Association promotes tracking, obedience and protection training, agility, search and rescue training

The Airedale was the pioneer for modern service-dog work.

and holds national workshops to develop the Airedale as a *working* breed. It favours a bigger dog too. Some Americans also breed black dogs and red dogs, not deemed acceptable by either the AKC or our KC. Our KC has, however, recognized the Russian Black Terrier, created by Russian geneticists utilizing Airedale blood – so a foreign terrier with a solid black coat is acceptable here, but not a native terrier breed displaying the black coat available from its own gene pool. Breeds like the Lancashire Heeler, the Dachshund, the Australian and Lakeland Terriers, the Bloodhound and the Pinscher are allowed to have either red or black and tan coats, but not the Airedale. This is hardly consistent, scarcely explicable and wholly irrational.

Design Issues

I am very disappointed by the Airedales I see in show rings, both here and at world shows. Their movement is restricted, especially by upright shoulders; the coat texture is woolly rather than hard, dense and wiry; the expression in the eyes is lifeless and compliant; the rear action lacks drive and the forehand is too 'fox-terrier' to be sound. I cannot understand the desire for a narrow front in a sporting dog that is hardly expected to 'go to ground'. Perhaps this is a penalty for the terrier classification. The strange pursuit too of a short back, even in the breed standard, is puzzling. Why does a hunting dog, around 2 feet at the withers, need a short back? I wonder if this desired requirement was simply copied from other terrier standards when the Airedale first came, later than some, as a breed onto the dog scene.

Nearly fifty years ago, the well-known Airedale judge Fred Cross was questioned on why he had awarded the challenge certificate to a bitch with what some fanciers considered to be a rather large head. He responded, admirably for me, with the words, 'She doesn't need to walk with her head!' Sound movement should always be a top priority in judging dogs. Fred Cross would not be pleased to see the high number of present-day Airedales that either step short in front or reach forward with a Hackney action, both caused by faulty front assemblies. But in so many breeds nowadays across the various groups, upright shoulders and short upper arms are giving dogs uncharacteristic, even flawed movement. You don't see many Foxhounds with these faults, as they have to function.

In America, the Southern/ROC Airedales, bred by Southern Drach Herrera in New Mexico, and all DNA-tested, come from old Mount View and Mooreland lines; she now has eight generations of solid-black, 27in, 90lb dogs, some having successfully hunted cougar and bear. For this she has received nothing but stigmatization and vilification from traditional Airedale breeders there. Not much prizing of genetic diversity in this breed! Which would you prefer, a sound strapping dog over the breed's weight limit or an officially acceptable unsound dog within the breed's stipulated weight? Why be prejudiced against really good dogs on weight and colour alone? Let two authorities on breeds of dog of eighty years ago have the last word on colour in this breed. Writing on early Airedales, Walter S. Glynn wrote: 'A real black and tan coat was not to be seen among them; all were possessed of the blue-grey colour, some darker than others'; while Theo Marples claimed, 'In the matter of colour, black-and-tan or grizzle-and-tan is the correct colour, but, as in the horse, a good Airedale can hardly be a bad colour.' Perhaps now is the time to concentrate not on colour but on good Airedales. This is an underrated, unfashionable, under-used breed truly worthy of promotion.

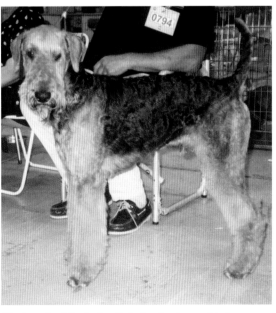

The show Airedale of today displaying the ultra-straight front now desired.

It is so good to learn that there are sporting people here, like lurcher and terrier owner Penny Taylor, who are well aware of this breed's field prowess and encouraging their use. In Hungary they are being used to hunt wild boar and for flushing birds where the bush is too thick for the pointers. I understand that Airedale-owning sportsmen can even train their dogs at 'boar-parks', fenced-off areas of woodland where the boars live free to roam. No doubt one day we will have their electronic equivalent here.

The Airedale terrier being an animal intended to travel fast it is essential to have a good 'roadway' between his legs, as in a horse; if he possesses this he is almost certain to be a good mover. As to coat, I like the head, front, and quarters, including the legs and feet, to be dark orange tan, and the saddle black, or only slightly grizzled; the texture of coat should be very hard, and lie flat.

Thorp's ideal Airedale Terrier from *The Twentieth Century Dog* by Herbert Compton (1904)

The tractability of the Terrier and the Airedale in particular may be judged by an advertising catalogue published periodically by a large Airedale kennel during the 1920s. This catalogue offered Airedales trained to suit the purchaser. The list of pursuits for which they could be trained was as follows: police work, farm dogs, for sheep or cattle; hunting dogs for bear, wolf, fox, deer, wildcat, lynx, skunk, coon, opossum, etc.; water retrievers for duck, geese, rail, plover and snipe; and of course dogs for the largest market, pets. From this listing it is apparent that there is little an Airedale cannot do…

The Book of All Terriers by John T. Marvin (Howell Book House, New York, 1971)

THE BULL TERRIER

Methinks, too, that the modern Bull-terrier has lost much of its character, and that touch of the devil which the old-timers used to display. Mark you, I do not mean savagery. No dog should be 'a savage', certainly not a Bull-terrier, which should be – and generally is – an affectionate and good-natured creature; but he should be able to take his own part when grossly insulted or assaulted. This trait should show itself in the dog's bearing and expression, and that is just lacking in some of the 'moderns'.

Dogs and I by Major Harding Cox (Hutchinson, 1928)

Bull Terrier depicted by W. Weekes just over a century ago; this illustrates the original head of the breed.

White Bull Terriers portrayed by Arthur Wardle in 1898 – handsome, unexaggerated dogs.

We once had a breed of dog, created here in Britain but eventually known throughout the British Empire, admired for its bravery, respected for the staunchness of its character, revered for its indomitable spirit and popular, not just because of these qualities, but because it was also robust, unexaggerated, sensibly constructed and stable in temperament. Once its dog-fighting ancestry had been bred out, this breed, the Bull Terrier, became rather more than the Bill Sykes of the dog world, with its blood being utilized to inject gameness into other breeds, from the heelers of Australia to the hunting mastiffs of Argentina. Referred to early on in its history as the bull-and-terrier, from its ingredients of terrier and Bulldog, this no-nonsense

Alken's depiction of the Bull-and-Terrier, c.1830.

breed seemed the perfect companion for growing boys and the feared adversary of house-thieves. Writing in the 1890s, the dog writer 'Idstone' reported: 'In the country house he is almost indispensable, as he is the resolute and determined enemy of vermin, and an efficient, vigilant guard to stables and outbuildings. His admirable form, [combines] in an exact proportion the frame best suited for activity, endurance, pace'. An outcross to the Dalmatian in its evolution gave the Bull Terrier an affinity with horses and the instinct to follow carriages.

The infusion of the English White Terrier's blood softened the dog-fighting instincts but the courage and stoicism remained. James Hinks of Birmingham is generally regarded as the creator of the all-white Bull Terrier at the end of the nineteenth century, with his sons continuing his work. It had, however, been the practice of working terrier enthusiasts to outcross their dogs to the Bulldog every fifth generation or so to instil gameness. Some early Bull Terrier breeders are also alleged to have used Whippet and Pointer blood to achieve the desired conformation. No breeder wanted his dogs to be called bulldoggy or whippety and so the shape of the skull assumed importance. Many people believe that the miniature variety of this breed is a manufactured addition, but the first Bull Terrier champion, Nelson, owned by S.E. Shirley, the first chairman of the Kennel Club, weighed under 16lb. Hicks himself had miniatures, one called Madman, weighing only 10lb.

Bull Terrier of today, showing no 'stop'.

Emergence of Type

The description of the Bull Terrier in 1896 produced by its breed club, established nine years earlier, specified the head 'should be long, flat, and wide between the ears, tapering to the nose, without cheek-muscles. There should be a slight indentation down the face, without a "stop" between the eyes'. Winning dogs at the early shows had heads roughly answering this description. A definite type emerged, based on a determined eye, a strong jaw and overall symmetry. Sketched by Arthur Wardle in the 1890s, the breed had a confident, athletic, self-assertive look about it, with the head of what might be termed a strong terrier. In *The Illustrated Book of the Dog* (1881), Vero Shaw described the head of the Bull Terrier as 'flat, wide between the ears, and wedge-shaped; that is, tapering from the sides of the head to the nose; no stop or indentation between the eyes is permissible, and the cheekbones should not be visible.' Prophetically, Vero Shaw complained about judges: 'We see, show after show, dogs gaining prizes in these classes which do not show one atom of *Terrier* character in their composition' and goes on to describe such dogs as 'cow-faced wretches'.

Detrimental Changes

The early years of the new century saw three major changes to this breed, which were each to have a significant effect on the breed. First of all came a striving to develop a better-shaped uncropped ear, which has given us the prick ear of today. Secondly, in a effort to

Bull Terriers Badger Hunting by C. Towne (c.1820); strong-headed dogs without exaggeration.

re-instil some of the gameness once famous in the breed, a back-cross to the coloureds (called Staffordshires) was undertaken, leading to the wider range of colours in the breed today. And, thirdly, in 1914, the first unwisely worded Standard of Perfection was introduced. This was the first time the words 'gladiator of the canine race' were used for the breed, now dropped in the recent KC review of potentially damaging descriptions. Sadly, the wording of the breed standard regarding the head changed quite dramatically. The Bull Terrier's head was henceforth expected to appear 'oval, almost egg shape' with a profile 'almost an arc from the occiput to the tip of the nose. The more down-faced the better'. For the first time in the long history of the dog, a breed was required to have an egg-shaped head. The reason for such a unique and unprecedented feature has never been stated. The Bull Terrier already had a clear identity and an established type when this rewording was agreed, so it could not have been to create a prototype.

Writing on the Bull Terrier before the Second World War, Hogarth described the foreface with this analogy: 'the curve of the profile should be "Roman",

as in, say, the Border, Leicester and Cheviot breeds of sheep'. So we now had a redoubtable British breed of dog, renowned all over the world for its guts and gameness, needing to have its head resembling that of a sheep. Why a breed created from a blend of Bulldog and terrier should suddenly need a foreface like a sheep has never been explained. If you took a pedigree Bull Terrier into a contemporary show ring without an egg-shaped head, you would be laughed out of the ring. Yet in 1926, a noted breeder, Mrs D.H. Robbs, edited a book entitled *The Bull Terrier Handbook*, published by The Perry-Vale Press, which pictured more than fifty Bull Terriers of that time, including such notable dogs as Ch Galalaw Benefactor, Ch Hades Cavalier and HK McCausland's Wildfire, as well as some from Mrs Robb's well-known Cylva kennel: not one of them featured the egg-shaped head demanded by the breed standard of that time.

The breed standard of the Bull Terrier, as authorized by the Kennel Club today, now includes under 'characteristics' these words: 'A unique feature is a downfaced, egg-shaped head'. This so-called 'unique feature' has only been a feature for seventy years or so;

Powerful prototypal Bull Terriers.

The Bull Terrier Fire Chief of 1901 by F.C. Clifton, with a balanced, symmetrical anatomy.

Lyndon Ingles's Bull Terrier Hinks at ten months, a beautifully balanced, athletic dog.

for fifty years before that it was not a feature at all. Such an absurd shape did not characterize the prototypal dogs; James Hinks, his sons and other early breeders – S.E. Shirley, E.H. Adcock, R.J. Hartley and J.H. Ryder would be greatly ashamed to see their dogs betrayed in this way. Tom Horner, who knew as much about Bull Terriers as anyone in the twentieth century, has written on this subject: 'The filled-up downfaced head is individual to Bull Terriers... No one knows exactly how it came into the breed, Hink's original white did not have it'. In other words, it was definitely not an original feature of the breed. It is an old tactic to invent new words in order to blur issues or try to justify the unjustifiable. The word 'downface' has no meaning; it was coined to legitimize an uncharacteristic, undesirable feature that developed in this breed. Horner also wrote: 'On balance it seems likely that the filled-up downface is the product of skilled breeding'. I am not sure that it wasn't the product of unskilled breeding by those without the touch of James Hinks and afraid to outcross to remove a strong alien feature cropping up in their stock. Far easier (and defeatist!) to authorize it. Then along came the Kennel Club and legalized it.

Perhaps cynically, one can detect the hand of either one wealthy dominant breeder, or a group of leading fanciers at that time, without the skill to prevent a certain shape of skull developing in their stock. Their predecessors would have probably used outside blood to correct such a tendency but in the modern world of the pedigree dog, such sacrilege cannot be permitted:

the gene pool is closed. This is in spite of the skilled, informed outcrossing practised by such master breeders as Millais, with the Basset Hound Brough, with the bloodhound Graham, with the Irish wolfhound and those who re-created the Cavalier King Charles spaniel. Such breeders never imagined for a moment that their dogs had been stabilized in a physical mould for all time. If alive, they would have bred for renewed type with whatever blood provided this. An outcross to the American Staffordshire Terrier, a beautifully symmetrical dog, with a balanced, unexaggerated head, could so easily restore true type in this most British of British terriers.

The simple fact is that this 'downface' should never have been allowed to develop in this quite admirable breed; it disfigures a famous dog, it attracts ridicule from the general public, it detracts from the symmetry and athleticism desired in such a breed and its mere existence exposes a breach of the original standard laid down by those who first developed this distinguished breed. It is an exaggeration, and as exaggerations tend to end up exaggerating themselves, in time the head of the breed will look quite monstrous. It is likely to 'morph' into a globe, with no protection for the dog's eyes and not enough room for normal teeth. Do we truly want a globe-headed Bull Terrier with its eyes popping out and poor dentition?

The dog-owning public is coming to its own conclusion. In 1972 there were twice as many Staffordshire Bull Terriers registered as there were Bull

Polecat and Terriers,
coloured engraving of
1835; this breed seems
to have lost its
sporting role.

Lord Brownlow's Bull Terriers of 1831 depicted by J. Ferneley – superb canine athletes.

Terriers; in 1988 there were three times as many; in 1998 there were four times as many. Twenty or so years ago, I wrote to one of the dog papers expressing my concern not just over the egg-shaped head, but also over the piggy-eyes and stiff movement prevalent in the breed. In response I got a very patronizing letter back from the most influential Bull Terrier breeder of the day, which in essence said, 'mind your own business, leave such judgements to us'. The well-being and conservation of our precious native breeds of dog, part of our national heritage, is far too important a matter to be left in the hands of breed-point faddists. Every breeder of pedigree dogs should keep in his mind the words of the great foxhound breeder 'Ikey' Bell, in *The Foxhound's Prayer*:

> Remember that your stewardship
> Spells trustee to our race.
> The duty now before you
> Is not to 'mess us up',
> And not go running riot
> To gain some silver cup.

Respecting the Breed

I go to 'alternative' dog shows, unlicensed by the KC, and see what are termed 'Irish Staffies' that look exactly like the old prints of our renowned Bull Terrier. Lyndon Ingles of Tredegar has kept the faith and perseveres with the classic type of white Bull Terrier; his dog, aptly named 'Hinks', is as good a specimen of the breed as you are likely to find. This breed used to be owned by gruff characters who didn't set much store on conforming – just as bull-and-terrier owners didn't in the nineteenth century! Our Bull Terrier is a very special British breed and it is being ruined by misguided show breeders who have no regard for the breed's classic physique and truly typical head. Any admirer of our native breeds of dog, especially one as characterful as this one, should frown when they see this travesty being paraded as the real thing. Come on, terrier-men of Britain, let's put this right!

Show breeders seem to overlook the fact that their breed was once very much a sporting terrier – long before it was a fighting dog. It is not right to perpetuate the gladiator and not respect the field dog. There is an abundance of antique prints and old paintings depicting the bull-and-terrier in action in the field. Breeders

need to look at the American Pit Bull Terrier to spot the genuine anatomy for the pit; whatever their misuse by man, this breed resemble powerful canine athletes, not waddling brutes. They are in fact more like the old depictions of the bull-and-terrier ancestors of the contemporary breed of Bull Terrier than the show Bull Terrier. It is vital for show breeders of Bull Terriers to think about what they want their breed to resemble – the fighting dog or the sporting dog?

> Previous to the time when my duties led to my living entirely in the jungles, I always kept one or two good bull-terriers for encounters with jackals, wild cats, etc. On the few occasions when I had the chance of using these dogs at formidable beasts they so distinguished themselves as to impress me with a high opinion of their prowess, and of their ability to overcome larger animals than might be thought possible.
> *Thirty Years among the Wild Beasts of India*
> by G.P. Sanderson (Allen & Co., 1896)

The Staffordshire Bull Terrier

The Staffordshire Bull Terrier is a very special breed, yet one still being punished by ill-informed legislators due to its fighting dog origins. Its famed courage, tenacity and stoicism, once prized in the fight-rings and specifically bred for, now counts against it. The breed is a victim of its own fanciers, with even a show breeder being convicted of dog-fighting offences. Those who misuse them seem to hide behind the good qualities in the breed, perhaps envying their dogs their courage and perseverance in adversity, whilst encouraging combativeness and savageness, often to exhibit their own desire for manliness. It is shameful to pose as being heavily masculine, willing to fight any taker and able to sustain pain unflinchingly, but only through your dog. The current craze for 'status dogs', in which young thugs parade their muscular dogs as trophies, at the same time very transparently exhibiting their own insecurity, lack of self-belief and inability to fend for themselves, is now receiving a police response. The canine victims, the dogs themselves, will often lose their lives; little lasting harm will come to their exploiters. Dog abuse can take so many forms but few breeds have suffered as

Bull Terriers of the Staffordshire type by E. Loder (1886).

American Staffordshire Terrier with superb shoulders.

A Staffordshire Bull Terrier depicted by G. Banham in the late nineteenth century, in repose but still hinting at great power.

American Pit Bull Terrier, a much maligned breed.

much from their own owners as the Bull Terrier from Staffordshire.

A colleague of mine, a great Stafford fan, has convincingly argued that the Stafford is the true bull-baiting dog, rather than the Bulldog, and if you look at depictions of dogs in the bull-baiting contests, they are shown far more Stafford-like than Bulldog-like. Bull baiting was very much a Black Country 'sport', as was organized dog-fighting at one time. But, as my colleague also argues, the dogs of the fight-pits were more like today's English Bull Terrier size than the smaller Stafford, although their weights did vary widely. The American Pit Bull Terrier, so widely misused, has an ancestry in bull terriers from Ireland rather than Staffordshire, if experts like Bob Stevens (*Dogs of Velvet and Steel: Pit Bulldogs – A Manual for Owners*, 1985), George Armitage (*Thirty Years with Fighting Dogs*, 1935) and Louis Colby (*Book of the American Pit Bull Terrier*, 1997) are correct.

Type and Size

Physical type has long varied in the breed. In his foreword to the book on the breed, which he edited in 1952, Major Count V.C. Hollender wrote:

There were so many dogs sold as Staffords in a boom after the 14–18 war, where Whippets, mongrels, and any small, smooth-coated dogs were used as sires. The modern-coloured Bull Terrier was revived in the same way, and one of the best breeders who ever lived (I refer to Harry Monk, of the Bloomsbury prefix) informed me that Greyhounds, Whippets, etc., were introduced in the modern product. Hence the light, leggy specimens that were first produced.

Is it at all surprising therefore that light, leggy specimens still turn up today, to be dubbed 'Irish Staffies' by their fanciers but worryingly attracting the attention of our leading animal charity as 'being of pit bull type'! If the men of Staffordshire can create their own type of bull terrier from existing stock then I can't see why other fanciers shouldn't be free to favour theirs. The size of the breed has long drawn debate.

Not surprisingly, a very different technique was required by the bull-baiting dogs from that of the fighting dogs used in the pits. A Staffordshire Bull Terrier dog should weigh between 28 and 38lb. In *Book of the American Pit Bull Terrier* Colby describes nearly all the most successful dogs in his many years

A well-bred Amstaff at a World Dog show.

A superbly-constructed 'Irish Staffie'.

in dog-fighting. His father John bred and sold around 5,000 dogs. He gives the weights of many of his fighting dogs: Pilot 27lb, Tiger 35lb, Boxer 33lb, Spring 31lb, Grip 29lb, Major 33lb, Pupsy 33lb, Peter 33lb, Tinker 38lb, Brandy 31lb, with the champion fighting dog of Mexico in 1922 weighing 39lb. Yet the RSPCA considers that an 'Irish Staffie' appreciably bigger than that poses a bigger danger than a dog the size of a pure-bred Staffie?

In his instructive but horrific book *Dogs of Velvet and Steel*, Bob Stevens writes phrases like: 'Lil...is in excellent shape... She is exactly on the weight she is supposed to be which is 36lb ... she has the ideal conformation for pit fighting' and 'the smaller dog is an *extremely* hard biter and very *powerful*'. In his book *Thirty Years with Fighting Dogs*, written in the early 1900s, Armitage writes of his lengthy experience with dog-fighting; he favoured a shorter-legged dog which went in low. Colby recommended a dog that he called the chest dog, which he considered the best style in the pit, which went in low with a 'boring-in style'. Why then does the RSPCA look out for leggy Staffies as an increased sign of being bred for fighting?

Writing in that admirable publication, *Celebrating Staffordshire Bull Terriers* by Steve Stone with Vic Pounds (Pynot Publishing, 2007), veteran breeder Jo Hemstock provides the view that: 'There is no real controversy over size. The Staffordshire Bull Terrier is

The 'Irish Staffie' type, full of sporting instincts.

Classic Staffie head (photo: Nicola Flynn).

a medium-sized dog that measures between 14–16 inches and weighs 28–38 pounds. Most of today's winners, and virtually all winning bitches, appear to comply closely with the limits set by the Standard.' Her daughter Sara, now an experienced judge herself, on an earlier page wrote: 'I would also say that the dogs of our preferred type have remained fairly consistent down through the decades and have survived both "bully" and "leggy" fads.' A judge at a championship show of 2008 did however state in the show critique, 'I would like to see more dogs closer to the 38lb mark as required in the Standard.' It is not always easy to find admiration from judges over the state of movement in the breed, a far more disturbing sign.

Temperament

One characteristic possessed in abundance even by the highly combative fighting dogs was their reliability *with people*; they were essentially family dogs, brought up with children. The ill-founded Dangerous Dogs Act of 1991, a knee-jerk response to dog attacks on humans, has victimized the Stafford, totally without sound reason, and entirely because the Kennel Club advised the Home Office to make the Act breed-

specific. Now, a thousand dead dogs later, they have changed their minds, without having the magnanimity to admit their crucial error. For any dog to be condemned to death because of its appearance alone is fatally flawed. Vets, despite not being trained to identify breeds of dog, RSPCA inspectors, despite being appointed to prevent cruelty *to* animals, and policemen with insufficient knowledge of dogs, have all been regarded as 'expert' witnesses in courts where blameless Staffords have been 'identified' as being 'of pit bull type'. Such activity has brought shame on our once-respected legal system. As with humans, it is behaviour which poses the threat, never appearance; the importance of temperament in the breed of Staffordshire Bull Terrier has never mattered more.

In *The Staffordshire Bull Terrier* (1943), breed expert H.N. Beilby BSc, a member of the Kennel Club, wrote in his chapter on character and temperament, of three types of Stafford: the outgoing, companionable type, the more introspective but more self-reliant type;

The Staffie type portrayed by L.G. Jadin (1805–82).

Two Staffordshire-type Bull Terriers and a Dachshund depicted by F. Adam (1865).

and the small group 'which is suspicious and of unreliable temper'. He comments that 'foolish and cruel treatment of a young dog can have the effect of turning an otherwise normal individual into a member of this [third] group, and there is little doubt that in past days many Staffordshires were so treated in a misguided effort to develop their fighting ability. I say "misguided" because a vicious dog is not necessarily a good fighting dog.' Neither is it ever likely either to make an acceptable pet, especially in a family. I believe that in the 1970s the RAF canine training school did a trial on the breed as attack dogs, perhaps because of their strong 'bite and grip' capability, but concluded that even training would not induce a Stafford to bite a human being.

Athletic Ability

One chapter in *Celebrating Staffordshire Bull Terriers* begins with:

> Among purebreds, the Staffordshire Bull Terrier stands out as being an athletic breed, a fact all too few

Staffords fanciers fully appreciate and those owning most other breeds seldom realize. The Stafford's athletic abilities remain a key factor in its continuing to be a *foremost all-purpose dog* and so bred-in-the-bone that not even many generations of being bred primarily for show has exerted much detrimental effect.

If you study the critiques from recent championship dog shows, where it is claimed that only the best appear, you see a different picture, however. Here are some of the judges comments: 'many exhibits carry far too much weight … many exhibits displayed a distinct lack of rib and forechest'; 'narrow fronts and bodies also upright pasterns'; 'shoulders and fronts have deteriorated alarmingly'; 'poor rear movement with many lacking drive'; 'I do feel that we need to work our way back to a correct blend of bull and terrier not one or the other'; 'rear movement was poor'; and 'I was quite alarmed by the number displaying features which depart so much from the Standard that there is a real possibility of breed identity being lost if we continue down this path.'

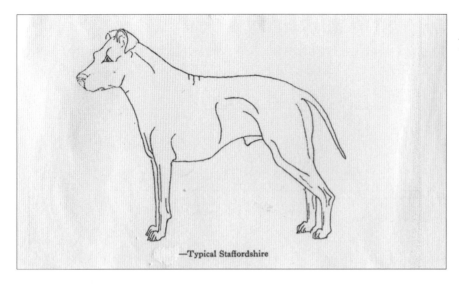

—Typical Staffordshire

Typical Staffordshire from H.N. Beilby's The Staffordshire Bull Terrier *(1943).*

Whilst it is good to see the honesty in such remarks, it is worrying to read such consistent criticism of some features over several years. I see Staffords in the show ring with very poor feet, feet more suitable for a Whippet, and they win! I see many without muscular development, which in this breed never looks impressive. An unfit, waddling Stafford looks dreadful and insults the heritage of the breed. A poorly constructed Stafford will never move well. Writing in the first issue of the magazine *The Stafford* in 1948, the respected breeder Jimmie Russ stated that:

> The foundation of the dog is the skeletal structure… Too heavy bone is usually coarse, and being heavy is slower in movement. Light bone on the other hand is fast but lacks strength. Aim for good, clean, straight bone, with neither frailty nor coarseness. Aim for quality, which is neither coarseness nor lightness. Your Stafford will lack the speed of a Whippet, but he will be surprisingly fast in the manner of a first-class welter-weight boxer.

That last phrase sums up this breed for me; the Stafford should be the welter-weight of the dog breeds, fit, muscular, fast on its feet, alert and full of vigour. This is a very special breed, whose blood is rightly prized in a number of other breeds or types. Staffordshire has given us a quite admirable breed of dog and one that needs our support more now than ever before.

Popularity brings another risk in its train. There is a class of breeder whom one might call the 'Exaggerationists', who, when told that the Staffordshire should have a wide skull, would proceed – without pausing to consider the reasons for this – to breed for skulls like Bulldogs, or cheeks like sideboards, which, if established, would completely spoil the balance, symmetry and usefulness of the breed. I have seen a few dogs of this type and they were invariably sluggish and slow, lacking in that alert vitality that is perhaps the most important asset of the variety. Remember the key-notes 'strength' and 'agility'; you can exaggerate both of those together (but not one at the expense of the other) as much as you like, but let us set our faces resolutely against the development of useless and unnecessary points.

The Staffordshire Bull Terrier by
H.N. Beilby (Blackie & Son, 1943)

CHAPTER 2

BREED DEVELOPMENT ELSEWHERE

The Scottish Breeds

The shepherds know the holes and caves where the foxes breed, and during the winter and spring these are all systematically visited. Two neighbouring farmers, perhaps, may join forces with the gamekeeper representing the shooting tenant. They will be attended on their visitation by ten or twelve little terriers of all sorts, upon whom the real burden of work falls. These dogs are a very mixed lot, not much to look at maybe, but keen on their work for all that…

A painting by G.M. Dundas from 1910, titled A Scottie; *the previous year the West Highland White Terrier had entered the KC's stud book.*

Dandie-dinmonts there are, of all colours, real Skye terriers – not the corpulent creatures of the shows, tousy as an unshaven poodle – smooth English terriers, Irish terriers, black Scotch terriers. And a hideous row they unite in raising.

Those words by D.L. Cameron, in a piece entitled 'Fox-hunting in the Highlands', and published in *The*

Dandie Dinmont Terrier of today.

Scottish Terriers of 1900, much less heavily coated.

An 1835 depiction of what appear to be the ancestors of Cairn and Scottish Terriers out otter-hunting.

Badminton Magazine in 1901, indicate very clearly an admiration for the working terriers used in Scotland, as well as a certain scorn for show dogs, even at that stage of exhibiting sporting terriers from Scotland.

Historic Type

For centuries, Scotland has had small rough-haired terriers, reference being made as far back as 1436 by John Leslie, in his *History of Scotland*, to a 'dog of low height, which, creeping into subterranean burrows, routs out the foxes, badgers, martens, and wild cats from their lurking places and dens.' H.D. Richardson, writing in 1853, refers to three varieties of Scottish terriers, one

'sandy-red and rather high on the legs' and called the Highland Terrier; a second, the same size but 'with the hair somewhat flowing and much longer, which gives a short appearance to the legs. This is the prevailing breed of the Western Isles of Scotland'; and a third, 'the dog celebrated by Sir Walter Scott as the Pepper and Mustard or Dandie Dinmont breed'. From this account, you could be forgiven for thinking of the Cairn, the Scottie and the Westie as one breed, with the Skye and the Dandie also featuring as distinct breeds at that time.

Colonel Hamilton Smith, writing in Volume X of *The Naturalists' Library*, published in 1840, consid-

Clydesdale or Paisley Terriers of 1894 by A. Wardle.

West Highland White Terriers by K. Rashleigh (1923), displaying the harsher coat.

ered the Scottish Terrier to be the oldest representative of what he termed the cur dog race in Great Britain, stating:

> Our diminutive modern terrier, particularly the Scottish or rough-haired breed, is therefore the race we look upon as the most ancient dog of Britain… and in no part of Europe has the rough-haired breed retained so completely as in Britain all the traits which constitutes a typical species. No dog carries the head so high…

Despite the Colonel's scholarly researches, I am forever suspicious of Victorian writers on terriers: the latter were utilized by working men, unlike gundogs and hounds, so, while whole libraries have been written about hounds, not many books were devoted to terriers in previous centuries and not every distinguished writer of those times was familiar with terrier work, terrier-breeding and terrier construction.

In *The Scottish Terrier*, published by *Our Dogs* in the late 1920s, W.L. McCandlish recorded that:

> The Macdonalds of Skye had a preference for longer coated dogs, and hence the development began which has led by selection to the modern Skye Terrier. The Malcolms of Poltalloch found a small dog with a short head most suitable, and latterly, having a family liking for cream or white-coloured ones, the development of the West Highlander commenced. The type from which the modern Scottish Terrier came was probably domiciled in the Blackmount region of Perthshire, the Moor of Rannoch, and surrounding districts… That there was no cross-breeding among the Terriers of the Highlands is improbable in dogs kept entirely for work by men not particular about pedigree or appearance.

For those zealots who seek an ancient line of pure breeding in their Scottish terrier, those words are of significance.

Loss of Capability

Have the terrier breeds of Scotland lost their sporting heritage? The West Highland is a show ring favourite; the Cairn has a loyal following, with, I understand, at least one working terrier backer; the Skye could be lost to us within half a century. The Scottie is still with us but like the others has no discernible working activity. The Dandie Dinmont has, I believe, a tiny band of working devotees. Do any of them deserve to retain their sporting terrier tag? Working use apart, do these breeds still retain the anatomy to work? I despair when I hear a show breeder of these worthy and long-established breeds declare that 'he doesn't want his terriers to go to ground, so why get het up about the ability to do so?' So much for respecting the origins of your breed!

The great chronicler of Scottish dogs, D.J. Thomson Gray, wrote in 1903:

> Fanciers of recent years have tried to alter the original type of Terrier, by trying to engraft on a short cobby body a long, senseless-looking head, to get which they had to breed dogs almost, if not quite, twice the size of the original, and to alter the formation of the head… This straight-face craze began in Black-and-tan Terriers, extended to Fox-terriers, is now contaminating the Collie, and is threatening our national Scottish Terrier. Coats are also getting softer and more woolly in texture… reminding one of a cat's coat instead of a pig's, the bristles which resemble the true coat of the Scottish Terrier.

Again and again in our terrier breeds, you detect the abandonment of working criteria out of breeder indifference or ignorance. The show critiques of today regularly comment adversely on the faulty texture in terriers' coats; but who will change the preferences of those who have never seen a working terrier braving the elements day after day?

Two authors, sixty years apart, but both writing on sporting terriers, Pierce O'Conor and Brian Plummer, did not write gushingly about terriers from Scotland. On the Dandie, O'Conor wrote, 'They are now, I fear, little used for work, "at the tods and the brocks", more's the pity. The show bench Dandie is rather too heavy and too low to the ground for an active working dog.' Plummer wrote of the Dandie, 'It is in fact a pity that nobody is prepared to exploit the working qualities of the Dandie Dinmont for the type is still ideal for working below ground.' On the Scottish Terrier, O'Conor wrote, 'Today, he is "a thing of beauty and a joy for ever" no doubt, but alas! a poor workman.'

Plummer wrote of this breed, 'As to when the Scottish Terrier was last worked is yet another moot point.' He quoted Lucas, who noted the inability of the breed to work as a pack.

In her book on the Cairn Terrier, published by *Our Dogs* in 1937, Florence Ross wrote:

> Since he came into prominence, the Cairn has found favour with English MFHs, their pluck and tenacity being sufficient to recommend a trial. One of the first to be engaged in this work was Crotal, bred and owned by Lady Charles Bentinck, and who worked regularly with Lord Charles, when he was Master of the Croome. The Grafton, Worcestershire, Meynell and Oakley all testify to their utility.

Cairn Terriers of 1928 by F.M. Hollams; very workmanlike.

She went on to quote from a Highland sportsman's letter, which read: 'I would happily pit a good working Cairn against any fox up the side of a long steep face of rock, with only roughnesses to use for foothold… the Cairn is often required to make its way into the fox's lair, by a circuitous route, amongst small spaces between rocks,' going on to praise their 'well turned out forefeet'. Well turned-out forefeet are not exactly favoured in today's show ring, although the breed standard does expect 'slightly turned-out' ones. Cairns which work are sadly not exactly favoured either.

Short-legged terriers dig by throwing the earth to each side of them; turned-out feet allow them to do this. Longer-legged terriers throw the earth backwards through their back feet and need straight legs to accomplish this.

Scottish Terriers at Work

But the Cairn Terrier is being worked by at least one enthusiast, using stock from the Cam Cairn kennels. He found they packed well above ground when used as a family or with kennel mates, praising their work

A Dandie Dinmont by H.H. Couldery (c.1885); stiffer-coated and lacking the topknot of today's dog.

The Scottish Terrier of today,
much heavier-coated.

in heavy cover and their scenting ability when bushing. Not surprisingly, Scottish keepers used the bigger leggier terriers on the moors and smaller shorter ones for going to ground. Much is made by show breeders of size, shoulder height becoming more important than hunting instincts. An experienced Highland keeper wrote in a 1914 issue of *Dog Weekly*: 'Give me a medium-length back Cairn, strong hindquarters, good feet and not too short-legged.' In the 1930s Madame de Parseval of Charmont, Senlis (Ouse) in France was hunting otters with her pedigree Cairns,

The Skye Terrier depicted in an 1830 engraving.

one a show champion. Terrier-man Alf Rhodes of Darton near Barnsley, who died in 2003, was using a Dandie called Cindy (born 1973) right up to her eighth birthday; he worked several terrier breeds but swore by her. Yet in the early 1920s Gavin Haddon's renowned earth-dog and grandson of the famous Yellow Dirk, perpetuating E.B. Smith's legendary Blackett House strain, was considered to be the last of the working Dandies. A gamekeeper called Archie Dalrymple was using Skyes in pairs against vermin and otter in the late 1940s, favouring a 9in dog, much shorter than the 40in nose-to-tail dogs of today. Were these the last workers in these breeds?

Show Specimens

In his book on hunt terriers, Lucas wrote, 'It must not be assumed that the bench has ruined everything. That pluck still exists in the right type of Highland terriers.' He may well be right but pluck without the backing of the appropriate terrier physique is not by itself going to make a worker. The excessive coats, elongated spines and weak back ends of the show Skyes, the under-muscled Westies and open-coated Cairns, along with heavily coated Scotties and their overdone heads, don't offer much of an enticement to sporting terrier-men. Any enthusiast wishing to try the terriers of Scotland as workers would need to exercise great caution before choosing pedigree stock. Show ring judges in their post-show critiques in recent years have commented on pinning-in at the front and movement too close behind in Cairns, weak muzzles, poor front and hind movement, woolly coats and thin feet in Dandies, out at elbow, narrow and poor fronts in Scotties, 'Queen Anne' fronts and weak hind movement in Skyes, poor rear construction, straight stifles and upright shoulders in Westies, and with one Crufts judge even stating that the Cairns at the world's premier shows were 'not of sufficient quality to be called show dogs'!

It is of interest to note what breeders of Skye Terriers were writing in past times. In *The Kennel Gazette* of January 1892, James Pratt wrote:

> Many of the winning dogs this year are bred simply for money-making purposes… They are only large, coarse brutes, with donkey heads and ears, and cannot boast of one single drop of Skye blood in their veins. Ask any aged Highland gentleman or gamekeeper if they ever saw in the West Highlands, 40 years ago, such dogs as were awarded the prizes at most of the shows held this year? I say we have not improved these dogs as working terriers. They ought to do a 'day's work' just the same as the hard-haired Scotch Terriers. Can many of them do this? Decidedly not!

A year later in the same publication, Thomas Nolan was writing:

> There are no doubt certain good old breeders who really believe that the Skye Terrier ought to be a largish dog of 20–25lb or more in weight… No doubt also the huge ugly Skyes that we are complaining of are to some extent a recoil from the pretty little 'toys' that sometimes disfigure the show bench… Most certainly we do not want any little toys on our Skye benches. But still less do we want any *big* toys – those great soft shapeless masses that a genuine little terrier of 16lb or 18lbs would demolish in a moment.

The Kennel Club still publishes its *Gazette* but would never print such hard-hitting comments today; that attitude is perhaps one reason why the same comments could be made today.

In his book on the Scottish Terrier, W.L. McCandlish writes:

Two Terriers by R. Hedley (1881); unexaggerated dogs.

Dandie Dinmonts portrayed by C. Suhrlandt in 1885, still viewed as sporting dogs.

Over the formation of the forelegs considerable discussion has taken place. In early show days the majority of dogs were very bent at the pastern, and such were often also out at elbow or at shoulder. As the breed came into the hands and under the judicial eye of persons accustomed to Fox and other higher-legged terriers, importance began to be placed on straight fronts.

Once a fad becomes acceptable in the show ring few individuals have the strength to oppose it, even on sound anatomical grounds. The imposition of too straight a front demands, in the interests of balanced, co-ordinated movement alone, a straighter stifle at the back, as extension is restricted and front and rear stride has to be in harmony. McCandlish went on to write: 'Of two Scottish Terriers with equal sense and equal vitality, but one strong at the pastern and muscularly coupled at the loin, the other weak at the pastern and long and slack in back, the former will retain his working abilities longer.' He was the great terrier expert of his day and his words are worth heeding.

The Way Forward?

Terrier authority John Winch, writing in *The Fell and Moorland Working Terrier Club Magazine*, once described the Dandie Dinmont as the 'crème-de-la-crème' of working terriers, yet a couple of decades later they are only patronized in the show ring. Does the effeminate-sounding breed title, coming as it does from a fictional sporting squire in one of Walter Scott's novels, put down-to-earth terrier-men off? This breed was once the choice of sportsmen in the Coquet Valley of Northumberland, where they rarely reached 15lb weight and were prized for their crisp, double-coated jackets.

The Cairn Terrier got its name from a 1907 show ring judge's objection to the title 'short-haired Skyes'; they were not called Cairn Terriers in Scotland before that. Rather than Westies and Scotties we so easily could have had Aberdeen, Pitterween, Poltalloch and Roseneath Terrier breeds, rather as we have Fell, Patterdale, Plummer and Lucas terriers now. Will some latter-day Brian Plummer come up with a revised working terrier from Scotland, perhaps in that stunning deep-red chestnut coat which once featured in Cairns, lacking the overcoats of the Scotties, the centipedal structure of the Skye and the entirely 'fancy' topknot of the Dandie! (A topknot does not feature on the terriers depicted in the old print entitled *Dandie Dinmont and his Terriers*.) It can be done: there are probably now more Plummer Terriers than Fox Terriers and more Sporting Lucas Terriers than Skye Terriers. What a project for a Scottish terrier enthusiast and what a rich heritage to call on.

Let the first thing aimed at in breeding be a dog that is palpably an active, intelligent creature, capable of doing a good day's work over rough country, and in all sorts of weather, and then endeavour to attain perfection in his appearance as a whole, and not as a conglomeration of points. If this be done, we need have no fear of the future of the sturdy little Hielander.
The Scottish Terrier by W.L. McCandlish
(*Our Dogs, c.*1928)

I think at the present time it behoves breeders and exhibitors not to forget that the Dandie Dinmont *is a terrier*. A great many of the failures of the breeder which are sold cheap as 'companions' are clumsy, heavy-looking, crooked-legged dogs, altogether unlike a terrier in appearance, and thus the general public get deluded into the idea that the Dandie ought to have crooked legs, like the dachshund, and that it is *not* a member of the terrier family.
Ideal Dandie Dinmont by E.W.H. Blagg,
from *The Twentieth Century Dog*
by Herbert Compton (1904)

Working terriers depicted by W. Jones in his Ferreting *(1840).*

I may here draw attention to the gradual drawing away from the Club's standard and to the breeding of dogs and bitches far too large. The natural occupation of the Scottish Terrier is to bolt – not worry – foxes and otters. How many of the present-day winners could get to a fox in a cairn? It would be interesting to have the weights of the principal winners of late years.

From the judge's critique at Leeds Dog Show, June 1891

Many of the winning dogs this year are bred simply for money-making purposes, their owners not caring for the list of points in any way, so long as they bring money into the coffers. They are only large, coarse brutes, with donkey heads and ears, and cannot boast of one single drop of Skye blood in their veins. I, and others, well know this. Some of their ancestors are supposed to boast of good pedigrees – but do not, and they are no more Skye Terriers than is a Clydesdale. Ask any aged Highland gentleman or gamekeeper if they ever saw in the West Highlands, 40 years ago,

such dogs as were awarded the prizes at most of the shows held this year? I say we have not improved these dogs as working terriers.

From 'The Review of the Year 1891 for Skye Terriers', published in *The Kennel Gazette* of January 1892

Scotland is prolific in Terriers, and for the most part these are long-backed and short-legged dogs. Such are the Dandie Dinmont, the Skye, and the Aberdeen Terriers, the last now merged in the class recognized at our shows as the Scottish, or Scotch, Terrier; but the old hard and short-haired 'Terry' of the West of Scotland was much nearer in shape to a modern Fox-terrier, though with a shorter and rounder head, the colour of his hard, wiry coat mostly sandy, the face free from long hair, although some show a beard, and the small ears carried in most instances semi-erect, in some pricked.

British Dogs by W. D. Drury (Upcott Gill, 1903)

SCOTCH TERRIER & WELSH TERRIER.
Mr. H.J. Ludlow's Alister. K.C.S.B. 21,414. Sire. Owner's Rambler K.C.S.B. 13,214.
Dam. Owner's Lorna Doone K.C.S.B. 18,626. Mr. J.B.Forsyth's General Contour K.C.S.B. 21,735.

Scottish and Welsh terriers of 1890.

(Why aren't these 'Terrys' ever mentioned in thick tomes entirely devoted to Scottish terriers? There is scope for further research here.)

The Welsh Breeds

The show ring has claimed the two Welsh terrier breeds, with the Welsh Terrier by name holding its place and the Sealyham under threat of extinction in the coming decades. Yet there are devotees still working their own brand of Sealyham, keeping the pioneer breeders' work alive; there are 'Welsh Wheatens' in the working field too.

The Sealyham and the Sportsman Lucas

The demise of the admirable Sealyham Terrier has been sad to witness over the years. With Kennel Club registrations going from 601 in 1914 to 2,617 in 1925, then from 936 in 1960 to a mere 43 in 2008, this breed has had its share of fickle fanciers. Eighty years ago, Pierce O'Conor, in his *Sporting Terriers*, was writing: 'It is to be regretted, however, that in the past judges have too often awarded the highest honours at shows to large, heavy, clumsy-looking animals to the great detriment of the breed... The real working type should not be extravagantly short of leg, and is comparatively light in bone with rather a long body.'

In *The Sporting Terrier* (1992), Brian Plummer noted, 'Sadly, one of the breeds that has been most damaged by the whims of breeders seeking to produce

Sealyham Terrier Show, 1913; the leggier type was often found in litters then.

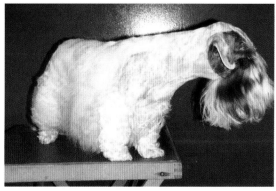

Show Sealyham of today.

Old-fashioned Sealyham Terrier.

animals solely for exhibition has been the Sealyham terrier'. The portrayals of this breed down the years indicate all too vividly the descent from spunky, active, lively earth-dog to chunky, less active specimen quite

Lewis Williams, a celebrated fox catcher of Powys, 1937, with his Welsh Terrier (from the Museum of Welsh Life).

unable to fulfil its basic function. If the registrations are anything to go by, all the show breeders have achieved is the obliteration of their favourite breed. And the Kennel Club, the self-appointed guardian of breeds of dog, have watched this happen. Once function is not bred for then the writing is on the wall for sporting and working breeds.

The famous terrier breeder Sir Jocelyn Lucas hunted a pack of Sealyhams from his famous Ilmer kennel but it was his disillusionment with the show Sealyham that inspired his experiment with an outcross to the Norfolk terrier, then little known outside its native county. His working lines had been based on a dozen 'mini-Sealyhams' from the Master of the Pembrokeshire Foxhounds, subsequently blended with the renowned Gladdish Hulke's stoat-hunting working terrier pack, which Sir Jocelyn bought. Seeking a smaller working Sealyham, he outcrossed in the early 1950s to a red Norfolk terrier (which he referred to as a Norwich or Trumpington terrier), and was so pleased with the litter that he attempted to stabilize the type. He later described this type as 'death on rats and rabbits'.

Seeking a Sporting Dog
Finding the show Sealyham too big, too cloddy, over-furnished, with disappointing temperament and whelping difficulties, Lucas sought a smaller-headed, harsh-coated, coloured terrier, which possessed both the physique and the character for hunting. He did not

care for the excessive coat and box heads of the increasingly popular post-Second World War show Sealyham. His 'new breed' had handsome red jackets and a perky assertiveness which he admired. His first cross Sealyham-Norfolks were mainly coloured, ranging from red-tan to wheaten and even black and tan. But the second cross produced a proportion of mainly white or white-bodied progeny. We have the Sporting Lucas Terrier with us to this day. Sir Jocelyn's descendant, Lord Lucas, is president of the breed club.

Writing on the evolution of the Sealyham in his book on the breed (Simpkin & Marshall, 1929), Jocelyn Lucas recorded:

> Just before the war, one breeder at least introduced a West Highland cross to reduce the size… Show wire fox-terrier bitches were also tried in later days in order to improve coats and fronts… Fifteen or twenty years ago few litters of Sealyhams were level or true to type. Nearly every litter consisted of one or two short-legged dogs, one or two medium ones, and one at least that tried to look like an Airedale as regards shape… There was a boom in the breed. Everyone in Pembrokeshire who had a bitch put it to a local dog, and the litter went to England… One breeder at least, a few years ago, tried a cross with the Clumber Spaniel to get heads.

„Brynhir Pardon',
appartenant à M. W. Robert, Chester. (Gravure extraite du *Stock-Keeper*.)

Welsh Terrier of 1904.

Captain Jocelyn Lucas MC with his famous Ilmer pack of Sealyhams, 1925.

Portrait of the Welsh Terrier type by F.C. Fairman (1877); note the cropped ears favoured then.

Against that background, is it at all surprising that even today we get heavy-boned, long-bodied, boot-box headed Sealyhams exemplifying the modern breed, to the despair of those who favour *sporting* terriers?

Establishing The National Breed

The other recognized Cambrian terrier and Welsh by name has long had a loyal show following, with around 250 registered in 1908, 1960 and 2000, rising to 360 in 2008. This appealing breed exemplifies the old rough-coated black and tan terrier once found all over Britain; England could well have claimed the type as hers too. Bigger than a Lakeland and smaller than an Airedale, the Welsh Terrier makes up in character what it lacks in physical identity. Once accused of being a wire-haired Fox Terrier in a different jacket, there have been accusations too of infusion of the latter's blood in this Welsh dog's development. The silhouette is markedly similar. It was argued that the old Welsh Terrier had a Chippendale front, poor shoulders, a big, coarse, apple head and big, round, bold eyes. The infusion of Fox Terrier blood allegedly produced a smarter-looking terrier but also introduced the long-muzzled head. Robert Killick, a distinguished breeder of Welsh Terriers, recently commented, 'After more than ten years in Welsh Terriers (my only breed) the result of a mating between my own three-generation bitch and my own four-generation dog produced a litter of three Wire Fox Terriers (and fine specimens) and one Welsh Terrier.' Past outcrossings, whether covert or overt, so often reveal themselves in the end.

At the Bangor Show of 1885, a group of Welsh terrier fanciers decided to approach the Kennel Club with a view to having their dogs registered as such. However, the north of England breeders of similar dogs wished their rights to be acknowledged too. In November 1885, to satisfy both parties, the KC agreed to enter in the Stud Book the classification 'Welsh Terrier or the Old English wire-haired Black and Tan Terrier Class 53'. Later, the fanciers of the English dogs failed to form a club and in time any reference to English terriers was deleted in registration and show documents. At a meeting of the Welsh Terrier Club in February 1890, the motion 'That no dog or bitch the sire or dam of which is a Fox, Irish, Airedale or Old

THE FIRST WELSH TERRIERS
Has the Welsh Terrier improved? At the top is "Dandy Bach" and below is "Dronfield Dandie," two Welsh Terrier celebrities of the eighties. It is interesting to compare these two with the Airedale and Irish Terriers of their day and to note the changes that have been made in all three breeds

Early Welsh show Terriers, 1920s; top: Dandy Bach; bottom: Dronfield Dandie.

English terrier shall be eligible to compete at any show…' was only narrowly defeated.

In October 1890, a Welsh Terrier stud dog was advertised in *The Kennel Gazette* as 'best-headed, perfect in coat and colour, best legs and feet, has a beautiful small ear, perfectly carried, is free from white; his only fault, by some judges: a trifle too big. Will not serve Irish or Fox-terrier bitches.' Such words would be both needless and unthinkable today, even if such an outcross were to be to the benefit of a sounder dog in any breed of terrier. I can understand the temporary short-term need to establish breed type in an emergent breed at that time. Over a century later, that long-sustained closed gene pool is not the best way to produce the healthiest, physically soundest sporting

Welsh Terrier of the 1930s; note the ramrod straight front legs and the stiff, close coat.

terrier; putting breed purity ahead of health and vigour is not only unwise but a form of calculated breed harmfulness, knowingly inflicted. In *The Kennel Gazette* of 1888, L.P.C. Astley, an experienced sporting dog judge, wrote: 'To my mind, the domed skull, low set ears, and large eyes of the Welsh terriers proper must certainly be improved by a judicious cross of the undoubtedly better-headed terriers of the

Welsh Terrier at Crufts, 1991; note the softer coat and longer leg furnishings.

north and centre of England.' He was seeking a better dog, not a cravenly perpetuated breed.

Fox Terrier Influence

The subsequent recognition of the smaller Lakeland Terrier by the Kennel Club in 1921 undoubtedly drew devotees of the English black and tan terriers, though 'Working Welsh' terriers of a separate type were still favoured. Writing in Compton's *The Twentieth Century Dog* (1904), the Rev. W.P. Nock recorded: 'The terriers are much too big, and many that are winning today are too red in colour and too long in body. In my opinion, too much is sacrificed for long heads, which are fox terrier heads, and are thus going away from the true old Welsh type.' In the same publication, W.S. Glynn was writing: 'In body formation and limbs he must be symmetrical; he must not be, as so many fox terriers are, all "front", and possessed of nothing behind the saddle fit to carry a mouse.' Time and time again, down the years, the influence of the Fox Terrier, as designed in the late nineteenth century, is regretted in so many terrier breeds. The unwise tendency in this breed to produce too long a head and too straight a front has been aped by other terrier breed fanciers too, to the loss of true type in their breeds, to the extent that this is now considered the real breed type by copy-cat exhibitors, anxious to perpetuate consensual thinking. It is time for some honest revision.

The Need for Conservation

Until the mid-1950s, two kennels still bred Welsh black and tan working terriers: the Ynysfor Otterhounds and the Glasnevin Foxhound pack. The former were kept free of KC-registered Welsh Terrier blood, being smaller, 14lb, 13in, box-headed dogs, much more like Fell Terriers. Interbreeding has probably contributed to the muted tan of the Lakeland being replaced all too often by the fiery red-tan of the Welsh dogs. The Welsh Terrier has been described as the terrier giving the maximum of pleasure with a minimum amount of trouble, but some terrier-men feel that they lack tenacity and committed prey-drive. Show critiques of recent years make disappointing reading, ranging from 'the quality of the breed has sadly deteriorated' to 'this breed is deteriorating in both quality and movement'. This is an attractive breed with a sound working provenance from its distant past, one deserving attention.

It would be an enormous pity if both these Welsh terrier breeds, the Sealyham and the national dog, slowly disappeared not just from public view but from the working role too. It is shaming that French sportsmen practising their '*venerie sous terre*' are using working Welsh Terriers in packs on fox and coypu, proudly parading them at their equivalent of our Game Fair, complete with terrier-pouches, spades and pick-axes. They arouse the admiration of every visiting British sportsman. It now needs a few patriotic Welshmen to rally to the cause and perpetuate the selfless work done by the pioneers in each breed. We lost the Welsh Setter; let's keep the Welsh Terriers!

The Sealyham terriers nowadays so much advertised, are too short-legged and broad-chested to properly negotiate rock crevices or surmount ledges underground... in many situations their build prevents them doing their best work. If we were asked to give a specification of such a terrier it would be as follows: Weight 15lb to 16lb; coat, thick and wet-resisting;

chest narrow, but not so much so as to impede the free action of heart and lungs, legs sufficiently long to enable the dog to travel above ground... jaw powerful but not too long...

Foxes, Foxhounds and Fox-Hunting by Richard Clapham (Heath Cranton, 1936)

Will he be a Welsh Terrier if he is to be like a Fox Terrier...? We have too many Fox Terriers already. Let the poor Welshman have his native terrier on different lines, if you please... I think the time has come for all gentlemen selected as judges to be able to distinguish the great difference between the Welsh terrier proper and the so-called, viz., the Black and Tan Wire-Haired terrier.

Writer calling himself 'Native Terrier' in *The Kennel Gazette*, February 1891.

In conclusion I would congratulate breeders on the great strides made in head properties and in uniformity of type, on the material reduction of undershot specimens, and especially on the wonderful coats one sees on these terriers. In this last particular I do not know a variety of terrier living that can touch the Welsh Terrier, ie for a good, hard, workman-like coat; but I would urge upon them the necessity of breeding better bitches, of breeding to the standard weight, and of continuing to keep clear of the Fox Terrier cum Hound cum Collie type.

Walter S. Glynn in *The Kennel Gazette*, January 1893

The Old English rough-coated Terrier by V. de Vos (c.1860).

The Show Sealyham is undoubtedly a very handsome, attractive animal, and when one compares the prize-winning specimens of today with those which were first benched at the Crystal Palace Show in 1910 the improvement which has been effected is truly astonishing. Many authorities argue that the craze for a powerful, and what is termed a punishing jaw, has been carried to excess, and, although this is to some extent true, there is now a decided tendency amongst most judges to favour a type free from very pronounced exaggerated features. Hence breeders are striving to produce a well-balanced terrier if possible of a weight rather under than over 20lb for dogs, and 18lb for bitches.

Fred W. Lewis writing in *Hounds and Dogs*, The Lonsdale Library (Seeley, Service & Co., 1932)

Gradually this form of sport [badger-digging] was discontinued… I wonder what sort of account our present-day Sealyhams would give of themselves if they were given the chance – everyone is concerned with their beauty for shows or their winning ways as pets nowadays – and sometimes I have wondered whether everyone has forgotten the breed's raison d'etre, and whether that is partly responsible for the fall from the great popularity of those early days.

Sealyhams by F. Chenuz (Ernest Benn, 1956)

The Irish Breeds

My father came from Limerick,
My mother came from York,
A half bred Yorkshire, blue and tan,
They hailed me as from Cork.
An Irish Terrier I was called
And sent on bench to show,
But oh! how little they believed
I should cause such a row.

Those words from *The Livestock Journal* of 1876 convey at once the fellishness of 'Erin's Dare-devils', as terriers from Ireland have been named. The red-golden coated Irish Terrier, the slate-blue coloured Kerry Blue, the soft-coated Wheaten Terrier and the harsher-coated Glen of Imaal Terrier have never been accused of lacking spirit. The wheaten hue is a common terrier coloration, being found in the Border,

Glen of Imaal Terriers at the Irish Kennel Club's show of 1933, now recognized as a distinct breed.

Lakeland, Norfolk, Norwich, Cairn and Scottish Terrier breeds, as well as the terriers from Ireland. I have never liked the breed title Soft-Coated Wheaten Terrier – no breed should be identified just by the texture or colour of its coat and there are plenty of wheaten terriers. Such a distinctive and admirable breed deserves a much more precise breed title.

All-Round Workers

When working in Ireland it was always of interest to study the farm dogs there; so many of them, ungroomed and unclipped, resembled the bouviers of Belgium, the Dutch Terrier or Smoushond and the stable dogs of Germany, the schnauzers. Going to work in Germany immediately after working in Ireland allowed me to keep a picture of Irish farm dogs in my mind when viewing their equivalents on mainland Europe. I have seen both schnauzers and wheaten terriers being used as herding dogs in their native countries and appearing interchangeable in form and technique. Once, at a world dog show I was convinced that the Bouvier des Flandres before me was a large Soft-Coated Wheaten Terrier from Ireland. Size apart, the appearance, the coat, the personality and the attitude were easily confused. I see similarities too between the Kerry Blue and the Laekenois of

Working Kerry Blue of today.

Belgium and the Schnauzer; perhaps the farm function decides form.

In Drury's *British Dogs* (1903) and Vero Shaw's *The Illustrated Book of the Dog* (1879), the Irish Terrier's prowess as a rabbit-dog is spelt out. The former states:

Without question, rabbiting is the kind of sport that the Irish Terrier excels at – the right dog in the right

Painting by 'Boxer' from 1836, showing the old type of ratting terrier and all-round farm dog.

Head study of Kerry Blue of 1928.

place, so to speak. A model Irish Terrier is a miniature Irish Wolfhound with a yellow-red coat, and, consequently, being built on these racy lines, he is by nature specially adapted for rabbiting in every way.

Shaw comments: 'Looking at them as workmen, rabbiting must first be mentioned… Rely upon it, their quick noses never make a mistake… It is only when one sees them at full speed that one can understand the necessity for insisting upon their peculiar build.' I always think of the terriers of Ireland as all-rounders, ready to pursue a chosen quarry, herd cattle or even sheep, go ratting in a barn or act as farm watchdogs.

Coats of Many Colours

Two hundred years ago a litter of terrier pups in Ireland could contain coat colours ranging from black and grey, red and tan to silver and gold, wheaten and white. At the first show to feature Irish Terriers, in Dublin in 1874, one winner was white, another black and tan and another grizzled blue. Selective breeding based on breeder and locality preferences concentrated the colour genes of terriers in Ireland into distinct groups, which were then perpetuated. Breeds reflected those preferences. Dr Carey, first president of the Irish Terrier Club, wrote in 1879, on colour: 'Red, yellow, wheaten or light brown inclining to grey. The best colour is orange tipped with red, the head slightly darker than the body and the ears slightly darker than the head.' The standard for the Irish Terrier today demands a 'whole-coloured' dog, with black shading

highly undesirable. Writing in Compton's *The Twentieth Century Dog* (1904), C.J. Barnett remarked: 'Thirty years ago there were many black and red terriers in Ireland, with very hard coats, but of course were not bred from. I only wish we had kept to it, and not thrown out the old blacks, as their coats were very, very hard.' It would be so good to see a really hard-coated *black* Irish Terrier once again.

The Kerry Blue is tolerated in any shade of blue with or without black points. The Glen of Imaal can be all shades of blue, brindle and wheaten. I have seen working terriers in Ireland with a shale-grey and a silver coat, with little hint of blue. A show was held in Limerick in 1887 with a class allotted to 'silver-haired Irish Terriers'. In *The Twentieth Century Dog*, published in 1904, Herbert Compton wrote, 'there was a terrier in County Wicklow (preserved distinct, and highly prized for a century) that was long in body, short in leg, and of a blue-black colour; there was a black terrier in County Kerry…'. Soldiers of the House of Hesse, serving in Ireland, may well have brought pinschers with them, which would have produced a harlequin and a red factor. H.D. Richardson, in *Dogs, their Origin and Varieties* (1847), wrote of the harlequin terrier in Ireland: 'In form, it is, as it were, a perfect English terrier; in colour it is a blueish slate-colour, marked with darker blotches and patches, and often with tan about the legs and muzzle. It is one of the most determined of its race…'. That does not sound like a true harlequin to me, but what has been called 'marled', like clay with a mixture of blue-greys in it. Blue-grey Neapolitan Mastiffs can display this mixture of grey shades. Water dogs, too, like the Poodle, can exhibit this chalybeous blue-grey coat. The romantic stories of dogs swimming ashore from Spanish ships near Tralee, sometimes featuring in fanciful Kerry Blue 'histories', may rest more fittingly in Irish Water Spaniel breed origins. Water dogs were ships dogs; terriers were unlikely to be. The terriers of Ireland have more in common with each other than foreign breeds.

Common Ancestry

It is likely that the modern breeds of pure-bred terriers from Ireland had common ancestors, becoming distinct breeds through county or locality specialization in coat colour and leg length. It could so easily have been that today's Glen of Imaal Terrier became known as the Wicklow Terrier and the Kerry Blue as the Limerick Blue. Irish Blue Terrier may well be a more apt title for the Kerry Blue. In 1919 a club was formed in Dublin to promote the interests of the Irish Blue Terrier. It was not until 1921 that the name Kerry Blue was finally formally adopted for the breed. The Irish Terrier, before the standard was revised at the end of the nineteenth century, could be bright red, yellow, wheaten or grey. Grey was subsequently omitted. Half a century ago, blue puppies still appeared in red and wheaten litters.

When I was working in County Down some forty years ago, I used to see what could be called straw-coloured terriers on farms there, really like coarsely bred wheatens. A while later I came across a painting of John Rawden-Hastings, son of the Earl of Moira, attributed to Robert Fagin, who died in 1812. In this painting there are two terriers, one remarkably like the rough-coated straw-coloured terriers I saw in County Down. The Earls of Moira had property in County Down and I wondered immediately if this portrayal was of an early wheaten terrier. At unofficial dog shows I see classes for what are called 'Irish Staffies', a

John Rawden-Hastings and local terriers, by Robert Fagan (c.1795).

leggier form of the Staffordshire Bull Terrier. Again my mind goes back to a painting (reproduced in Chapter 1), this time to John Ferneley senior's Nelson and Argo, Lord Brownlow's Bull Terriers. The dogs portrayed are exactly like today's Irish Staffies. John Ferneley worked in Ireland in the early nineteenth century; this painting was dated 1831. Lord Brownlow's ancestors descend from Anne, sister of John Brownlow, Lord Viscount Tyrconnel of the Kingdom of Ireland. Today's Irish Staffies may have distinct ancestry too, although this emergent type gets little but scorn from the pedigree world. I cannot see why a group of fanciers shouldn't prefer a leggier Staffie; a century ago a comparable group in Staffordshire broke away and created their own breed.

Irish Staffies

The RSPCA is suspicious of Irish Staffies, claiming they are substitute Pit Bulls. This is hardly credible: the old dog-fighting men, as Fitz-Barnard, Stevens, Armitage and Colby point out in their books on them, never favoured a leggy dog, believing from experience that it allowed opponents to get under them. But when did facts ever interfere with the pursuit of innocent dogs under the discredited Dangerous Dogs Act? A longer-legged Irish Staffie would be better described as an 'Irish Bull Terrier' so that the height and weight limitations linked to pedigree Staffordshire Bull Terriers didn't lead to assumptions of their misuse in dog combat. The Bull Terrier does not have weight and height restrictions in its KC breed standard. The loose title Irish Staffie is not a recent innovation. Forty years ago in Ireland I used to hear of the Norford or Northern Ireland Staffordshire Bull Terrier, usually a dog with blue in its coat, rather like the Blue Paul in Scotland. The red tan dogs were called Dublin Reds. Terriers at Irish country shows were once divided into Sounders or earth-dogs and Strong Dogs or dogs too big to go to ground, like Kerry Blues and Wheatens. Terrier tests have been favoured in Ireland for some years, even by the Irish Kennel Club.

Sadly, as in England, dog-fighting was widely conducted in Ireland until banned, but still persists in some areas. Irish, Wheatens, Kerry Blues and Glens have all been used 'in the ring'; fighting dogs not 'good' enough for the ring were often relegated to the independent field trials, where gambling also played a

Field Trials

The Teastas Begg, or small test, involved the hunting of either a rabbit in a field (a scenting test) or a rat in a stream (a catch and kill test). The Teastas Mor, or large test, involved the use of a live badger in an artificial set; an earth-dog was used to drive the wretched badger into a further 'shore' or widened tunnel, so that a strong dog could be tested on it from the other end. The bigger terrier then had to draw the badger in under six minutes, whilst remaining totally mute, silence being associated with courage. Around 1966 public opinion rightly brought an end to these cruel acts but clandestine tests may well be still going on. Independent field trials held sixty years ago by the Working Terrier Association of Ireland led to accusations that Kerry Blues were being crossed with bull terriers from England. The original IKC tests were for pure-bred dogs only, rather as gundogs can gain their working test certification. At one time no Glen of Imaal Terrier was allowed to become a full champion without its Teastac Misneac, or dead-game certificate.

major role. I understand that American Pit Bull Terriers were tried at both activities but not favoured because they were simply too frenetic, giving voice freely and being too frenzied. Irish travellers told me that they regarded a dog that made a noise a coward; Staffordshire Bull Terriers were apparently renowned for their silence during combat. Sectarianism even reached this so-called sport: a famous bull terrier of

Working Irish Terrier with a slate-grey coat.

Kerry Blue Terrier of today.

Glen of Imaal Terrier of today, strongly made and harsh-coated.

the 1970s in the Portadown area was called the 'Red Hand of Ulster'.

I read that the thugs of Northern Ireland now seek the American Pit Bull Terrier as their 'status dogs' more than ever before, the ban under the DDA having bestowed even greater street-cred on their mis-

guided illegal ownership. They also seek crosses between Dogos Argentino and Bull Terriers, big strapping white dogs or a blend of Rhodesian Ridgebacks and American Pit Bull Terriers. This has not surprisingly given the local tabloids the chance to rage about devil-dogs and an ever-present danger to

Irish Terrier of today,
balanced and hard-coated.

the public from any bull terrier-like dog. The Ulster SPCA has sadly gone down the 'breed not deed' avenue, leading to perfectly innocent family pets being seized, much to the distress of their owners. I doubt if the DDA and legislation in its wake in many countries has actually contributed anything of value to dog control. I am sure it has contributed a great deal to the needless destruction of hundreds, if not thousands of blameless dogs, purely on account of their breed or appearance.

Distinctive Breeds

Whatever their breed title, whether registered as a breed or not, the native terriers of Ireland should be treasured. Each one is very different from the other. I do hope that the Irish Wheaten, as I prefer to call the breed, doesn't fall victim to its profusion of coat, which seem heavier here than in Ireland. With soft-coated in the breed title, Ireland's 'gentle terrier', as I've heard it dubbed, and with more of them in America (where grooming can be obsessive) than in Ireland, their working instincts deserve more attention than their grooming needs. Dr Declan Looney has some excellent working Wheatens, with excessive coat not featuring in his stock. Some of the American dogs are not only groomed excessively, but appear to have acquired a strange high-stepping rear action, perhaps from exaggerated angulation.

The Kerry Blue will always be distinctive, but I've seen them with large thick ears, short on the leg and heavier in the skull than previously at shows. Their coats seem to be becoming heavier too. I've seen working Irish Terriers featuring a woollier coat and a white brisket in Ireland, the outcross to the Wire-haired Fox Terrier possibly manifesting itself. I always look for a racier build in them, with a good arch over the loin and a good length of body. The Glens have their own style, with strong bone, distinctive front legs and plenty of attitude. I am told that the Sporting Glen Club in Ireland has 120 members, with a dozen people still working the breed. I was told of Red Ned, a famous working Glen of the 1950s, and that around the same time the Earl of Rocksavage had two formidable Glens on his estate in Ireland. You underestimate the terriers of Ireland at your peril!

> Oh, I've no time for the lap-dog kind,
> I'm not that sort of a chap.
> Give me a jolly good chase down wind,
> Or the joy of a cheery scrap.
> I'll hold my own with the best of them,
> I'll fight till my bones are cracked,
> For my coat is red and I'm Irish bred,
> And darned well proud of the fact.
>
> Quoted in *The Dogs of Ireland* by Anna Redlich
> (Tempest, 1981)

Soft-coated Wheaten Terrier of the show ring.

Declan Mooney's working Wheaten.

Irish Terriers.
Champion Dogs: B.A. (first), grand head, expression, good body, and a better height on the leg than Michael (second) with his fair head and character, softish coat of better colour than the winner; they are both 'awful', worst feet I ever saw. Ballyhooley (reserve) all wrong in head and character, grand legs and feet and hard coat. St. George, soft in expression, coat, bad in loin with good front. Begum, common and too thick, good in coat…

> From the judge's rather outspoken critique
> on Irish Terriers, Kennel Club's Show
> at Olympia, July 1889.

The modus operandi of a novice is too frequently to purchase from some unscrupulous person a snipey-faced, weedy little bitch, or a big, ungainly, flaxen-coated specimen of very doubtful blood, that bears no affinity to an Irish Terrier, except perhaps in colour, and then plank down his money for the service of a stud dog of totally different outline and character, in the full expectation that the mating will strike the happy medium in the size and quality of the progeny, simply because the sire is a good dog. This is diametrically opposed to the laws of practical breeding, and only brings sad disappointment to the experimenter, wastes his time and money, and stocks the country with mongrels that should never see the light of day.

> *British Dogs* by W.D. Drury (Upcott Gill, 1903)

The Lesser Known Breeds

What's in a Name?

The list of terrier breeds recognized by the Kennel Club could have looked so very different. In place of famous breed names like the Sealyham, Scottish, Welsh, Irish, Border, Norfolk and Parson Russell terrier, we could so easily have ended up with the Trumpington, Cowley, Bewcastle, Elterwater, Suffolk, Will Norris and Squire Poole terrier. In the early nineteenth century, many localities, even some valleys, had their own favoured type of terrier, some of which became swept up in a distinct form we now call a breed. A comparable situation occurred in other types of dog in other countries, as the mountain dogs of Switzerland – Bernese, Appenzeller, Entlebucher and Great Swiss – illustrate. The setter breeds provide another example of surviving breeds representing today the much wider range of colours and types that existed in the last century, like the milk-white Llanidloes, the liver and white Naworth and Featherstone Castles, the tricolour Lord Lovatt and the Earl of Southesks and the jet black of Lord Ossulstons.

Inspired individuals often determine whether the distinct type of terrier they develop and promote survives both the test of time and a lack of like-minded supporters. We could now be hearing of Capheaton, Heysham and Letts Terriers if their devotees had possessed the single-mindedness of breeders like Lucas

THE EARLY IRISH TERRIERS
The Irish Terrier also has been altered by the Fancier since its most important days. On the top we see Mr. E. A. Wiener's Ch. "Brickbat" (the finest Irish Terrier ever seen—so they said at the time), its ears cropped, and below we have Mr. Pim's noted dog, Ch. "Play Boy," another of the greatest dogs of its day

Early Irish Terriers, from the1920s – the best dogs of their day.
Top: Ch Brickbat; bottom: Ch Play Boy.

Arthur Wardle's depiction of Other Working Terriers (1896); the white dogs (foreground) are two 'Cowley Terriers', with Fox and Sealyham Terrier blood.

Norfolk Terrier in black and tan, F.M. Hollams (1948).

and Plummer. Mrs Royds of Heysham, a quite experienced breeder, once decided to create her own breed of terrier, somewhere between a Pembrokeshire Corgi

and a Cairn Terrier, smooth-coated and short but straight-legged. Her prototypal dogs were very attractive, allegedly resembling the Swedish Vallhund, a small cattle dog from Sweden, filling the gap between the leggier Fox Terrier and the shorter-legged Scotties. She even aroused the interest of the Kennel Club in this 'new' breed. But sadly when she mated within her new gene pool she just lost type, being left with a mixture of bad Cairns, poor Corgis, unacceptable

Norfolk Terrier type by A.J. Batt (1888).

A Norwich Terrier, owned by Mrs Fagan, 1930; this would later be called a Norfolk Terrier.

A 'Jones Terrier', owned by Mrs Fagan.

A 'Jones Terrier', owned by Mrs Fagan.

Patterdales and an undesired Heysham phenotype. She reluctantly abandoned her dream.

The Trumpington Terrier

The Trumpington Terrier was an ancestor of the Norfolk and was sometimes called the Cantab Terrier since the undergraduates of Cambridge prized them so much. Small red-tan terriers were once favoured in East Anglia, a Master of the Norwich Staghounds called Cooke establishing a strain of his own. A character called 'Rough-rider' Jones, who had been in Cooke's employ, took another hunt position in Leicestershire and took some of what were termed Red Norfolk Terriers with him. Frank Jones had arrived from Ireland with a brace of Glen of Imaal Terriers and quickly acquired a Trumpington Terrier. He purchased every red-coated whelp he could, from a mating between a Dandie Dinmont crossed with a Smooth Fox Terrier and what was described as a cross between an Aberdeen Terrier and a Cantab Terrier. He had a head for business and eventually exported a number of his terriers to America, where they became known as the Jones Terrier. Various American hunts used them, finding them excellent stable dogs as well as fearless earth-dogs. Jones got his foundation stock from a terrier breeder called Hopkins, who actually called his dogs Trumpingtons; he favoured a 14lb dog, red or yellow tan and not 'too strong-headed'. Like Lucas he linked the big head with heavy bone, undesired in a working terrier. Many of these dogs had their ears cropped before the practice was made illegal.

Unplanned Creations

In 1984, an unplanned mating between a hunt terrier belonging to a former Master of the Middleton Hunt and a local rat-catcher's dog produced an unexpected litter. One of these pups, a tan with black points and a smooth but thick coat, found a home at Capheaton Hall in Northumberland. In due course, this dog produced two litters, the first to a black and tan dog, the second to a local huntsman's dog. From this actually unwanted liaison came a bitch called Bramble, who had two litters of eight, eventually establishing a dynasty of nearly forty of this type in the county. A foot high at the withers and preferred in tan with black points, they once featured on the label of a locally brewed beer, Terrier Ale. Small terriers of this type are found in many Fell Terrier litters but do not always breed true to type. Further back in the 1950s, a breeder called Dora Sendall produced what she termed her 'Crunchie' line of terrier, a handsome golden-coated long-haired Toller-like terrier, going on to develop this type past three generations. There was more than a hint of the old Norfolk red decoy dog behind this line, but they sadly did not survive.

Planned Creations

Letts Terriers

More seriously, Martin Letts developed his own brand of hunt terrier up in the Cheviots, whilst Master of the College Valley and North Northumberland Hunt. He settled on a line from an old-type Sealyham bitch from local huntsman Jack Howells crossed with a Jack Russell. For some forty years he went on developing this type, famed for their constitution and stamina, and subsequently used by the Middleton Hunt as hunt terriers, who found them intelligent, biddable and robust, able to run with the hounds, rather than travel with the terrier-men. Lett's terriers are long-legged and rough-haired, a weatherproof coat being essential in the country they hunt. They can feature black, tan or black and tan markings but are favoured in mainly white jackets. They are bred for work and not sold as pure pets without a working potential use.

A determined-looking Fell Terrier of today.

Patterdale Terriers

Patterdale Terriers, the black (usually, but dark red and chocolate varieties can also emerge from the black genes) form of the Fell Terrier, and the more varied but still distinctive Fell Terrier itself, could be described as local variants of the better-known Lakeland Terrier. The Patterdale, now recognized in America (where it is used on possum, raccoon and groundhog, as well as for baying the wild boar) as a separate terrier breed, as is the Sporting Lucas Terrier and soon perhaps the Plummer Terrier too, comes from the eastern slopes of Helvellyn at the southern end of Ullswater. The most famous breeder of Black Fells or Patterdale Terriers is Brian Nuttall of Cheshire, who inherited his father's

A workmanlike Patterdale Terrier of today.

famous strain, and has now passed them on to his son Craig. If Cyril Breay of Kirkby Lonsdale in the Yorkshire Dales, Maurice Bell of Hawes and Frank Buck of Leyburn engineered the Black Fell, then Brian Nuttall perfected the strain, relying on Border Terrier blood in his breeding programmes. Frank Stacey of the Holme Valley Beagle kennels also had some excellent dogs, as did Jack Smith of Midhope Stones in Yorkshire.

Promotion of Types

Lakeland Terriers are known to produce a black whelp from time to time, with Willie Irving of the Melbreak Pack producing some notable ones. Black terriers were traditionally bred at Grasmere and Windermere. Whether it is the Lake District or Norfolk in past centuries, black whelps can result from red to red matings and colour prejudice should never condemn a good dog. A black English terrier would make a welcome addition to the coat colours of our native breeds. A tan terrier with black points and a close coat, like the Fell Terrier, would add variety to our terrier range. It might only take just one dedicated wealthy fancier to strongly promote such a breed, perhaps to replace the lapsing pedigree breeds, like the Skye and Sealyham.

Not much has been written about the terrier types which did not achieve KC breed status, mainly because terrier work was not a job for the educated monied classes who could have written books about them. As a consequence, it is probably easier to research just one setter breed than all of our lost terrier breeds, such is the disparity of written material. In *The Terriers* (1896), a volume in his *Modern Dogs* series, Rawdon Lee does make reference to the little-known types of terrier found then. One of his illustrations is by Arthur Wardle and depicts *The Other Terriers*, with two of those featured being Cowley Terriers. The working terrier fraternity of Rawdon Lee's time could have provided evidence of ten or twenty additional 'breeds'.

New Working Terriers – the Plummer and Sporting Lucas

Sadly, a comparable depiction in recent times would be more likely to feature Schnauzers, Pinschers, Dachshunds and the German Hunt Terrier, such was the domination of breeds originating in Germany in Britain in the 1990s. But now, just in time, as the new millennium unfolds, the working terrier breeders, who never follow fad or fashion, are at work again. Just as a *working* Clumber Spaniel, half the weight of the show dog and with sounder hips and eyes, is being promoted, so too are restored working Sealyhams and Bedlingtons, a resurrected Lucas Terrier, recast as the Sporting Lucas, and a new breed, the Plummer Terrier.

Sporting Lucas Terriers.

The distinctive Plummer Terrier of today.

An inquisitive brace of Sporting Lucas Terriers.

The Plummer Terrier, named after its creator, schoolmaster-turned-writer, the late Brian Plummer, author of at least a dozen books, mainly on lurchers and terriers, is steadily gaining ground. Between 11½ and 13½in at the shoulder, smooth-coated, with a head displaying signs of both Bull Terrier and Fox Terrier ancestry and a striking fiery tan colour with white finching, these dogs were developed in a hard school and now breed consistently true to type. There is a breed club, a stud book going back to the early 1950s and an annual show in July. The breed club is affiliated to the British Field Sports Society and John Winch, a Northumberland barrister with a long interest and high standing in working terrier circles, is its president.

The Lucas Terrier was described by its creator, Sir Jocelyn Lucas, famous for his Ilmer kennel of Sealyhams, as 'death on rats and rabbits', and this too is no ornamental breed. Seeking a smaller working Sealyham, Sir Jocelyn outcrossed to a red Norwich Terrier, and, finding the crossbred puppies attractive he set to in an attempt to stabilize this type. The Sporting Lucas Terrier enthusiasts of today are completing his unfinished work. They are producing hard-jacketed, foothigh, strong-headed terriers, either white-bodied with darker markings or coloured-in body, all shades of brown, black and tan and grizzle and tan. They are fearless without being fighters, and, thankfully for terriers bred from game stock, not – in the words of their breed standard – 'overly noisy'.

Ironically, it was Sir Jocelyn Lucas's disillusionment with the show Sealyham that inspired his outcross to the Norfolk. Finding them too big, too cloddy, over-furnished and with disappointing temperament and whelping difficulties, he sought a smaller-headed, harsh-coated but not excessively coated input and went for the then scarcely known (outside their native county) Norfolk Terrier. His working lines had been based on a dozen 'mini-Sealyhams' from the Master of the Pembrokeshire Foxhounds, subsequently blended with the renowned Gladdish Hulke's stoat-hunting working terrier pack, which Sir Jocelyn bought. The Lucas Terrier struggled on until the early 1990s but then lost type and virility and Brian Plummer's advice was sought, leading to the use of Sealyham blood.

The breed has since been relaunched on the same formula as Sir Jocelyn used: small Sealyhams mated

Two Lucas Terriers bred by Jocelyn Lucas, who crossed small Sealyham bitches with a Norfolk Terrier.

Norfolk Terrier of today.

with two carefully chosen Norfolks, plus the blood of a surviving Lucas dog. The breeding programme has now been operating for a decade and the type desired just about fixed. Brian Plummer was very much the guiding hand behind both these quite exciting new entries to the working terrier breed lists. His knowledge of genetics, his extensive experience with working terriers and his intellectual energy has given us a chance to regain our international reputation as working terrier breeders. His dogged persistence in producing his own breed after many setbacks and mishaps is a lesson to all would-be dog breeders.

Both the Plummer Terrier and the Sporting Lucas Terrier enthusiasts observe a written and approved breed standard and have sensible breeding plans. Most of the Plummers have been sired by working terriers owned by professional terrier-men working for fox-

Norwich Terrier of today.

hound packs. They have exceptional noses and it would be difficult to find better ratters. One is being used to track deer, rather as the Germans use their 'teckels'. They can display what French huntsmen would term '*excessivement meurtrier*' or be, more euphemistically, determined vermin-killers. They are certainly not dogs for elderly spinsters in Reigate!

The Advantages of Independence

Sadly the well-intentioned, skilful breeders of these two carefully bred terrier breeds will get no official encouragement here. We are too busy recognizing the newly introduced Cesky Terrier, produced overseas from our Sealyham's blood. Yet the terrier breeds are essentially British, very much part of our sporting heritage. Paradoxically, this indifference from above may, in the long run, turn out to be no bad thing. The show ring has reduced so many of our native terrier breeds to over-coated lapdogs, usually with upright shoulders and lacking that suppleness in the back that is so important to an earth-dog. The critiques from show ring terrier judges in the last decade or so make my point for me.

Here are some examples. West Highland White Terriers (at Crufts 1996): 'The other faults I found appalling were the number of very dodgy mouths, along with very poor construction. To think these dogs had to qualify in order to enter Crufts leaves me speechless.' Cairn Terriers (at Crufts 1995): 'I was very disappointed with the movement of our own dogs which caused me great problems. I was also disappointed yet again to see a number of untypical heads and, surprisingly, unacceptable or suspect mouths, even in some exhibits who have won well.' Parson Jack Russell Terriers (at Crufts 1995): 'Some do lack bone and there were thin feet.' Glen of Imaal Terriers (at Crufts 1995): 'it was a surprise to find so many bad mouths at such a show as Crufts. Also there was some hint at deformity of the ribs.' If these are the KC-registered pedigree terriers, which qualify for Crufts, what are the rest like? These dogs will have been bred from, with their descendants now spreading their faults.

Yet if the Plummer and Sporting Lucas Terrier devotees seek official recognition for their dogs, however unwise that may be, they will receive little but scorn, including some from individuals breeding the

*The Norfolk type,
captured by G. Armfield
(c.1850).*

dogs described above. These two emerging terrier breeds are too precious to be put at risk; the step from show ring debut to being the most popular breeds for puppy-farmers, as Westies and Yorkies now are, is a worryingly short one. I see some Parson Russell Terriers at KC shows, which could still work, but I also see some that are shelly, slab-sided, too short in the back and with poor feet and snipey muzzles. The

*Yorkshire Terriers depicted by W. Harrowing (1891) – much more
terrier-like, much less Toy dog than nowadays.*

movement of so many terriers at KC shows is desperately worrying, but then how can any dog move well when it's strung up on too taut a lead with its front legs only skimming the ground?

Pedigree Health

Pedigree terrier breeders are becoming much more knowledgeable about health problems in their breeds. Inherited defects in popular terrier breeds such as Scotties, Westies and Cairns are well documented, but the minor breeds have their problems too. Research carried out by Dr Martina Ruchti in Switzerland showed that 80 per cent of Norwich Terriers were affected by an upper airway problem. A further 16 per cent were suspiciously affected and only 4 per cent were clear. Another researcher, William E Schultz, DVM, suggests that as many as 95 per cent of dogs of this breed have everted saccules, lumps of tissue located between the vocal folds and the outside of the larynx. These are worrying percentages; breeds with a small gene pool have to be eternally vigilant – and honest about problems, some of which come not from close-breeding but from breeding for an untraditional, undesirable template.

If you look at the early photographs of the prototypal dogs in just about every KC-recognized terrier breed (with the notable exception of the Border Terrier and perhaps the Cairn) and then compare them with contemporary dogs, you will soon see how far they have wandered from their own original type. With a closed gene pool in every KC-registered breed, how can this divergence be remedied? With so many worrying inherited diseases manifesting themselves in our pedigree terrier breeds, what breeding programmes are being scientifically planned to breed them out – such as outcrosses to other more virile breeds? We need the enlightened approach of individuals like Brian Plummer if informed initiatives are to be undertaken.

Our breeds of dog came to us as the result of the single-mindedness, commitment, dogged determination and skill of individuals, not clubs or committees. I take my hat off to the admirable individuals who are striving to produce the Sporting Lucas and Plummer Terriers; unlike many of us their efforts will still be appreciated long after their time is up. With the KC registration lists increasingly dominated by foreign breeds, it is so encouraging to see British dogs being championed, to see British terriers being promoted and to see working capabilities being respected. Every terrier breed, to justify the name, must be bred with the *ability* and the anatomy to work, even if they are not required to do so.

There is growing up in this country at the moment at least one generation that has never experienced the joy of working a hedgerow with a pair of happy terriers, never witnessed the excitement of ratting in a barn or, as Brian Plummer's terrier pack used to, in a maggot factory! No teenager with his own terrier is ever going to complain of being bored. Anyone brave enough to own a Plummer Terrier is going to have to love a challenge! Anyone wishing to own a highly individual Sporting Lucas Terrier will be wanting to join a quite admirable group of true terrier lovers on a most worthy quest. Here's to the future success of the Patterdale, the Fell, the Plummer and the Sporting Lucas Terrier and those associated with their emergence.

There are lovers of the hard-bitten 'earth-dogs' who still keep these strains inviolate, and who greatly prefer them to the better-known terriers whose natural activities have been too often atrophied by a system of artificial breeding to show points. Few of these old unregistered breeds would attract the eye of the fancier accustomed to judge a dog parading before him in the show ring. To know their value and to appreciate their sterling good qualities, one needs to watch them at work on badger or when they hit upon the line of an otter. It is then that they display the alertness and the dare-devil courage which have won for the English terriers their name and fame.

Dogs and All About Them by Robert Leighton
(Cassell, 1914)

Old English Wire-Haired Terriers
The entries in these classes were not many, but everything must have a beginning, and no doubt there will be a much larger entry next time. In the over 20lb class a rare good stamp of terrier turned up in Adam III. This dog has a long, powerful jaw, well-placed and right-sized eye, lean flat head, wonderful shoulders, and straight front, round bone, good feet, with a stout pad under them, and a fair coat; his ears are a good size, but he would not carry one of them, and is not of a taking colour; he would be the better for a bit more strength of loin and thighs, but is altogether a capital terrier.

Report from the Kennel Club Show at Alexandra Palace, February 1889. Fox Terriers, Welsh Terriers and Airedales were judged in their own classes; this class did not survive and England lost a terrier breed.

Old English Terriers
Much the same dogs have been carrying off the prizes throughout the year, with one exception of a new face in Boughton Curio, who was bred by Mr A E Clear and brought out at Birkenhead. This dog is a beautiful terrier, with very few faults indeed; but it is a great pity that he is a Fox Terrier bred one. Notwithstanding this, he can very easily defeat any of his own sex in the breed. Welsh Terrier breeders are now closely approaching us in type of head, which was before the only difference that an ordinary visitor to a show could see between the two breeds, and it will therefore soon be practically impossible to tell one breed from the other.

From the 'Annual Retrospect, the Breeds in 1892' in *The Kennel Gazette*, January 1893.

These were the dying days, as a breed, of the old black and tan rough-coated terrier of England. This 'Annual Retrospect' in *The Kennel Gazette* provided a most valuable summary of the state of a breed and is much missed. This publication does not print such critiques nowadays, concentrating instead on praise for show dogs that have won. The Kennel Club of England did little to conserve the Old English Terrier, but their Terrier Group now embraces four Irish, five Scottish, two Welsh and even a newly created terrier breed from mainland Europe.

Terriers Abroad

Most of the terrier breeds are quintessentially British. But nowadays we can read of Rat Terriers as a breed in America, the Brazilian Terrier and the well-established Australian Terrier, as well as the misnamed Tibetan Terrier. French and German writers of previous centuries have made reference to dogs functioning as terriers, not just Dachshund types but Pinschers and Schnauzers too. We may have captured the terrier breed market but not the terrier function. The Dutch have re-created their Smoushond, with a distinct terrier appearance. The German Hunt Terrier has fanciers here; the newly created Cesky Terrier is finding favour here too. The Boston Terrier is not an earth-dog although it does have a bull terrier ingredient in its ancestry.

The Smoushond of Holland.

The Cesky Terrier.

Chien aboyeur (pour sangliers); *the baying dog, for wild boar.*

The old type of Boston Terrier of 1904.

The Pinschers

The Doberman Pinscher and the Giant Schnauzer are, like the Airedale and the Russian Black Terrier, not exactly earth-dogs, but the smaller pinschers and schnauzers were farm and stable vermin controllers, just like our native terriers. The smooth-haired Austrian Pinscher has many similarities with our emergent Plummer Terriers. The Franks had a small dog they called the *bibarhund* or *biberhunt*, literally 'beaver-dog'. From these came a type referred to as rattlers, both smooth and rough haired. Later came the Rattinpintscher, literally a dog that nips rats, and in time the breed type we know as the pinscher and schnauzer, literally a dog with a bearded muzzle, developed. The German authority Richard Strebel, writing in his massive 1903 work, *Die Deutschen Hunde* (German Dogs), recorded that: 'There is little to say about the history of the German Pinscher. Illustrations of the breed are rare. It does not appear in old oil paintings. He occupied such a menial position, so unimportant, that artists felt it not worth their while to depict him for posterity.'

That statement echoes the omission of both pastoral dogs and terriers from English paintings of past

Austrian Pinscher.

centuries. In some old English dictionaries, the word pinscher is defined as a dog breed, a short-haired English Terrier, black and tan terrier, rough or wire-haired terrier. Some authorities state that the pinscher originated from stock brought back from England by German workers and that a cross with the French

An English print from the 1800s of a terrier-like dog called 'Pinscher'.

Early Schnauzers; note the much more terrier-like appearance of these harsh-coated dogs.

The Ratonero Bodeguero from Andalucia.

griffon-type produced the rough or wire-haired variety, to become known as the Schnauzer. Interestingly, there is an old English print from the early 1800s depicting a notable bull-and-terrier of that time, with a definite Continental look to it, called 'Pinscher'.

European Interest and Field Use

In Ireland, the unusual smoke-grey coat of the Kerry Blue Terrier has been linked with the Harlequin Pinschers of the soldiers of the House of Hesse, who were stationed there. In Kay's *Portraits From Nature* (*c.*1810) there is an illustration from Scotland of a Pinscher. In the coastal areas of the Scottish Highlands lived men who served as mercenaries in German armies, and the Pinscher may have been imported by them. As far as the German Hunt Terrier is concerned, the reverse may have happened. When I was working in Germany nearly fifty years ago, an old German Forstmeisster told me that his grandfather had imported English hunt terriers to control vermin. International boundaries have never been barriers to the dog trade.

In France, the Société Centrale Canine and the Réunion des Amateurs de Fox Terriers have instituted the Coupe de France de Broussaillage – flushing game above ground. Smooth Fox Terriers there are recognized not just below ground, but for their aptitude for hunting above ground, flushing out wild pig from thick undergrowth and their persistence and boldness in the drive. German Hunt Terriers, Jack Russells and Welsh Terriers are used, as well as the Fox. Points are awarded for performance during the search (15),

flushing and voice (20), drive and pursuit (10) and reaction to gunfire (5). Judges can multiply the scores according to the dog's overall showing, so that a total of say 40 could be increased by doubling or even tripling the score to 80 or 120. Grades are awarded for 125–150 points (excellent), 100–125 (trés bon) and 75–100 (bon), with 50–75 earning an honourable mention. How good it would be if such terrier working tests were to be introduced here, if only to reveal the braggers!

The Tenterfield Terrier from Australia.

Terrier Derivatives

The past popularity of the Fox Terrier has led to derivatives appearing even further afield. In America the Rat Terrier and the Toy Fox Terrier (not a smaller Fox Terrier but a newly created breed, with Chihuahua and Manchester Terrier blood), both recognized breeds, have been developed. In Andalucia, Spain, the sherry houses and wine shops use another Fox Terrier derivative, the Ratonero Bodeguero, to keep rats under control in their store rooms. The Rat Terrier, developed allegedly from crosses of Smooth Fox Terrier and the Manchester Terrier, comes in three sizes: 14–23in, 10–14in and under 8in in the miniature form. The larger sizes were once used in rat-baiting contests, but are most famous for achieving huge totals of rats killed on farms, with the record set at around 2,500 rats killed in an infested barn over a seven-hour period. They are used by American hunters on squirrel, coon, possum and ground game, as well as in tracking wild boar and deer. Beagle blood has increased size, scenting and hunting skills; Whippet blood has provided the source for the blue and brindle colours. The 10in-high Toy Fox Terrier is still used as a rat killer, having lost little of its tenacity in its reduced form.

The Shelburne Terrier was developed a century ago, in Vermont, USA for work with the Shelburne Foxhounds. The original stock came from a Sealyham–Wire-Haired Fox Terrier cross, with a dash of Norfolk Terrier and later an infusion of blood from what were termed 'Jones Terriers' after their Leicester breeder. Red became the favoured colour, but a back-crossing to a Sealyham restored the white coat. They were described as weighing around 12lb and eventually featured all the terrier coat colours, revealing their mixed origin.

The Sealydale – from Airedale and Sealyham blood, hence the composite name – was developed in South Africa just after the First World War by Miss Bodmer. Looking like Jack Russells and lacking any trace of Airedale blood, they became popular amongst local sportsmen as vermin catchers but never became established as a distinct breed. Both the Shelburne and the Sealydale illustrate the reliance on British terrier blood when a sporting terrier was desired.

The Japanese Terrier, 12–13in high, is also called the Nippon Terrier, Mikado Terrier and Oyuki or

Australian Terrier.

snowy terrier, but is essentially a companion dog. The Brazilian Terrier, also called the Fox Paulistina, is used to control vermin on ranches and estates and is derived from imported Fox Terrier blood, weighing around 15–20lb; in their native country they come second to the Filas in numbers of registrations. The Tenterfield Terrier in Australia, around a foot high, can be confused with a Jack Russell, but the head is narrower and finer, and the bone heavier and the build stockier. It is not known outside Australia.

Well known outside Australia, however, is the national terrier, the Australian by name. With more than fifty registrations each year here, this terrier breed originated in Tasmania around 1800, where

The Shelburne Terrier, depicted in 1930 by F. Vow.

A Schipperke from 1930 – more like terriers than the other groups of recognized breeds.

German Pinscher in Stuttgart, 1904.

little vermin-destroyers, weighing around 10lb and bearing striking blue sheen coats with tan under-markings, became valued. Once known as the broken-coated blue and tan terrier, it is said to have Skye Terrier blood for colour of coat, length of body and shortness of legs, Scottish Terrier blood for harshness of coat and Dandie Dinmont blood for the topknot. There are claims too of Yorkshire terrier blood and the introduction of Irish Terrier blood to stabilize the red colour. It could be that the major input came from the old black and tan rough-coated common terrier of England, taken to Australia by settlers. At 10in high and around 14lb weight, I am impressed by those I see at shows, but I am not aware of their working use by any reputable terrier-men, which is a pity. In *Australian Barkers and Biters* (1914), Robert Kaleski writes these words on the terrier need there: 'There is generally in the Australian bush a need for a small ver-min-dog – to kill rats, rabbits, foxes, bandicoots, etc… The best dog for this is, of course, a small smooth-haired Terrier; and the best of the smooth-haired Ter-riers is the "Foxie". It is ironic that the blood and performance of our Fox Terrier are rated more in Aus-tralia, Japan, Brazil, North America and southern Spain than here.

There is a distinct terrier look to the Belgian breed of Schipperke, used as a vermin controller on barges there; they are sharp-witted and quick-moving, with an alert expression and a terrier-like attitude. Coming from the old province of Flanders, they were popular along the canals of Belgium and Holland and have been credited with the first one-breed dog show, one set up by guild workmen in 1690. Strangely our Kennel Club puts this breed in their Utility Group, with the Schnau-zer and its smaller variety, but puts the German Pinsch-er in the Working Group and its smaller variety in the Toy Group. The German earth-dog, the Dachshund, is considered by them to be a hound.

A German Hunt Terrier – it could have been from English stock.

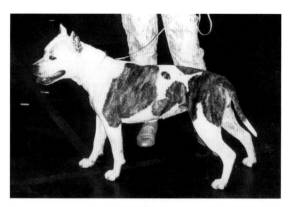

An impressive American Staffordshire Terrier, carrying the head of our old Bull Terrier type.

The German Hunt Terrier is gaining ground here and has a distinct Lakeland Terrier look to it. Welsh and Fox Terrier blood has been claimed in the development of this attractive little sporting dog. As always with German native breeds their breeding is well stewarded and an underground test mandatory for breeding stock.

The Smoushond of Holland has much in common with the old German rough-haired Pinschers but still throws black and tan progeny, with some experts claiming an infusion of English terrier blood in their development. Wherever terrier-like dogs appear in the world an origin in British terrier stock is likely; the reputation of British terriers is rightly acknowledged by dog-breeders all over the developed world.

The American Staffordshire Terrier

British terrier stock was very much involved in the origin of the American Staffordshire Terrier, a breed developed there and from the same root stock as the American Pit Bull Terrier. The American Staffordshire Terrier, or Amstaff, is now highly popular in continental Europe but is unlikely to be favoured in Britain because of the Dangerous Dogs Act, which judges a dog's behaviour on its physical construction. Amstaffs do look like Pit Bulls. I have seen them at half a dozen world dog shows from Helsinki, Budapest and Vienna to Brussels, Dortmund, Oporto and Lisbon. Two aspects of their appearance there stand out: firstly they were for me the best breed there for physical soundness and secondly every single one of them had a stable, equable, quite admirable

temperament. Their conformation was a model for many breeds: the breed uniformity was remarkable – each one looked as though it had come from the same dam! They may well have been the best-bred dogs on display. They resembled our old Bull Terriers as depicted by nineteenth-century artists, and represent the unexaggerated, eminently sound, canine athleticism desired by our ancestors in their vermin-controlling terriers. Their blood would improve our waddling, egg-headed Bull Terriers and provide good breeding material for those seeking bull-lurchers. For such admirable dogs to be denied to dog men here by ill-founded, poorly drafted legislation is lamentable.

A show of ratting terriers was held in the Palais de l'Industrie at Antwerp in July, and is worthy of record as being the first show held in Belgium by a specialist club. The entry of 156 included 16 dachshunds, 13 Schipperkes, 40 fox terriers, 2 Skyes, 6 bull terriers, 3 Yorkshire terriers, and several toy griffons, with a few white English terriers and black and tans, in addition to a nondescript variety class … on the second and third days the visitors were treated to grand ratting contests, which are very popular in Belgium. There were no English exhibitors present…

The Kennel Gazette, August 1888

The Teckel

The Badger Dog and the Badger Hound

I have written that terriers as earth-dogs are very much a British creation, although pinschers and schnauzers, and especially the German Hunt Terrier, are terrier-type. But the Dachshund, classified by the Kennel Club as a hound ('*Hund*', although very similar to our word 'hound', actually just means 'dog'; the German word for hound is '*Bracke*'), in its working role or Teckel use, is very terrier in function. Much is made in show dog histories of the Dachshund of clandestine terrier blood infusions, especially the Dandie Dinmont contribution, but I can find no proven use of terrier blood in the creation of the Dachshund. The development of the wire hair was aided in 1925 from Dandie blood by Lt Klaus Graf Hahn of Potsdam, but the centre of working use was the Harz mountains, where *Dachswurgers* (badger-destroyers) were treasured, and where one can find intriguing references to a *Lockhundlein* or little decoy dog.

A far more compelling version of the Dachshund's ancestry traces its descent from German foothounds, like the Dachsbracke. In the early 1800s, a Prussian forester called von Daacke was increasing the Dachshund's scenting ability by outcrossing to his Hanoverian Schweisshunds, producing red dogs with black masks and an eel stripe along their backs. Small foothounds were favourite sporting dogs in western and central Europe in past centuries: the Drever in Sweden, the Steenbrak in Holland, the Sauerland Hound or Steinbracke, as well as the Dachsbracke, in

The Kaiser with his Teckels at Hubertusstock, 1892.

A Teckel, acting as tracker, with a Schweisshund, acting as scenter, in the German stag hunt.

Dachshunds portrayed by A. Wardle (c.1898).

The Dachsbracke is the badger hound.

Alpine Dachsbracke, 'Erzgebirglers' from the Erz (Ore) Mountains near the Czech border.

Dachshunds eyeing a rabbit, by J. Hartung (c.1875).

Germany and the Jura Niederlaufhund in Switzerland. There is a variety called the Alpine Dachsbracke, found in the Erzgebirge mountains near the Czech border, known locally as the 'Erzgebirgler', usually in a rich tan. Most of the Swiss hound breeds have a smaller, shorter-legged Niederlaufhund variety, illustrating the genetic tendency in these foothounds. Our English Basset, bred by the packs and the result of a Harrier outcross, is our equivalent hunting hound.

As the Basset Hound demonstrates, these small hounds can throw crooked-legged dwarf offspring, with the show ring favouring the latter and sportsmen going for the straight-legged variety. The Dachsbracke, or Badger Hound, represents the latter, with the Dachshund or Badger Dog representing the former. Crooked-legged dwarfism is a genetic freak, an abnormality called achondroplasia, inherited recessively. As breed depictions indicate down the years, such a genetic sidetrack exaggerates itself over time, leading to the harmful elongated backs and the disabling legs of the show ring specimens. In the Dachshund front, the whole forehand structure is reduced in bone length, the elbow action arc being actually *above* the brisket line. Not surprisingly, Dachshunds and, say, a sighthound breed such as the Saluki, move very differently from each other. Dachshunds are the only breed with the shoulders positioned so high above the brisket, or keel, as breed fanciers like to term it. The Dachshund is predisposed to intervertebral disc disease because of its conformation, with disc disease occurring in young dogs as well as in old.

R. Strebel's 1905 portrayal of the wide variety in Dachshunds, all showing the high head carriage.

Size

Described in its sporting past as a *Dachskrieger* or badger-warrior, with the lower to ground specimens called *Dachskriecher* or badger-creeper, any Dachshund would have to be some dog, physically and in spirit to tackle a badger. Every earth-dog needs remarkable agility to work underground, both to manoeuvre and to dig. The anatomy alone of the show ring specimens would preclude such activity. Hunt terriers tend to be 12–14in at the shoulder and weigh around 14lb, because that is what enables their function. The ideal weight for a Dachshund is 20–26lb, while the miniature varieties are around 10lb – not much for badgers to fear there! For a 10lb dog, practically legless and with an exaggerated weakened spine, to be called a 'badger-dog' is absurd; 'badger-breakfast' would be more accurate!

Soundness

In one of his invaluable books, R.H. Smythe, himself a vet and exhibitor, wrote, in *The Dog – Structure and Movement* (Foulsham, 1970):

> So far as their spines are concerned the most unfortunate are the long-backed dogs, especially the Dachshunds. The abnormal length of spine between the wither and the croup is unsupported at its centre so that undue strain falls upon the intervertebral articulations and the intervening cartilaginous discs. It has been said that the normal life of dogs of this breed is fourteen years, but the spine is good only for five years. Although Dachshunds tend to suffer at intervals from disc trouble with temporary recoveries, the tendency is for ultimate paralysis to develop at a comparatively early age.

Dog breeders shouldn't need veterinary advice to breed soundly constructed animals, just affection for their breed and simple humanity.

My concern over long-backed, short-legged dogs, the exaggerated show specimens rather than the Teckels, relates to the strain on their spines on the move. Unlike longer-legged, shorter-backed breeds, the dog's weight is not supported continuously by the legs. The hind legs are just not long enough to place the hind feet close to the fore feet while moving. The spine therefore bears the weight unsupported and the consequent strain must be appreciable. Vets complain of seeing Dachshunds in their surgeries who are only a year old but have 'five-year-old spines'. 'Sausage dogs' can be endearing to many, but back pain to all is best avoided, and could so easily be in this breed by breeding for a shorter back and lengthier legs.

Sporting Dachshunds

Encouragement comes in the form of the Teckel, the sporting Dachshund, so like a shorter-legged Basset Fauve de Bretagne, or chestnut Basset of Brittany, a most engaging little hound. Teckels have been used extensively for deer work, both in stalking and tracking. They were introduced to the UK in the 1970s, with the UK Teckel Stud Book Society founded in 1999. There are over 580 Teckels registered with the society to date. The Ryeford Chase is a private pack of thirty couple Griffon Vendeen Bassets and uniquely ten couple Teckels, started in 1974 and willing to hunt all over the country. I have heard the smaller Teckels described as *Dachsels* or *Kaninchen*, used as rabbit dogs, on the continent, where nine distinct tests are conducted to test hunting skills, including a water trial. The wire-haired variety is favoured by hunters from Poland to Slovenia. Colours recognized by the Stud Book Society are black and tan, chocolate and tan, red, brindle and dapple.

Earth-Dog Tests

The vast majority of the UK Teckels are used for deer work and so most of the nine working tests don't apply but their existence displays a commendable, genuine desire to perpetuate a working breed. The German working tests include ones for gun-shyness, underground work (hold at bay not kill), tracking a 1,000m boar blood trail and specific tests to bay boar, deer and fox. Earth-dog tests are conducted both in France and North America, designed to test terriers and Teckels under the ground using tunnels, pipes and artificial burrows. Earth-dog tests in the USA involve a junior (instinct) test, where the dog has to traverse a 30ft-long, wood-lined, underground tunnel with three 90-degree turns and 'work' the prey (caged rats) for at least sixty seconds. There are more realistic tests for the Senior and Master Earth-Dog titles. I understand that the Irish Kennel Club has now formulated a working test for Dachshunds, consisting of four parts, all to be taken on the same day. There are 25 points available for each part, with a pass mark of 50 out of 100, even if no marks are scored in one part. The first part consists of tracking, following a 300–400m trail, which is two to three hours old, with points allotted for searching ability, accuracy, obedience and endurance. The second part is going to ground,

C. F. Tunnicliffe's depiction of badger dogs in the 1950s.

Teckels in the hunting field.

Terrier-like 'boar-finder' used in the German boar hunt.

Dachshunds, 'bred to be warriors', by A.H. Mackeprang (c.1875).

through a tunnel, with points for willingness to enter and speed. The third part is for obedience, with points for staying with the handler in sight, recall and lead-training; the fourth part involves a gun test, although a temperament test may be substituted to appease the anti-gun lobby. Could we not copy this sort of test for all our earth-dogs?

> The kind of dog used for hunting the boar is quite different to what I had expected to meet with… In the country through which I have travelled the hunters never make use of any other than a kind of hound, of a cross breed between the yellow blood-hound and a small dog called a dachshund or dachslein – badger hound – which is, in fact, a terrier with very crooked legs, but possessing in a very great degree both the appearance and fine nose of the beagle… He is a small dog, but varying in size, as do our terriers… There are some also with straight legs, but they are not considered of so high courage as the crooked-legged ones, and are chiefly used for unearthing the fox and badger.
>
> Leading article in *The Kennel Gazette*, February 1884.

(It is of interest that the straight-legged ones did the digging; a great deal is made in the United States of the advantage of bent legs for Dachshunds when digging.)

> Duckmanton Winkle (vhc) was in wretched condition. Jack Twopence (hc) has a good skull and set on of ear, but his long thin legs, and sharply pointed muzzle, put him out of any keen competition. The others need no comment; they were nearly all cripples.
>
> From the Dachshund judge's critique from the Kennel Club's 35th Show, April 1891

> I think we should guard against lapsing into any feeling of satisfaction as to the very long, very loinless, and very jointless type of which there are now too many, a type too painfully like those clever Chinese toys for children, made of jointed pieces of wood in the semblance of a crocodile. Moreover, we ought also to guard against those many weak-jawed Dachshunds who could hardly hope to compete with a sparrow, and would probably be unequal to the task of carrying a straw for twenty yards in their poor little pinched and beak-like jaws.
>
> *The Kennel Gazette*, February 1893

CHAPTER 3

THE ESSENTIALS OF THE SPORTING TERRIER

Sound Movement

Short Limbs

The great expert on the conformation of the dog, who was active in the middle of the last century, was vet, exhibitor and sportsman R.H. Smythe. In *The Examination of Animals for Soundness*, he wrote, on dogs: 'Intermittent lameness in the hindlimb is very frequent from patellar causes in the short-limbed dogs (Cairns, Sealyhams, West Highlands and Scottish Terriers). It will also be observed whether the dog "hops" occasionally on one hind limb with the opposite foot held off the ground momentarily (a sign of patellar subluxation).' If he were writing today he would more likely cite Jack Russells, as I see so many which 'carry' a hindlimb every few strides. This is not a good sign because these dogs are so often bred from, and their characteristic movement is considered almost a charming breed feature. Even canine sportsmen need sound knees, however, so there has to be more than a 'hop and a skip' to terrier movement.

Sporting terriers in pursuit by F. Paton (1892).

Dogs with short legs have long been a feature of man's association with sporting, working and companion dogs. Breeds with particularly short legs, like the Dachshund, the two corgi breeds and other heelers, the various Basset Hound breeds, any number of

Fox Terriers moving well, by F. Paton (1892).

Duck hunting with two Fox Terriers and a Bull-and-Terrier, 1835.

terriers and many Toy dog breeds, have been favoured for quite some time by any number of people. There is a worry, however, that in those breeds the shortness of the legs has been more and more exaggerated, to the detriment of the dog. Some breeders of such dogs are resentful of measures being planned on mainland Europe to counteract extreme shortness in a dog's legs, pleading that their particular breed has 'always looked like that' and is not uncomfortable. There is of course a huge difference between small dogs with proportionately short legs and bigger dogs made appreciably shorter by the absence of leg length.

In May 2003 I judged a show for Plummer Terriers, having, a few years before, judged the annual show of the Sporting Lucas Terrier Club. On each occasion I was mainly going over dogs that worked for their living, hunting ground vermin, many of them owned or bred by professional terrier-men. Not one of them was exceptionally low and long, they were not desired to be; rather they had an anatomy that allowed them to function underground – an eel-like flexibility based on a strong, supple spine. If professional terrier-men see no value in exceptionally long and low earth-dogs, why does a KC committee based in Piccadilly think it knows better? If function does not justify the exaggerated form of a breed of dogs and if vets condemn the conformation being sought, how can the endorsement of unusually long and low dogs by the KC justify their declared purpose of 'improving dogs'? If you compare illustrations of Skye, Dandie Dinmont and Sealyham Terriers of one hundred years ago with those of today, I don't think the word 'improvement' is appropriate. Terriers with no leg length cannot move freely.

Importance of Shoulders

On the subject of shoulders, the late Tom Horner, who knew a thing or two about terrier movement, wrote:

> If the upper arm is short and/or steep, the angle between it and the shoulder blade will be much greater – more open than the desired 90 degrees – with the result that the elbow will be brought forward on the chest and the possible length of stride of the foreleg will be reduced. If shoulders are also steep the angle will be greater still and the stride even shorter.

Plummer Terrier eager to move.

A brace of working Sealyhams.

Wire-Haired Fox Terriers by Sir George Pirie (1863–1946); their front assemblies allow sound movement.

Small terriers with a shortened front stride are now almost the uniform exhibit in our show rings. It is extremely tiresome when this draws admiration from TV commentators at Crufts, who describe them as 'simply flowing over the ground' – perhaps because they can't walk naturally!

When a dog's shoulders are too upright they tend also to be narrower, shorter and bunch the muscles, giving a coarse look. This in turn shortens the neck and artificially lengthens the back, producing an unbalanced dog. Breeds like the Skye and the Dandie are now longer in the back and shorter in the leg than their ancestors. Working hunt terriers are usually a little longer backed than their show ring opposite numbers but for a good reason: the long, sloping shoulder tends to accompany the slightly longer back, while the pursuit of a cobby terrier, with the shorter back, encourages the more upright shoulder. Dogs required to work underground need flexible backs so that they can work in confined spaces. Most show Fox Terriers would have some difficulty manoeuvring underground because of the construction now apparently sought in them.

In his book on the Border Terrier (1991), Walter Gardner has written:

The well-laid on shoulder allows for great range and liberty of movement. On the other hand, when the shoulder blade is lacking in correct obliquity and is too upright, it usually lacks the desired length and therefore muscle attachment. The movement is therefore contracted, and the action short, cramped and lacking in elasticity.

It is this short, cramped, restricted forward movement that so many small breeds demonstrate in the ring and even get rewarded for. Walter Gardner goes on to state, 'it is unfortunate that many of those who are judging dogs have never had the opportunity to judge any other type of stock'. Certainly, working horses are often stocky in build but display superbly placed shoulders. This feature is prized in the horse show ring. So many of the pioneer judges at dog shows were pony judges too.

Movement in the Show Ring

A jaunty carriage, a blur of legs moving at high speed and a perky determination from a small dog in the show ring often brings unwarranted admiration – unfailingly from the fawning, uncritical TV commentators at Crufts. Most very small pedigree breeds that

I see in the show ring display poor movement, usually stepping short in front with little forward reach and lacking any power from their lower hindquarters. Once judges accept such limited movement as characteristic then an inbred fault is on the way to becoming sealed in the gene pool. That is very bad news for small dogs. I can understand, without approving, poor movement in Toy breeds being condoned, as so many have anatomical designs that create such an undesirable manifestation, but unsound movement in small terriers is worrying. These are *sporting* breeds. The sporting terrier is part of Britain's great sporting heritage and even the smallest of them must be a real terrier, in build and in attitude. Exhibits from any sporting breed should be disqualified in the ring for poor movement.

Critical Comments

What have show judges actually been saying about movement in the pedigree terrier breeds in their critiques in the last decade? Here are some from 1997: Border Terriers: 'Movement is still a problem'; Border Terriers (at Crufts): 'Sadly, movement left much to be desired'; Dandie Dinmont Terriers: 'Hind movement in some was very bad'; and from Crufts 2000: Airedale Terriers: 'Movement is shocking'; Kerry Blue Terriers: 'Two main faults appeared ... and rear movement'; Sealyham Terriers: 'I found ... bad hind movement'.

The four Crufts reports are the most worrying, for how do exhibits that display poor movement actually qualify? Who would want to breed from such dogs? But terriers that qualify for Crufts are rarely *not* bred from; this is a worry. Who are the allegedly skilled breeders, breeding to the standard, who are producing these dogs with such unsatisfactory movement? Are they judges as well? The Border Terrier is expected to have movement sound enough to follow a horse. The Dandie Dinmont Terrier is expected to have a fluent, free and easy stride. For these two breeds of sporting terrier to have even disappointing movement is a poor comment on some contemporary breeders.

If you accept that movement is a manifestation of sound anatomy, why are poor movers not thrown out of the ring? When I watch the judging even at working terrier shows, I still see weak pasterns, turned-out toes (acceptable in short-legged terriers but not the leggier specimens) and loose elbows up front, and cow hocks, bowed hocks, and too close or too wide a hind action. Poor shoulder placement and straight stifles and hocks are the cause of much poor movement in working terriers. Such functional dogs should move 'as square as a box', as the great terrier-man O.T. Price would have put it. This means an action that is free, with appreciable but not long strides, parallel at both ends – showing the pads of the hind feet, with obvious drive from the hocks, a level topline – retained on the move, with the tail on top, a determined carriage of the head and a definite air of bossiness.

Movement Faults

We may not want our small terriers to move like ponies but we should try to ensure that they are able to lead active lives. A tiny Norwich, a sturdy Scottie, a cocky Cairn or a jaunty Jack Russell should, each in its own way, move soundly. It is not in the best interests of such dogs for them to be allowed to get away with poor movement or be judged as if sound movement didn't matter at all. Faulty movement rooted in the forequarters is more serious than in the hindquarters. The centre of gravity of the terrier is situated just behind the front legs. Some of the longer-legged terriers experience the wear and tear of 'pounding', in which the front foot touches the ground before the forward thrust, providing locomotion in the dog, has been expended; this creates physical stress.

Long-standing faults in Dachshunds have been short necks, upright shoulders and loose elbows. Not surprisingly movement in the breed has long been a weak spot. The high head carriage helps this breed, but it has to take an awful lot of steps to get anywhere.

Unless the head is carried high, the appropriate muscles will not be able to pull the upper arm and then the whole foreleg forward to its full extent. Judges need to watch a dog moving across and then towards them and establish that the two forelegs are being brought *well* forward from the shoulders and the elbows. Any dog that 'marks time' is incorrectly constructed. Insufficient angulation between the pelvis and the spine, high-placed hocks and straight stifles contribute to a short back stride and can be detected from a stilted action. But if that stilted action is actually admired, the fault is effectively condoned.

Small dogs with small bones, just as much as bigger, heavier dogs, need sound construction to lead a healthy, happy life. 'Stepping short' on the parade ground is a deliberately artificial movement and a surprisingly tiring one; stepping short in the show ring too should be regarded as artificial, unnatural and undesired. All dogs can only move with the construction bestowed upon them by their designers and breeders. I suspect, with some sadness, that breeders will continue to do their own thing, whatever the effect on the dog. Terriers in the show ring tend to have non-existent fore-chests, their front legs too far forward on the body, barrel-straight vertical front pasterns, allowing little spring or give, especially when the dog jumps, and little bend in their front pasterns when on the move. Straight-stifled breeds can produce what has been termed a 'sickle-like' action, where the rear pastern doesn't completely open at the hock.

For me, the Soft-Coated Wheaten and Kerry Blue Terriers often feature too long a second thigh, which can cause the hind-legs to over-extend, in a tiringly high bicycle-pedal action, in order to retain coordination with their shorter front legs. The Norwich Terrier is becoming too short-bodied and stocky, whereas its sister breed, the Norfolk Terrier, is longer in the body and a better mover. Compactness doesn't mean too short-bodied. In the show Bedlington, the feet are closer than the elbows, to produce what in horses is termed a 'fast-trotters front'. Does a sporting terrier need such a front? Construction affects balance and balance affects movement. Proportions relate to breed type, balance, function and movement, both when the dog is walking briskly and cantering.

In *An Eye for a Dog* (Dogwise Publishing, 2004), conformation expert Robert W. Cole writes that: 'There are six terrier breeds that, due to their specialized forequarters, do not move at the same trot in the same manner as normally constructed breeds. These six terrier breeds are the Airedale, the Lakeland, the Smooth Fox Terrier, the Wire Fox Terrier, the Irish Terrier, and the Welsh Terrier.' He comments on the stress given in the descriptions of such breeds to the power coming from the rear, undermining both the need for strength up front and a balance between the energy emanating from both front and rear assemblies. He also emphasizes the need for 'a show of pads'

Different breeds – same quest.

Hunt terrier – built to move well.

when the dog is moving away, stating that a 'no-show' can indicate the dreaded sickle-hock. I see all too many show ring terriers with short steep upper arms, upright shoulders, straight stifles and narrow chests; they are no longer sporting terriers.

Flawed Winners
What I find especially baffling at KC dog shows is how dogs are awarded tickets when they breach their own breed standard, whoever has approved it. If you examine the wording of the KC breed standard of the smaller terriers on movement you find highly commendable wording. The Cairn is expected to have 'very free-flowing stride. Forelegs reaching well forward.' The Dandie Dinmont is required to have 'a fluent, free and easy stride, reaching forward at the front', and a stilted gait is highly undesirable. The Glen of Imaal has to be free in action. The Scottie has to have a smooth and free movement. The Skye's whole movement is termed free and active. The Westie's must be free, with the front legs freely extended forward from the shoulder. So far, so good.

If you then spend time studying these breeds in the ring, what do you find? I see them, almost invariably, with short upper arms and upright shoulders which limit their reach and give them a fast, chopping, stilted, abbreviated front action with nothing free about it. Yet these dogs win, even at Crufts! The profusion of coat in some of them gives the illusion of their flowing over the ground – but then so too do millipedes. The extent of a dog's front stride is controlled by the length of its upper arm and the angulation or slope of its shoulders. The too-fast, short-reaching, chopping

The Earth Stopper, depicted in 1924 with his highly mobile terriers.

action of so many small terriers in the ring has almost become the norm. A good judge would notice that there is nothing free about such an action – the dog has to take two or three steps when one should do. Not surprisingly, this affects hind action too.

A canny judge will ask for small dogs to be moved slowly so that the true quality of the gait can be revealed. Just as the flying trot conceals a multitude of sins in the German Shepherd Dog, so too does the blurred, too-hasty, millipede-like leg movement in little dogs with little legs.

Breeding for the Future
In an emergent breed, like the Plummer and the Sporting Lucas Terrier, breeders have a one-shot opportunity to breed working terriers that could be envied the world over. Others are departing from soundness; now is surely the time to breed for the breed and not the wallet, and establish the basis of a breed that respects its own breed standard but ensure that dogs lacking working instincts are not bred from. Any fool can breed charming little dogs that resemble tail-less squirrels, or white-coated Yorkies fit only for the bed-warming role. Breeding a working terrier is surely a joyful challenge: does it *want* to work? Does it have an anatomy that *allows* it to work? Will those who come after us respect our work?

We live in times that threaten the very future of our sporting breeds. This means that without a loyal, well-intentioned, selfless, honourable band of breed fanciers to safeguard its future, many a breed will go to the wall. Sporting breeds will only survive because their survival is planned – and their ability to move soundly is ensured.

To achieve correct movement it is necessary to have the bones in the right places, of the right lengths and proportions to each other and held in place by tight ligaments and the right quantity of muscle... A dog's conformation is quite a complicated affair and movement cannot be judged by looking at it from just one or two directions. It must be looked at from in front, from behind and from the side... Looked at from the side the forelegs should reach well forward, irrespective of their length, without too much lift, 'cutting the daisies' as the horse people say... A long, smooth stride is what is wanted, reaching well back before

Sporting terriers have to be active, agile and athletic.

leaving the ground as the dog moves forward. Similarly, from the side the hind legs should reach well forward without too much lift, and well back, working all the time in co-ordination with the forelegs, with the drive from behind very apparent.

All About the Bull Terrier by Tom Horner (Pelham, 1973). Tom Horner was perhaps the best terrier judge of his generation, judging all breeds, not just the Bull Terrier.

Running with the Hounds

In the early part of the twentieth century, Major Harding Cox was a prominent figure in the canine world, both in the show and the hunting sphere. In 1928 he wrote a fairly forthright book on dogs, entitled *Dogs and I*, which had much to say on terriers. He ridiculed the whole concept of breeding leggy terriers capable of running with the hounds, writing that: 'The theory anent [concerning] Fox-terriers running with Fox-hounds is a fatuous one.' He considered that such misguided thinking resulted in long-legged, badly constructed terriers no longer capable of being earth-dogs. It is significant to note the physical type of today's terrier breeds which have survived the quest for terriers that can 'follow the hunt', such as Fox and Border Terriers.

On Fox Terriers, Harding Cox wrote:

All of a sudden there arose certain wiseacres in the ranks of Fox-terrier breeders who laid down a law, which went near to ruining the breed for good and all. They declared that the type which hitherto had been accepted *must* be scrapped, and that breeders *must* at

Ikey, a working terrier, carried on the saddle; from a painting by J.I. Chamberlain.

Border Terriers with Otterhounds, by Vernon Stokes (1938).

once set about producing dogs which would be fast enough and possess sufficient stamina to *run with hounds*! Goodness only knows how they expected a Terrier of even 22lb to run with Fox-hounds and live with them when driving at score on a holding scent! The whole thing was of course impossible, and the theory utterly ridiculous; but there it was! The benches were soon disgraced by long, leggy Terriers… for a long time, the insistence upon exceedingly narrow fronts made shallow chests, weak ribs and 'wedged' quarters inevitable!

He would not be amused by show-bench Fox Terriers today.

Dual-Purpose Dogs

In the breed standard of the Border Terrier, under the characteristics description, there is the phrase 'capable of following a horse', which is often interpreted as a requirement for the breed to run with the hounds. But the breed was often employed with foot-hounds not the mounted field. The physical needs of an earth-

The terrier-man of the Bicester Hunt, showing their then approved way of conveying a terrier.

Hunt Terrier with hounds (1900).

dog and a running dog are in conflict. I wonder if originally a phrase like 'able to follow the hunt', that is, to support the hounds once the quarry had been located as being underground, was used for terriers working with foot-hounds. The country over which the hunting took place, and where Border Terriers were used, was not always suitable for mounted huntsmen. In similar country, the Scots and the Cumbrians never sought a leggy terrier, able to run with the moving hunt. In his book on terriers of 1896, Rawdon Lee wrote: 'Some of the terriers follow hounds regularly, and are continually brought into use, not only amongst the rocks and in rough ground of that kind, but in equally or in more dangerous places – wet drains or moss holes, or "waterfalls", as they are called in Northumberland.' Not much scope for mounted huntsmen here!

An interesting point was made by a breed correspondent 'GL' in the Border Terrier breed notes in *Our Dogs* half a century ago:

They wanted a dog which could follow a horse. Here I think is something which is inclined to be misunderstood by many people. One must bear in mind that the horse in the Border counties would not be the same type as that used for hunting the flatter areas,

Hunt terrier with Foxhounds: Gone to Ground *by J. Emms (1882).*

but would be more often than not the cobs of the farmers, more noted for their stamina and their sure-footedness than their speed … the term 'follow a horse' is not intended to mean that a dog has to keep up with a hunter at full gallop … it means that the dog must have enough leg to enable him to cover the rough and hilly areas of the Border counties, and must be able to keep up with the horse under these circumstances.

Yet so many breed fanciers today overstate the requirement for their terriers to be able to 'run with the pack', a different concept entirely.

In his informative book on the Border Terrier (1991), Walter J.F. Gardner queries, 'How many of the world's top athletes are short-legged or short-backed or both? How many animals which go to ground or can gallop and stay long distances have a short back?' It is a question to be answered by Border Terrier devotees. There are obvious conflicts between the anatomy of a scenthound, even a foot-hound, and that of an earth-dog. It would be a challenge for any breed-designer to set out the blueprint for a sporting dog that could do *both* effectively; galloping and digging demand different physical qualities. How can you construct a terrier for which the show bench requires a short back whilst the working role demands a longer one; when the latter expects an animal designed to work underground, with ease, and some fanciers want them to be able to run with the hounds?

Running with the Pack

In the July 1999 issue of *Hunting* magazine, Martin Scott set out some interesting facts on hunt 'journeys', for example: on the 1973 Christmas Eve hunt of the Cottesmore, hounds covered 14 miles in one hour fifty-five minutes; in November 1983 the Bicester bitches in Cottesmore country had a four and a half mile point, and twice that as they ran, in seventy minutes; the Galway Blazers hunt managed 15 miles in under an hour and a half and there was a Heythrop hunt in 1971 which ran for nearly three and a half hours over 24 miles; in 1990, the North Cotswold had a run of 9 miles in fifty minutes. Any terrier attempting to accompany hounds at such a pace would need longer legs and bigger lungs than most terrier breed templates decree. Hounds are bred for pace; terriers are bred to dig.

No doubt a gutsy terrier will do its utmost to keep up with galloping hounds if asked to, but why impair its earth-dog capability by expecting it to run with hounds too? It imposes needless handicaps on the dog as a terrier, and in striving to be a hound as well, produces a composite anatomy unfitted for both roles. Both terriers and hounds can be designed for a specific hunting country and quarry but dual-purpose can so often result in 'not fit for purpose'. Daniel tells us of a match run in 1874 for a huge stake, in which a quite small terrier ran a mile in two minutes and six miles in eighteen minutes. He doesn't record whether the dog was any good underground! Sir Jocelyn Lucas's view was that 'most foxhound packs have a terrier man mounted or on foot, but in some of the wilder countries terriers run with the hounds and, although outpaced, always seem to cast up when needed.'

In *Fox-Hunting from Shire to Shire* (Routledge, 1912), Cuthbert Bradley, or 'Whipster' of *The Field* magazine, wrote:

For many years the Belvoir had a noted fox-terrier, named Bluecoat, running with the pack; a dog with a wonderful character for work, who never tired in the longest day's hunting. Bluecoat was about as game as they make them… A nearly all-white dog with a few blue ticks in a strong working coat, he was a good stamp of hunt-terrier, rather short in the neck, but good over the back, and through the loin. Known all over the Leicestershire and Lincolnshire district

Bluecoat, the hunt terrier that ran with the Belvoir.

where the Belvoir hunt, he soon established a reputation for work and gameness, keeping up all day with the pack.

Clearly a terrier running with the hounds in this instance worked well, but Bluecoat was an outstanding animal with legendary gameness. Appropriately, if sadly, he drowned swimming after a rat, but not before siring some excellent offspring.

There is a quote in Rawdon Lee's book on Fox Terriers by a Captain Handy, a Cotswold sportsman: 'Now in these fast days, sportsmen cannot wait for a fox to be got out, and the order is "find another one"; hence the use of fox terriers to run with hounds has been discontinued, and the breed has not been kept up at Badminton.' In his *Encyclopaedia of Rural Sports* (1870), Delabere Blaine wrote:

> Terriers, we have already stated, were formerly very commonly used to accompany packs of foxhounds for the purpose of unearthing the fox… They were usually of a medium size; if too large, they were unfitted for penetrating the sinuousities of an earth, or creeping up a confined drain; if, on the contrary, they are too diminutive, they cannot keep pace with the hounds of the present day … in some few packs, however, both large and small terriers still accompany the dogs.

A Question of Size
Fox Terriers were not always of uniform height, even in the show ring. From 1876 and for a decade after, there were separate classes for dogs over and under 18lb, and for bitches over and under 16lb. At a show in 1875, one of Rawdon Lee's winning dogs weighed under 15lb. There was more concern over construction than size itself. Rawdon Lee wrote:

> There are judges who have recently gone to extremes in awarding honours to these so-called 'narrow-fronted' terriers. Such have been produced at a sacrifice of power and strength. Most of these very narrow-chested dogs move stiffly, are too flat in the ribs, they are deficient in breathing and heart room, and can never be able to do a week's hard working the country, either with hounds or round about the badger earth or rabbit burrows.

The show ring Fox Terrier of today would have depressed him, required by its breed standard not to exceed 15½in at the withers, with an ideal weight of 18lb (slightly less for bitches). The Border Terrier, on the other hand, is required to weigh from 13 to 15½lb, and, according to its KC-approved description, to have 'the stamina to keep up with a horse, in order that he will be there when he's needed'. A Foxhound is around 24in at the withers and a man needs a horse to keep pace with one. Foot-hounds like Beagles are not expected to match a horse's pace but be 13–16in at withers. Leg length affects an animal's pace and the number of strides it takes affects its stamina. My own feeling is that hunts were accompanied by two sizes of terrier in some places, with some pre-positioning of smaller terriers, but that eventually the improvement in Foxhound breeding produced a hound too fast for any terrier to run with. In the country where the Border Terrier was used, the hunt was not able to conduct fast pursuits, so the terrier's pace was not so significant.

In *Hounds* magazine in the late 1984/early 1985 issues there was an interesting exchange of views on this subject. 'Babbler' wrote an article in which he stated:

> When I have asked why terriers don't run with hounds any more I have received a number of rather unconvincing answers. Perhaps the most curious was: 'It stops the hounds drawing properly'. Are the terriers so much better at drawing than hounds? Or are the modern Foxhounds really so lazy? – neither surely. Perhaps an answer more to the point is, 'There aren't those sort of terriers around any more'. To some extent this is true. There are not many around, for you need a long-legged terrier with plenty of stamina and probably weighing 16lb and such a dog is all too often reckoned as not able to go to ground nowadays. 'Too big?' Well, they were not too big before the war.

This brought several responses, one from 'BB' of Gwent:

> I have always been of the belief that you can use a small terrier anywhere, but you can only use a big terrier in a big place. Even in the Fells, where outside of which, it is always believed that they use a large leggy

type of terrier for their rocky rugged country, the small dog is preferred…having had three days hunting in the Fells this season, I find they like a terrier to be under thirteen inches at the shoulder.

Paul Fermor wrote in from Ivybridge in Devon to state that:

At the Dartmoor Hunt, we frequently run a terrier with our hounds. A terrier fairly well up on the leg is needed in our country of over 100 square miles of bleak desolate moor, without any roads. The disadvantages are several, but the advantages outweigh them – generally! When running a terrier with the hounds, one has no choice whether to enter him in the earth or not. Hence there is a real danger of getting him stuck in an awkward place. That's no fun

6 or 8 miles from the nearest road! The advantages are obvious. No waiting for ages for the terrier-man to catch up with us … one of our terriers hunted five days out of eight calendar days last season.

As always in the hunting field it's the country that decides.

My favourite author, Beckford, writing a little less than one hundred years ago, says that he 'prefers the black or white Terrier'; but some, he says, 'are so like a fox that awkward people frequently mistake one for the other. If you prefer Terriers to run with your pack, large ones at times are useful, but in an earth they do little good, as they cannot always get up to a fox.' For my part, unless a Terrier is small enough to go to ground, I see little use in him; and the perfect Terrier

Fox Terrier kennelled with Foxhounds, by J. Emms (c.1880).

should be able to make short cuts, and keep up with the Hounds, or be planted amongst the farmers at different points – of course, I mean fox-hunting farmers – so as to be handy when required…

> *The Dog* by 'Idstone' (8th edition, 1893)

Formerly it was the custom to add a couple of terriers to every pack of foxhounds, so as to be ready to aid in bolting the fox when he runs into a drain, or goes to ground in any easily accessible earth; the stoutness of the terrier enabling him, by steadily following on the track, to reach the scene of operations before it would be possible to obtain any other assistance. This aid, however, in consequence of the increased speed of our hounds, is now dispensed with, and the old fox-terrier is out of date, or is only kept for the purpose of destroying ground vermin.

> *The Dog in Health and Disease* by 'Stonehenge' (1867)

It was at one time common to have Terriers of two sizes with a pack of Foxhounds; the larger ones to run with the pack, the smaller kept at places convenient to the earths, to be ready to bolt the fox from holes too small to admit of the larger Terriers entering. The greatly increased speed of our modern hounds has banished the Terrier from the covert as companion and co-worker with the hounds. So far back, however, as the end of last century, the small-sized Terrier was looked upon as the finer race, and most valued.

> *British Dogs* by Hugh Dalziel (Volume II, 1888)

I am very glad to think that during the past year our Terriers, taken as a whole, have not increased in size. To my mind, the whole essence of a Terrier for work is in the fact that he should be small, active, strong, but lithesome [lissom]. Let us breed him as long and as flat in his shoulder blades as we like, as strong and as long in his quarters and second thighs as we like, but let him be a Terrier in size. He won't be able to live with hounds if they run, I admit, nor would he if he were twice the size; but let the run be as long as it may, or a fast twenty minutes, our friend, if trained to hunt fox and not rabbits, with his heart in the right place, will be upon the scene within ten minutes or so of Reynard going to ground, and will then be able to do

his work if required to do so, a great deal quicker and more easily than his lumbering big brother.

> From the Fox Terrier critique of the Wolverhampton Show, reported in *The Kennel Gazette*, December 1893.

For the terrier to be carried by a Hunt servant is in my opinion the most useful method, because he arrives quickly and full of fire and go, and fresh. Another method is of course for the terrier to be taken by the Hunt runner, who is seldom there, except on a ringing sort of day or a cub-hunting morning: and a third method is to allow a terrier or two to run with the pack. This I never allowed; it makes hounds flashy and wild and the terrier is blown and probably useless … it is nice to have a choice as to whether a terrier shall be put to ground or not; with a loose terrier you have no choice.

> Charles McNeill, Master of the Grafton and then the North Cotswold, writing on *The Hunt Terrier* in The Lonsdale Library, Volume VII, *Fox-Hunting* (1930)

The Anatomy for Work

'First of all make certain that you have the sort of terrier whose build will enable him to do his job effectively and with ease to himself.' That quaintly worded but still telling advice was offered over seventy years ago by the field sports enthusiast and working terrier devotee, Major G.B. Ollivant, in *Hounds & Dogs*. What build does enable the earth-dog to do his job

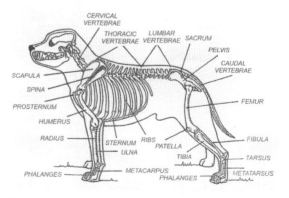

Canine skeletal terminology.

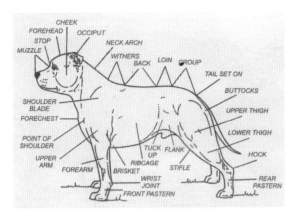

Canine surface terminology.

not only well but more easily? O.T. Price, that much-loved old terrier-man, who sustained his own type of terrier from 1896 to the 1950s, opted for a dog 'twelve inches in height, about three and a half in breadth and weighing about twelve pounds'. 'I like a narrow eel-like terrier,' he used to counsel. Certainly his favourite dogs Tartar and Worry and his little bitch Twinkle, famed over many counties, were on these lines.

Around 1880, the best terrier judge of that time, Edward Sandell, measured around forty of the top hunt terriers, revealing some interesting dimensions. The averages were as follows: height 14½in, weight 17–20lb, neck circumference 12¾in, span of thorax 20½in, span of loins 18½ins, hock 4½in from ground;

and shoulder (leading edge) to root of stern 13½in. A measurement from point of shoulder to point of buttock would have given a length of around 14½in, the average height of these dogs. The most successful dog at that time was Carlisle Tack (grandson of the Rev. John Russell's bitch Fuss), who was all white, 17lb, and described by Rawdon Lee as 'built on racing lines almost, without any lumber about him, and with powerful jaws'.

Geoffrey Sparrow, in his classic *The Terrier's Vocation*, goes for a dog 'weighing from twelve to sixteen pounds, with a strong jaw – not snipey like the show breeds – a good back, neck and shoulders, and fairly long legs. The length doesn't matter. They can be folded up while bad shoulders cannot'. He would not have liked the Fox Terriers in contemporary Kennel Club show rings, with their upright shoulders, lack of forechest and short bodies. If they could actually get underground, they are unlikely to re-emerge!

Terrier-men tend to be forthright characters ever ready to give a view on the ingredients of a perfect working terrier. In *Field Sports* magazine of June 1952, veteran terrier-man R.R. Stopford was writing:

> General conformation is a subject of much argument, but to commence with, I always look for a dog with a strong, thick tail, carried slightly below the horizontal, since it is my contention that a tail turning up, no matter how sharply, is a sign of weakness in the spine.

The classic terrier phenotype.

Typical terrier pose: F. Paton's portrayal of a nondescript terrier, 1902.

Maud Earl's 1905 depiction of three famous champion Fox Terriers: Donna Fortuna (described as 'perfect'), Dukedom and The Sylph; they are noticeably more muscled than today's dogs.

Viewed sideways on, the body should be square-shaped (excluding the head and tail) with a short thick neck and good depth of rib. So long as this squareness is apparent, the legs will be in proportion. It matters not as to cat or hare feet. Provided there is no undue breadth to the chest, there is no particular advantage in a short-legged variety, since it is a fallacy that the shorter the leg, the easier to ground. A fox stands higher at the shoulder than any dog of equal weight and can turn round comfortably in an eight-inch pipe. The answer lies in the simple fact that the correctly proportioned dog pushes forward his forelegs and relaxes the shoulders when he is going to ground, using the hind legs as the sole means of propulsion, while the short-legged dog has developed a broad chest and cannot adapt himself to the alternative procedure.

Built for Work

What should 'a working construction' be based on? The original working Fox Terriers were barrel-chested and featured a fairly straight stifle and hock; the longer tibia and well-bent hock of the show ring terrier of today is not much use underground. But an even bigger difference lies in the shoulder angulation and depth of chest. Show Fox Terriers almost without exception display upright shoulders and slab-sidedness but deep chests; none of which helps an earth-dog. Nor does the short back of the pedigree Fox Terrier, which reduces flexibility and overall suppleness. It does, however, produce a more compact-looking, showy type of dog. Longer-legged terriers like the Fox dig by throwing the earth back under them; they therefore need straight front legs, but retaining spring in the pastern. Short-legged terriers dig by throwing the earth out to each side of them; they therefore need an outward-turning foot. Both need a 'digging design'.

The craze for long heads in show terriers, exemplified most clearly in the smooth Fox Terrier, is rooted in the misguided belief that length gives power. You also hear the expression, 'plenty of heart room', as though the dog's heart enlarges when it is exercising. Plenty of *lung* room is desirable, especially in terriers that run with the hounds. But it is rib-space that gives a dog lung room, not depth of chest.

I'll go back to Major Ollivant for a challengeable description of the physique of his terriers:

The conformation I have always found the best for a Working or Hunt Terrier is that which approaches the nearest in build to the short-backed, short-legged hunter... like the short-legged hunter he must have long, well laid back, sloping shoulders, a short back and big long galloping quarters. This conformation will make him stand over a lot of ground, in spite of the fact that his back is short and not long.

As he didn't specify proportions, it is arguable what he really meant by the word 'short' in connection with backs. Most wild creatures that live underground have been shaped by nature to have relatively long backs. Far too many pedigree terrier breeds are now too short-backed for an earth-dog but some too have exaggerated hindquarters, with the hindfeet having to be positioned way beyond the croup when standing naturally. This is not useful to the dog.

In his informative book on the Border Terrier, Walter Gardner makes an interesting observation:

I have found that there is a close relationship between the height of a well-proportioned animal and the length of its head. This is not an original observation: the French hippotomists [horse-dissectors] regarded the height of a well-proportioned horse to be two and a half times the length of the head, a relationship which seems relevant to Borders as well. This is not surprising if one considers that if you put a long head on a Border then you require to increase the animal's height to balance the body. If the dog is very short, you require to reduce the head, again to balance the body.

It's a pity that Walter Gardner wasn't in Sealyhams! Proportion is important when considering a terrier in the ring; symmetry is key to activity and the application of body strength in the field.

As dog-show exhibitors without working experience gained the ascendancy, these arguments were forgotten. In time, a judge like MacDonald Daly, despite owning coursing greyhounds, was advocating Fox Terriers with the physical desiderata for show ring success. The long muzzle, short back and upright shoulders are easily spotted, even from the ringside, and sadly are now the norm, held as the perfect earth-dog blueprint, the ideal anatomy for a sporting terrier. The smooth, uninterrupted line from throat to the toes, ramrod-straight pasterns and sickle hocks may be rewarded in the show ring; the working dog needs a flexible torso, excellent angulation in its limbs and

'digging feet', often manifesting themselves as well-turned-out feet, not admired by many Crufts judges!

Forequarter Power

For me, the first point of real quality in a dog lies in clean, sloping shoulders. Well-placed shoulders give a perfect base for a proud head carriage. They provide, too, the balance between the length of the neck and the length of the back, preventing those disagreeable dips in topline which mar the whole appearance of a dog. I have learnt, over the years, to start any judgement of the shoulders by considering the position of the elbow. If the elbow is too far forward, then the dog is pulling, not pushing, itself along, not capitalizing on the drive from the hocks, thighs and loins. In his video on the pack hounds, Captain Wallace states that the shoulders are controlled by the elbow. He is worth heeding.

It is only when the scapula and the humerus are of the right length *and* correctly placed that a dog can achieve the desired length of stride and freedom in his front action. Sighthounds can have their upper arms 20 per cent longer than their scapulae. In terrier breeds they tend to be equal in length. Dogs with no forward extension are nearly always handicapped by upright shoulders and short, steep upper arms. A dog of quality must have sloping shoulders and compatible upper arms to produce a good length of neck, a firm topline without dips, the right length of back and free movement on the forehand. Even when there is a discernible curve in the topline, as in the Borzoi and the Bedlington Terrier, well-laid shoulders are required to produce the correct topline, with the arch in the spine starting in the correct place. The correct Borzoi and Bedlington 'arch' position is over the loins, to enable the dog to bring its hindfeet forwards, in front of the chest when galloping, without any restriction from the ribs.

Feet

From time to time, a committee of the Kennel Club looks at the wording of breed standards, in an attempt to avoid harmful end effects on dogs from unwise written anatomical designs. The words on feet should receive their urgent attention. I am against a dog's feet being described in its breed blueprint as large, small, a different size fore and aft (as in a number of terrier standards) or being unhelpfully worded, as in the Irish Terrier's, whose feet have to be 'tolerably round' and 'moderately small'. At least the breed standard of the West Highland White Terrier asks for feet which are proportionate in size; so should every breed standard. I once sat at the ringside of a working terrier show and watched the judge award prizes to exhibits that had appallingly splayed feet – flashy-looking terriers all owned by the same exhibitor, but unsound ones too.

Feet are a vital part of the dog's anatomy, more important than 'bite', colour of coat, length of coat, set of tail, length and carriage of ears and pigmentation. Dog show judges should murmur to themselves 'no foot, no dog,' before they begin their duties, advancing 'feet first' in every ring. Before writing 'movement disappointing' in the critique, a judge should ask 'did I examine the feet?' The feet may not exactly be the mirror of the soul but the soles of the feet can so often reveal the quality of the dog. For me the judge's scrutiny should start at the feet of the exhibits. At least the dogs judged by them can actually walk off with a prize! I always look at the wear on the dog's pads when judging: excessive wear on one part of the pads indicates incorrect construction. The soundness or otherwise of the foot can affect the balance of a dog. If the heel-pad is not sharing the body weight of the dog with the toe-pads, then the latter are bearing extra weight and this will in time weaken the toes. The dog's knee will absorb what the toes haven't the strength to do. This is why at the turn of the century, when Foxhounds were favoured with massively timbered forelegs and a fleshy, contracted, bunched-up foot, so many stood over at the knee, to reduce the jarring. Such hounds had their weight all on the forehand, which in turn led to their shoulders becoming more upright. There is a danger in the pursuit of round, over-compact, knuckled-over, bunched-toed feet. No foot, no dog!

Common Faults
Short Backs
Writing in *Hounds* magazine in 1987, experienced terrier-man Tony Kirby stated:

> Arguments between terrier-men as to the length of leg, close or long coupled between the front and back legs and general size are often held around the show

rings. My personal preference is a terrier with a length of leg so that it stands about 13–14in at the shoulder – in other words not as tall as I believe some show terriers are becoming. Close or long coupled? I definitely prefer a terrier long in the back. What animal that lives below ground is short backed? I cannot think of one. Certainly the fox has a long back in relation to its overall size to enable it to twist round corners and make it more agile. The general size of a terrier depends on the type of earth to be tried but it should be a balanced size.

In every animal walking on four legs the force derived from pressing the hind foot into the ground has to be transmitted to the pelvis at the acetabulum, and onwards to the spine by way of the sacrum. In over-angulated dogs the locomotive power is directed to an inappropriate part of the acetabulum. In addition, in order to retain the required degree of rigidity of the joint between the tibia and the femur, other muscles have to come into use. In the over-angulated hind limb, the tibia meets the bottom end of the femur at such an angle that *direct* drive cannot ensue. The femur can only transmit the drive to the acetabulum *after* the rectus femoris muscle has contracted, enabling the femur to assume a degree of joint rigidity when connecting with the tibia. This means that the femur rotates anticlockwise whereas nature intended it to move clockwise.

Excessive Angulation
Excessive angulation in the hindquarters, with an elongated tibia, may, to some, give a more pleasing outline to the exhibit when 'stacked' in the ring. In the long term, however, it can only lead to anatomical and locomotive disaster. In his instructive *The Dog – Structure and Movement* (1970), vet, exhibitor and sportsman R. H. Smythe wrote:

> There is however a difference between a little angulation and the excessive angulation which is now becoming so fashionable. The side effects of excessive angulation are only now beginning to be understood and there is a distinct possibility that in time to come it may be necessary to take steps to breed out excessive angulation to prevent the development of a race of cripples.

Bedlington Terrier hybrid; not the handsomest dog but a worker.

I hope that breeders of Kerry Blue and Wheaten Terriers have read this valuable book. Such angulation destroys the ability of the dog's forelimbs and hindlimbs to work in harmony in propelling the body. Yet I have heard it argued by breed specialists at seminars that it will increase the power of propulsion operating through the hindlimbs and on through the spine. If it did, the racing Greyhound fraternity would have pursued it with great vigour. I have heard a dog show judge praise an over-angulated dog because it 'stood over a lot of ground'. So does a stretch limousine but it requires a purpose-built construction to permit that luxury. The way in which an animal carries its weight really does matter.

Poor Proportions

In, say, a Welsh Corgi or a Fox Terrier the centre of gravity lies farther back than in the Bulldog, which means that in the latter far more weight falls on the forefeet than upon the hind ones, with the muscles of the shoulder and the thorax being called upon to do more work in moving the body than those of the loins, quarters and second thigh. This means that the Bulldog's weight mostly lies in front of the midline, whilst in the Fox Terrier and the Corgi, the front and hind halves weigh about the same. In those terrier breeds where the tail carriage is considered significant, like the Fox Terrier, the sacrum must lie parallel with the ground or even very slightly elevated at the rear. When this elevation is not excessive, you expect to see a back which appears short and an erect tail. When the elevation is overdone, you find a 'gay' tail, with the tip well over the back. This is often a feature in Airedales. The seeking of a short back, made even worse by a short body, leads to problems.

Fell Terriers – superbly built for their role.

In an article in *Shooting Times* of December 1981, Dan Russell wrote:

> I have been reading with great interest the standard laid down by the Jack Russell Club of Great Britain. By and large it is excellent, but there are two provisions about which I have reservations. The first is that the standard says the tail should be set on rather high, carried gaily, and be in proportion to body length, usually about four inches, providing a good handhold. It is the 'carried gaily' bit that I don't care for… I have seen very few real workers which carried their tails gaily. Your real dyed-in-the-wool worker usually carries his tail parallel with the ground or even tucked in behind his hindquarters.

He associated a gay tail with a yappy terrier. He went on to state that a real working terrier never shows well, being deeply bored by a ring appearance. Following the docking ban you do see some unsightly tails on show terriers; the set of tail is related to the pelvic slope, affecting, in turn, hind movement and the transmission of power.

In many terrier breeds a long neck usually goes with well-inclined shoulders because the cervical and dorsal bones are equally lengthy; but whilst the neck must be long and the scapula well inclined, in keeping with these elongated vertebrae, the dorsal bones, and especially the lumbar ones, need to be unusually short so that the body too is short. The difficulty for breeders is to get both these contradictory features present in the same dog!

Cobbiness

In the Lonsdale Library's volume on fox hunting, Charles McNeill OBE, Master of the Grafton for seven seasons and of the North Cotswold for five, writes:

> As all terrier-men know, a good way to get a real hard, wiry, weather-resistant coat is to cross a wire with a smooth… A nice little short-legged terrier is best, he is not too heavy to carry, but he must not be wide in front. A tall terrier with good shoulders and narrow front will get to ground better than a small cobby one, but a small dog, with narrow front and good shoulders, with a long lean head, is the ideal huntsman' terrier.

Many show ring terriers are expected to have a cobby build, some arguing that it makes for a smarter-looking exhibit; cobbiness, often accompanied by a short body, is of no help to a terrier underground, where he needs the greatest flexibility of spine he can be given. In his *Foxes, Foxhounds and Fox-Hunting* (1932), the great fell hunter Richard Clapham wrote:

> The make and shape of a terrier have everything to do with the dog being able to perform his work properly. His conformation may vary a good deal, particularly as regards length of leg and width of chest, so that type varies with the nature of the surroundings in which the work is done… What is wanted is an all-round type, capable of doing good work under a variety of conditions. If we were asked to give a specification of such a terrier it would be as follows: weight, 15–16lb; coat, thick and wet-resisting; chest, narrow, but not so much so as to impede the free action of heart and lungs, legs sufficiently long to enable the dog to travel above ground with ease to himself; teeth level, and jaw powerful but not too long; ears, small and dropped close to the head, so that they are less likely to be torn by foxes.

Surely we all seek a working terrier with a build that allows him to be 'at ease with himself'?

Dan Russell, in his admirable *Working Terriers* (1948*)*, states:

> Fourteen pounds should be the weight to seek for… Length of leg does not matter a great deal. A long-

White Lakelands, built for work.

legged dog can get down a surprisingly small hole if he is narrow chested... The dog to refuse instantly is the one with loaded shoulders or turned-out elbows or a wide cobby chest.

The Difficulty of Creating a Breed Standard

The Rev. John Russell's own description of his ideal terrier as manifested in his renowned Trump is worth quoting:

> Her colour was white, with just a patch of dark tan over each ear and a similar dot not larger than a penny piece over the root of her tail. The coat, which was thick, close and a trifle wavy, was well calculated to protect the body from the wet and cold. The legs were straight, short and thick, and the feet perfect, while the size was equal to that of a full-grown vixen fox, that is to say, her weight was about twelve pounds. Her whole appearance gave indications of courage, endurance and hardihood.

It is interesting to compare the great man's words with those of the standard first proposed by the PJR Terrier Club. This early official club blueprint stated: 'Coat – rough, a trifle wiry or smooth. Dense with belly and undersides not bare... Forelegs – strong and straight with joints in correct alignment. Elbows hanging perpendicular to the body, working free of the sides.' I'm not sure I want a dog answering to that description! There was no indication of what the dog's general appearance should be like. Any pedigree Parson Jack Russell dog that was less than 13in at the shoulder could not meet the requirements of the early official KC breed standard. This was subsequently altered to read 'lower heights are acceptable', provided that the exhibit is capable of being spanned behind the shoulders by average sized hands. This proviso could mean that a 13in terrier with a short, narrow ribcage might become acceptable, not sound attributes in a working terrier or any sporting dog.

I'm not surprised to read the judge's critique at the 1996 National Terrier Championship show which states: 'I'd hoped to find more of the West Country original Parson types but sadly, there were few who looked like them. We seem to be moving towards a modern day PJRT which wasn't at all what was intended when the club was revived some ten years ago.'

In the same vein, William Baker, one of the breeders who developed the Sealyham, has put on record:

> In my opinion, no Terrier for underground work should be coarse in his shoulders, but my experience teaches me that nature decrees that a certain width of chest is always there in the gamest of them. The Sealyham of today is verging on a fancier's craze — straightness, length of head, great bone and cloddiness. If these are carried to excess, goodbye to him as a working Terrier.

Prophetic words!

Judges' Verdict

At a recent Crufts, the Lakeland Terrier judge used these words in his show report: 'On the whole the standard of Lakelands at this show were [sic] not of a very high standard, some nice ones, some not so nice, and some absolute rubbish.' I do hope those working Lakeland terrier-men who resort to show dog blood occasionally choose wisely! The myth of the association between pedigree and quality is surely finally acknowledged by sportsmen of all styles. At the Scottish KC Championship show a year ago, the judge recorded:

> When recognition of the PJRT took place I was under the impression that we were going to preserve the look of this old type of working terrier, it now seems that some breeders with no knowledge of, or regard for, the traditional type are determined, with the help of judges with no breed type experience, to change completely the character and look of the breed.

That, in comparatively few words, sums up very aptly what happens to terrier breeds in the KC show rings. The Patterdale, the Lucas, the Plummer and any others heading towards KC recognition should beware: performance is soon second to prettiness. Another judge at a different show gave this report: 'I was disappointed with the quality of my entry, too many had heavy cheeks, absolutely foreign to the Standard.' This is hardly the most valuable yardstick for passing judgement on a breed designed to work!

When judging the build of a working terrier, let us be guided by the wise words of Major Ollivant, writing more than seventy years ago: 'A terrier that has to work underground must have his heart in the right place; then if his body permits him to do so, he will get there like the good sportsman he is.' The only reason why we have working terriers to breed from nowadays is that countrymen who were real terrier-men kept their heads over many years and ignored the financial allure of the KC show rings. I salute them.

> Fanciers of recent years have tried to alter the original type of Terrier, by trying to engraft on a short, cobby body, a long, senseless-looking head, to get which they had to breed dogs almost, if not quite, twice the size of the original, and to alter the formation of the head. This straight-face craze began in Black-and-Tan Terriers, extended to Fox-terriers, is seen in Bedlington Terriers, is now contaminating the Collie, and is threatening our national Scottish Terrier.
>
> D.J. Thomson Gray, the great expert on the Scottish breeds, writing in *The Bazaar* magazine, 1895

It would be true to say that no show champion of twenty years ago – certainly in the terriers, and in most other breeds as well – would stand a chance today. In the terriers, at least, their heads would be described as 'coarse'; and none of the old champions, so highly regarded so short a while ago, would, of course, be 'standing up on his toes on stiff and useless pasterns'.

> *The Domestic Dog* by Brian Vesey-Fitzgerald
> (Routledge & Kegan Paul, 1957)

The Terrier, unlike other dog breeds is basically a digger. For this reason most Terrier breeds have been modified to effect a compromise in bone structure which permits digging as an essential effort. To this end the Terrier's shoulder bones have slightly different proportions than those found in a runner, for example, a Greyhound. This does not mean that the fundamentals have changed. So many persons think that a 'Terrier' front requires an upright shoulder and that Terriers should walk with stilted and stiff movement. This is incorrect but the idea may have been spawned by the frequently used term 'straight Terrier front'. This does not mean an upright shoulder; it refers rather to a modification of the racing or running front, where a shortening of the upper arm relative to the shoulder blade has been accomplished. This structural deviation offers better digging power through increased leverage. The lay-back remains unchanged.

> *The Book of All Terriers* by John T. Marvin (Howell Book House, 1971)

The Make-Up of the Sporting Dog

The Terrier instinct is bred into every Terrier worthy of the name. How many can recall the amazing aptitude their dog has for killing a stray rat that foolishly crosses its path? Others can remember the fight of one of their Terriers to finish a woodchuck. Still others have seen the rare conflict between a Terrier and an otter, a rugged battle but one in which Terrier spirit usually prevails. Thus, today's Terrier, no matter what the breed, still carries in its veins the blood of conflict and the instinct to do the job. Let's not change his conformation so that these traits and instincts cannot be used.

> *The Book of All Terriers* by John T. Marvin
> (Howell Book House, 1971)

Handsome is as Handsome Does

Ugly little varmint or cute little canine fashion model? Couch potato or crouching tiger? Scarred canine miner or handsome reduced hound? What should a sporting terrier look like? Does its anatomy truly matter, or is its spirit more important? In *Sporting Terriers* (1926), Pierce O'Conor wrote: 'That the fox terrier of

Victorian engraving entitled Tantalization, *illustrating the predator drive of the terrier.*

Working terriers of 1840, unexaggerated and sporting.

The head of a 1900 Smooth Fox Terrier, showing the immense keenness to work.

Head of an 1893 Smooth Fox Terrier, exhibiting the sporting eagerness of the terrier family.

today is a great improvement, in so far as looks go, on his predecessors of forty or fifty years ago is beyond question, though whether he is better suited physically or morally for work underground is a matter of opinion.' If O'Conor were alive today, I think he would use stronger words and would not be a happy terrierman.

In *Field Sports* magazine in 1949, in an article entitled 'The Hunt Terrier Man and His Dogs', old terrierman Fred F. Wood wrote of his kind:

There is also another attendant to the pack, the terrier man… then look at his little companions, maybe a couple or a couple and a half of terriers, not much to look at perhaps, the show terrier-man might call them ugly little mongrels, but there is no mongrel about them, many of their pedigrees have been as carefully kept as those of the hounds, not for their

Smooth Fox Terriers hunting rabbits in America in 1900, showing a strong desire to hunt.

appearance, but for their qualities. They have to be constructed of bone, wire and whip cord, and have coats that will keep out cold and wet and then on top of that be brave as lions, if they are to do the work they are called upon to do … So think of those little terriers … they will stay and fight their fox until he bolts or they are dug out, that requires pluck.

Waiting to Pounce *by T. Blinks (1883); the Bull-and-Terrier beyond the Fox Terrier is almost Boxer-like but still packed with sporting terrier instinct.*

It was fear of their terriers losing their working anatomy, and especially their 'pluck', which steered working terrier enthusiasts away from the show ring.

Geoffrey Sparrow wrote, in *The Terrier's Vocation* (1949):

> Some years ago there was a wire-haired dog at the Crawley and Horsham Kennels which was one of the best I ever saw; he had rather a shy way with him and couldn't abide a lot of raucous halloaing, nor would he enter a hole unless he wanted to. The first time I saw him at work out hunting, they couldn't get him to go at all and were just going to give it up when someone said: 'There's a heck of a noise underneath where I'm standing.' Well, it was quite obvious he had waited his time and then gone into another hole, got up to his fox and was busy at him. At the beginning he looked abject, mean and utterly lacking in courage, showing how deceptive a dog may be.

I have had comparable experiences with infantry soldiers, especially countrymen; judgements made on outward appearances don't count for much when the real tests come.

Terrier Senses

The key senses of a working terrier: sight, hearing and 'feel', or touch, matter very much to an earth-dog. The great American expert on dog behaviour, Clarence

J. Pfaffenberger, in *The New Knowledge of Dog Behavior* (1963), wrote:

A dog can hear much higher and lower sounds than a person can. His sense of smell has never been satisfactorily evaluated, but it is so superior that we do not yet know its workings. A dog's eyes are different from ours. One very valuable quality is his ability to practically photograph motion. Where we might be aware that something moved, a dog will know just where it moved.

In this connection, it is worth noting the words of Dugald Macintyre in *Field Sports* magazine in 1949:

Terriers are smart dogs, and I had more than one which did remarkable feats. There was the West Highland White who, assisting farm collies to chivvy the hares out of an oat-field which was in the process of being reaped – after some hares had escaped, lay down by the gate of the field, and so secured several. The collies could only see what was 'before their noses', but that terrier was a bit of a thinker. The same terrier could be lifted up in one's arms to point out a distant hunting stoat, or to make him understand that he was to go to a bridge and cross it, to get to at the holt of an otter.

Terriers may lack height but we must never underestimate their ability to pick up movement far, far better than we can; it would be unwise, too, to play down their sheer canniness, as Macintyre indicates.

Hardness

Hearing the expression 'gamest of them' applied to early Sealyhams resurrects an old worry of mine. Having read of the method used by the celebrated Captain John Tucker-Edwardes to 'prove gameness' in the terriers when fashioning the Sealyham as a distinct breed, it has always appeared to me the perfect recipe for producing brainless canine psychopaths. I cannot understand his fame as a terrier-man if the stories about his 'selection tests' are true. Terriers, which, when not at work, are expected to kill captive polecats are not likely to appeal to those terrier-men who also keep ferrets!

In his book *Working Terriers* (1948), Dan Russell writes:

The very best terrier I have ever owned was one of these Border-Sealyhams. He weighed 15lb and was immensely strong. For four seasons running he did his two days a week with hounds, during which time I dug eighty-three brace of foxes with him and he bolted goodness knows how many, twenty badgers and three otters; in all that time he sustained no injury beyond an odd nip or two and never missed one day's hunting.

I have never heard a proper terrier-man admire a dog that was too hard. O.T. Price, a great terrier-man in his day, once advised: 'Don't let your terrier get too hard. Remember that a terrier's job is to bay the fox, not fight it.' According to Dan Russell, 'the hard dog is as big a nuisance as the coward. He spends half his working life in hospital.' I am reminded of the story of the idiot who returned a young terrier to its breeder as a 'waste of space' because it declined to slaughter a neighbour's tomcat which he had put into a barrel with his newly acquired pup to 'see what it was made of'. The pup, which had been raised with farm cats in his barn birthplace, went on to prove himself as the bravest of dogs.

In an article in *Hounds* magazine in 1987, that most knowledgeable of field sportsmen, who wrote under the *nom de plume* of 'The Gaffer', stated:

I have seen many big dogs shockingly scarred and marked simply because in a tight place they could not

Classic terrier form in F.M. Hollams's 1947 painting.

get back from the fox, thus they became very hard and are useless for bolting. Give me the smaller narrow terrier with brains and character that can get in a small place, stand back and make a lot of noise. Those are my sort! I have bred and worked them for the last fifty years and it always pleases me when there is a call for one of the 'Gaffer's' little bitches.

Writing in *Field Sports* magazine in June 1952, working terrier expert R.R. Stopford stated:

> As time goes on you will know just what sort of noise he makes against different opponents. No dog fights mute, but some have the aggravating habit of baying at a rabbit when there is a fox or a badger in the same earth! For this reason many experienced diggers will not use their dogs for rabbiting, but provided you have not got a fool of a dog he will tend always to seek out the most dangerous opponent. A terrier that stays underground until he kills, or is physically exhausted, is a real nuisance and a danger to himself.

Major Ollivant wrote that 'the terrier's pluck must not be the bravery of the Bull Terrier that goes in regardless of consequences, but the brave, fearless kind of pluck that knows its own danger, and yet has the grit to stay there'. How much aggression to build in is important – if you use Bull Terrier blood to strengthen the head, you risk producing a holy terror that could be a blessed nuisance! When I hear of working terrier-

men utilizing show dog blood to achieve a physical point, I recall the words of Geoffrey Sparrow on this subject: 'but then she had a working pedigree back to the nineties on both sides. The real blood must be there or the pups are sure to throw to soft lines.'

Symmetry

Working terrier enthusiasts will never show great interest in precise measurements, exact proportions or wordy descriptions of anatomical features, but balance, symmetry, correct proportions and physical soundness really do affect function and therefore performance in a hunting animal. Terrier show judges may prefer to judge entirely by eye and experience, but is this enough? A seminar of sporting terrier judges to bring on the younger judges would surely be of value. It would be interesting to hear, at such a seminar, what terrier show judges' decisions are actually being based on: gut feeling, their own preferences, previous winners, knowledge of anatomy? I attend seminars run by the Sporting Lucas Terrier Club, in my role as breed advisor, and am always willing to argue my views at such an event, whether on conformation or colour.

In his piece in *Field Sports* magazine in June 1952, R.R. Stopford also wrote:

> The weight for all types of work should not be more than sixteen pounds, and preferably about fourteen. Colour, looks and length of coat are personal considerations, but the more white there is the better, because a conspicuous colour has its advantages when shooting in thick cover. Another controversial point is the length of muzzle. A long nose is useful for ratting, but takes heavier punishment underground; moreover, it is but rarely accompanied by a strong wide jaw, so that, on the whole, we may say the shorter the better.

He would not like the head of today's Fox Terrier, but it is of interest to see the high priority he gives the colour of his dogs' coats.

Coats

Terrier-men have long held prejudices about the colour of their dogs' coats. You only have to look at some terrier breeds to see that colour makes the

A hunt terrier Highdown Peter of the Chiddingfold, strongly made and truly wire-coated.

The author addressing a terrier seminar.

breed: West Highland Whites, Kerry Blues and Plummer Terriers for example. In his insightful *The Mind of the Dog* (1958), vet, exhibitor and sportsman R.H. Smythe wrote:

> Conformation, physique and hair colour appear to exert less influence on temperament than these same features are believed to do in the case of humans. One cannot truthfully claim that black dogs are more sensible, more trustworthy or more lively than white dogs or vice versa. A Kerry Blue is usually vivacious and high-spirited, sometimes truculent; a blue Bedlington is often sensible and gentle in disposition. A red Irish terrier may exhibit the characteristics attributed to his countrymen, but a red Irish setter may be mild and law-abiding. Any differences are obviously associated with the breed rather than with the colour of the coat.

On a practical level, however, being able to see a small bushing dog in close cover may matter a great deal.

Coat texture seems to matter for some, not in its weatherproofing qualities, but in its association with stubbornness. In his underrated *The Understanding of a Dog* (1935), Lt Col G.H. Badcock, a highly experienced trainer of dogs, wrote:

> Why should most smooth Fox-terriers be so much more biddable and easy to train and correct of faults

than the wire-haired variety? There is a curious tenacity of purpose about these broken-haired breeds that makes them extraordinarily difficult to correct of faults… I have a larger percentage of failures with insubordinate wire-hairs than any other breed.

I personally would value 'tenacity of purpose' in a working terrier, but Badcock knew more about training dogs than I do!

Inclination to Hunt

A writer with plenty of experience in training terriers, the late Brian Plummer, wrote in his *Secrets of Dog Training* (1992):

> Terriers, despite their small size, are sometimes far from easy to control. In addition to the fact that most terriers still retain a strong inclination to hunt any type of animal or bird whose scent crosses their paths, the majority are particularly eager to take offence from another dog… terriers do need a great deal of exercise to sublimate their working instincts.

A number of researches into defensive behaviour and pain sensitivity have revealed appreciable differences between breeds. Terriers were found notably, but hardly surprisingly in view of their role, very resistant to pain relative to other dogs. This demands more patient training so that a young terrier doesn't actually perversely welcome 'punishment' but can be guided by firm consistent direction and its desirable persistence retained.

In *Working Terriers* (1948), Dan Russell wrote:

> The real working terrier is usually very self-contained; he keeps himself to himself and does not fight with other dogs unless in self-defence. I always think this is because he knows he gets into enough trouble in his life without going to look for it. In any event, the quarrelsome brute is generally a coward. Watch your dog at the meet. You will have him on a lead, but hounds will come around and sniff at him. If he is of the right sort he will stand his ground quite quietly, although he may give a warning growl when hounds crowd him or get too familiar, but he will show no signs of fright or panic.

These are wise words; sporting terriers need to be self-confident, steadfast and with stable temperaments. All show and no 'go' is of no value whatsoever to a sporting dog.

Genetic Factors
Genetic predispositions in breeds of dog are rooted in their function. The American psychologist Stanley Coren wrote a book about matching breeds to human personalities. He listed dogs in seven categories according to their psychological make-up. The Airedale Terrier was the only terrier breed listed as independent, perhaps its hound blood manifesting itself. He listed as 'self-confident' breeds: Irish, Scottish, Welsh, Yorkshire and Fox Terriers, but would not have known of many working types of unregistered terrier breeds. He listed the Skye Terrier quite separately under the 'steadfast' types, perhaps a reflection of their long breeding for show ring boredom!

It is important to keep in mind that a dog is *not* just like any other animal, but very much a creature of humans, an artificial animal in many ways. It is an animal that has been shaped and fashioned in its behaviour and appearance to suit human desires. With the possible exception of the domestic cat, a dog is probably better equipped mentally than any of the other domesticated animals, yet its perception of other living things and objects around it is restricted

by the conditions and emotions of the moment. It is a modern cliché that dogs are ruled by instinct. In reality, compared with the lesser animals that do function mainly by instinctive action, the dog seems to possess rather a limited number of instincts that cause it to operate. A number of psychologists and behaviourists have commented on this.

In his enlightening book *Understanding Your Dog* (Blond Briggs, 1972), the distinguished veterinary scientist Michael W. Fox writes:

> The inheritance of behavior and temperament is complex, for the characteristics of a breed comprise a combination of several independently inherited traits which are modified by genetic factors. No trait is inherited as such; genetic factors are transmitted by inheritance, but the traits themselves are modified by interacting genetic and environmental factors. Training and early experience greatly influence these traits, and it is the selection of traits which facilitate easier training to perform particular tasks that differentiates one breed from another and individuals within the breed.

Well-selected breeding stock is more likely to produce progeny that can assimilate training and respond to experiences. Genes are facilitators, not directors.

Early Learning
The pioneering animal behaviourist Dr Konrad Lorenz has coined the phrase 'instinct-training conditioning', in which an innate, or instinctual, predisposition to respond is reinforced or shaped by experience. Following a trail and discriminating it from others, and the ability to catch, kill and even consume prey efficiently, exemplify this. The innate predisposition to follow enticing scent and to pursue small moving objects is seen in all young pups, as they explore their environment and 'play-hunt'. These activities expose them to experiences from which they benefit by instigating and improving their ability to track and hunt. Early learning enormously assists the young terrier to 'cash in' on its genes. Early experiences can be lasting ones, for good or bad. The making of a terrier comes from such early learning; the make-up of the terrier allows it to benefit the most.

Terrier breeders should always be seeking 'the whole dog', not pursuing one feature obsessively and excessively whilst accepting others not entirely beneficial. As Darley Matheson noted in *Terriers* (1922): 'Quality of front is greatly sought after by breeders, but a beautiful front ought not to be allowed to overshadow poor hindquarters.' This over-emphasis of one physical feature to the detriment of others is a curse. Some terriers are judged on their 'spannable thorax' whilst their stuffy necks, weak loins, short bodies and thin feet are overlooked. Some tolerate frenetically barking terriers, furiously striving to attack any dog within reach, mistaking such character weakness as terrier-temperament. The sound production of a terrier is about the whole dog, never the blinkered obsessive seeking of perfection in one area or the blind overlooking of undesirable traits. There is one area, however, which should always be emphasized in sporting terriers, and it is in their spirit, not their build: without 'attitude' no working dog is ever going to succeed. The character of a terrier is everything.

The Need for Field Testing

I believe that it is entirely fair to state that of all the types of dog ruined by the effects of the Kennel Club-approved show rings the Terrier group has suffered the most. This is sad for a number of reasons: firstly, the Kennel Club was founded by sportsmen, with the Rev. John Russell an early member and Fox Terrier judge; secondly, the breeders of those terrier breeds recognized by the KC boast of the sporting ancestry of their dogs – and then dishonour it; and, thirdly, some quite admirable breeds of terrier have been degraded, even insulted, in this way. Discounting the Airedale, never an earth-dog and more a hunting griffon, and farm dogs like the Kerry Blue and Wheaten Terriers, which were all-rounders rather than specialist terriers, all show terriers should only be called full champions if they have passed an underground test.

In the United States, they are shaming us by conducting such 'gameness' tests, ranging from 'Introduction to Quarry' and 'Junior Earthdog' to 'Senior Earthdog' and 'Master Earthdog'. Introduced by their

Terriers at Work, *Arthur Wardle's 1906 portrayal of Fox Terriers out rabbiting; all breeds of terrier should have the make-up for their sporting role.*

kennel club, the AKC, in 1994, in the Introduction test, the terrier (or working Dachshund) has two minutes to enter a 10ft tunnel, negotiate a 90-degree turn and 'work' (that is, bay, growl, lunge or dig) the quarry (sometimes a caged rat) for thirty seconds. The American enthusiasts say that 'you put a dog down the hole but you get a terrier out of it'. In the Master Earthdog test, acting in a brace, a dog has to follow a 100ft scent trail to a hole, which is intentionally a false one, investigate the false den without giving tongue, then navigate 30ft of tunnel only 9in square, three 90-degree turns, a false exit, a constriction point and an obstacle.

The French have their clubs practising '*la venerie sous terre*', working under licence on badger, fox and coypu using wire and smooth Fox Terriers, but also featuring Teckels, Fell type and smaller hunt terriers. They proudly parade at the French Game Fair at the chateau of Chambord near Tours each year, with their gleaming spades and polished pick-axes, even badger-

tongs. Writing in *The Countryman's Weekly* in November 2004, Jeremy Hobson stated:

> It seems strange to have to visit France to see the best examples of working terriers. Long-legged smooth-coated Jack Russells are extremely popular and almost all conform to the likeness of Trump (the terrier Russell bought from a milkman in 1819)… deep-chested, straight-legged and with powerful shoulders, a stud dog from one of these packs would, I feel, benefit many strains being bred in the UK today.

Seventy years ago, Pierce O'Conor was advocating something similar. He described the French apparatus for trying terriers: a wooden conduit 7½in wide,

TERRIER TRIALS

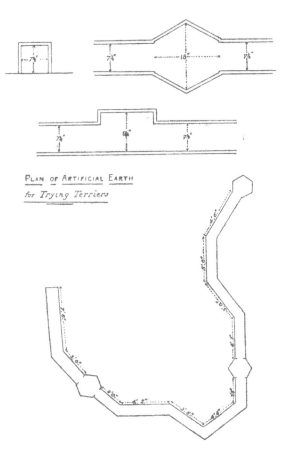

A Border Terrier follows the scent through the tunnel. The top and sides of the tunnel are made of wood but the floor is earth.

Pierce O'Conor's design for an underground test ground for terriers.

sunk in the earth, with passing chambers, just over 50ft long. Terrier-testing underground is so much more a basis for judging than any 'beauty show'. It tests, however artificially, the working instinct and character of the dog. It is both surprising and disappointing that there's no underground testing of terriers at game fairs and country shows. It would cost little to install the equipment needed for such essential tests of terrier function. Come on, Game Fairs of Weston Park and Ragley Hall, lead the way!

Forbidden fruit is always sweetest, and breeders of show terriers are never tired of dinning into one's ears that their dogs are workers as well, and bred on the right lines for make and shape, but they lose sight of the fact that while they have been breeding them for straightness, they have acquired a giraffe-like length of leg, and while breeding them for appearance and show-points they have lost all their individuality, intelligence and stamina.

> Arthur Blake Heinemann, writing on
> Hunt Terriers in *The Field*, October 1912

These old working terriers were tough and strong. They had to be because their daily life consisted of facing cornered animals which they had to kill or bolt. The fighting underground was savage and the terrier was expected to succeed or die – and many of them did – either through bites or by being trapped under the earth. Courage or 'gameness' was the quality most prized by the terrier breeders and cowardly dogs were very rare indeed because a terrier showing the slightest trace of fear was quickly destroyed and never used for breeding. The old types were also swift and some were known to have covered over six miles in thirty minutes – a very good time over rough country by a comparatively short-legged animal.

> *The Book of Terriers* by C.G.E. Wimhurst
> (Muller, 1968)

But now for the terriers, a most important and indispensable adjunct to a pack of otter hounds; for on every occasion where strong holts or underground drains are met with, on them it will depend whether a trail is to end in a find or not. The process of ejectment, generally a bloody one in close quarters, it is their duty to serve. The terrier, therefore, should be hard, wiry, and by no means too big in size; otherwise he will not only be able to work a narrow drain, but by scraping back the earth to get at the otter, he will dam the water behind him, and so, if not rescued, be drowned.

> *Hunting* by the Duke of Beaufort (Longman, 1886)

Showing the Sporting Dog

Judging Standards

Do terrier shows have any value? Is the judging at terrier shows really producing the true winner, actually rewarding the best dog present? Terriers can achieve a reputation above the ground as well as below it; but is it fairly earned? The bigger types of dog, especially those with a close coat, are probably easier to judge, both for a sound construction and for movement, than a small terrier, especially one with a profuse coat. It is disappointing to stand ring-side at a working terrier show, especially when a so-called 'hunt terrier-man' is judging, and see all manner of faults being rewarded by his placements. A one-eyed, heavily scarred, three-legged terrier may be the best working terrier in the county, but a show is all about appearance not reputation. I have actually seen a terrier win a first prize whilst suffering from a luxating patella; but that was at Crufts.

Of those who argue that such a show is just a beauty contest and the condition of the dogs an afterthought, let me ask these questions. Firstly, when did you ever

Winning Bull Terrier of the 1980s.

Bedlington show winner of today.

Early prize-winning Bull Terrier: Young Victor, first at Crystal Palace, Manchester, Darlington and Glasgow.

Early prize-winning Bedlington Terrier: Tartar, first at Crystal Palace, Crook and Aberdeen.

see a national beauty queen with a spare tyre and podgy limbs? Secondly, what is the point of having a serious hobby if you don't take it seriously, especially if you want to win? Thirdly, if exhibits are expected to be in 'show condition', why are judges taking a different view? I was also disturbed to watch four successive classes of one breed being judged without the exhibits' feet once being examined. The bite of each dog was checked and infinite care taken over the comparative assessment of the entry. But feet are crucial to working dogs, more important even than mouths. Why does the organization inviting the judge invite such an inadequate individual? Shouldn't every exhibit at any dog show be in show condition?

Show Quality

What is actually meant by the expression 'show condition'? The Kennel Club's *Glossary of Terms* defines condition as: 'Health as shown by the body, coat, general appearance and deportment. Denoting overall fitness.' Not brilliantly written but the last phrase is the key one. Frank Jackson, in his most useful *Dictionary of Canine Terms*, defines condition as 'quality of health evident in coat, muscle, vitality and general demeanour'. Harold Spira, in *Canine Terminology*, describes it as, 'an animal's state of fitness or health as reflected by external appearance and behaviour. For example, muscular development'. The Breed Standards and Stud Book Sub-Committee at the KC inform me that 'show condition' indicates an expectation of 'a dog in good health as indicated by good coat condition, good muscle tone, a bright eye and up on the feet', adding that any competent judge would know this. One thing is inescapable in the interpretation of these definitions: condition means fitness, as demonstrated in the dog's muscular state.

Why then, at major dog shows, both KC-sanctioned and country shows, are the judges of sporting terrier exhibits rewarding dogs in poor muscular condition and quite clearly *not* fit? Is it ignorance, incompetence or indifference? Some of the judges I have watched in recent years simply did not know soft muscle from hard and seemed incapable of detecting the absence of muscular development. I shudder to think where this will lead us! Judging livestock is essentially a subjective skill based on what you see in the entry, not what the exhibitor wants you

A view of the National Terrier Club's championship show at Olympia, 1947.

to see. Rather than a reaction to the animal before you, it is more a conscious action to relate the animal presented to you in the ring to the beau ideal for that particular breed.

Physical Condition

If we are going to accept at KC dog shows unfit exhibits lacking muscular development as challenge certificate material, then novice exhibitors are being given a wholly undesirable impression and standards have already become unacceptably low. We are in effect betraying the work of the skilful pioneer breeders who handed these fine breeds down to us. That apart, where is the pride of the breeders, owners and handlers concerned? Who admires a puny, unfit, under-developed dog or an obese, flabby one? These breeds were designed to work. What sort of encouragement is this to those admirable exhibitors who spent hours getting their dogs into real show condition?

In his informative *The Practical Guide to Showing Dogs* (1956), Captain Portman-Graham wrote:

The fact that a dog is structurally sound is not in itself sufficient to ensure that it will always win at shows. It is of paramount importance that it must be ... at the highest standard of condition. Perhaps one of the

biggest advantages which dog showing confers on the dog as an animal is the care which must be bestowed upon it.

If unfit dogs with poor muscular condition can win at dog shows, then the whole argument that such shows improve dogs or serve to display breeding material is totally destroyed. Dogs that are inadequately exercised and merely wheeled out for the next show should be identified early by any competent judge and

Wire-Haired Fox Terrier at Crufts in 1991.

quickly thrown out of the ring. Are our current crop of judges up to this? I see plenty of under-muscled terriers in working terrier show rings.

The estimable Portman-Graham went on:

Exercise is a vital consideration in maintaining any breed of show dog in bloom, health and vigour... When one watches the beautiful muscles of a racehorse one sees a similarity between a dog's muscles which have been developed correctly and naturally, and ripple in movement. Yet there is evidence of lack of muscular tone and development in many show breeds today.

He would not have liked the entries in show rings today. Surely such shows should be didactic not merely epideictic; in other words, they have a role in teaching those wanting to learn, not conducted literally just for show. A dog show, properly conducted, should attract exhibitors not exhibitionists.

In his book on the Sealyham, Sir Jocelyn Lucas made the same point:

Never show a dog unfit. If he is thin and out of coat, or too fat, it must militate against success. Dogs are judged by their appearance on the day of the show, not as to how they were a month before or will be in a month's time. A champion shown out of condition may be beaten by a moderate dog put down in good trim, the latter being henceforth advertised as having beaten Champion X.

Judging Working Anatomy

The terrier judges at Crufts in 2009 had some worrying comments in their critiques on the exhibits there: Sealyhams – 'Rear movement was a major concern to say the least… Toplines were not good, too many were weak and dipping;' Glen of Imaals – 'I was constantly trying to balance my ideal type with movement' (type in breeds does matter but movement reveals real faults); Wire-Haired Fox Terriers – 'I was disappointed to see so many heavy heads and large eyes' (no sporting terrier breed needs a heavy head or large eyes); Bedlingtons – 'I am greatly concerned at the lack of quality in the dogs currently being shown;' Parson Russells – 'Poor movement is still very much in evidence, with plaiting, paddling and a general lack of coordination readily seen;' Irish Terriers – 'Movement in general was disappointing, looseness in fronts and a lack of drive behind;' Borders – 'Many nice dogs lost out because of a lack of muscle or flat feet.' Sporting terriers with such faults at a show where, it is claimed 'only the best of the very best' are shown is disturbing; these dogs will all be bred from.

Pedigree livestock is still judged to a scale of points; pedigree dogs are no longer. Subjective judgements can bring fine differences of opinion to the fore. But for a sporting terrier to win a prize in any ring with upright shoulders, splay feet, a wry mouth and a stiff inflexible torso, as I witnessed recently, is more than depressing. If countrymen can't judge a dog these days, what hope for urban judges at Kennel Club shows? If the terrier shows at such prestigious venues as Harrogate, Ragley Hall and Weston Park are to remain valued and their winning dogs revered, the basic elements of a soundly constructed sporting terrier need to be understood. The gamest of earth-dogs still needs a working physique to perform.

Winning brace: C. Ormond's Lakelands, Tess and Bren.

Winning working terriers: on the judge's left is D. Hannah's Border Terrier pup Roy, on the right is D. Winder's Lakeland Terrier pup Gravel.

Working terrier in the ring; exhibits at such a show are in much better condition than those at KC shows.

The Limitations of Pedigree

In his valuable two-volume *The Dog Book* (1906), the underrated Scottish writer James Watson describes quite scathingly those in the world of pure-bred dogs who fail to realize that a pedigree is only a piece of paper. He records a conversation with the great Irish Terrier breeder of one hundred years ago, William Graham, who cast his eye over a show entry of his time and declared: 'Some men show pedigrees; I show dogs and take the prizes.' Vero Shaw, the distinguished canine authority of that time, gave the view in a show report that, all too often, the pedigree was worth more than the dog. To this day you still hear an indifferent animal excused on the grounds that it 'has a good pedigree'. As James Watson observed: 'No one with any knowledge of the subject will breed to a dog merely on pedigree ... a good dog makes a pedigree good, and not the other way.'

There used to be a saying in dog breeding circles: no animal is well-bred unless it is good in itself. I haven't heard it spoken of as a received wisdom for some years. Much more important than the names on the written pedigree is the ability to 'read' it, translate the names into physical content. As the great Scottish Terrier

breeder, W. L. McCandlish wrote in his book on the breed: 'The names in a pedigree form are merely ciphers, designating certain groupings of features and certain sources of blood, and pedigree is of no value unless the breeder can translate what these ciphers mean.' Yet even some quite experienced dog breeders get dazzled by names on forms, rather than by dogs, supported by blood from distinct ancestors. The eminent canine geneticist Malcolm Willis has written: '*Never* does pedigree information become more important than information on the dog itself.' We must always value dogs that are good in themselves.

Champion and runner-up: left: M. Steel with Lakeland Terrier Bob; right: R. Wilson with Border Terrier Holly.

Working terrier enthusiasts will never show great interest in precise measurements, exact proportions or wordy descriptions of anatomical features. But balance, symmetry, correct proportions and physical soundness really do affect function and therefore performance in a hunting animal. Terrier show judges may prefer to judge entirely by eye and experience, but is this enough? A seminar of working terrier judges to bring on the younger judges would surely be of value. It would be interesting to hear, should that happen, what terrier show judges' decisions are being based on. Rosslyn Bruce, in his book on the Fox Terrier, has written:

The author judging Plummer Terriers at Belvoir Castle.

> One reason for the existence of a Show is that any exhibitor may obtain the unbiased opinion of experts. Therefore, it is necessary not only to follow the judging, but to try to understand the reasons why a dog is rejected. There is no reason at all why the judge should not be approached, when judging is over, and asked about his awards.

Whenever I judge at a terrier show, at the end of judging, having asked the organizers if I may do so, I gather the exhibitors together and explain what I was looking for in the entry, what faults I found and my overall impression of 'the state of the breed' as seen that day. They may not agree with my placings but at least they are aware of my reasoning in coming to the decisions I did; that I believe is their right when entering a terrier under me.

> The greatest tragedy that can ever befall a breed is to become purely a fancier's dog... breeders must aim not merely at producing a good-looking dog, but also a workman. The cloddy dog who gets tired after walking half a mile, and who is too slow to catch a rat is a danger to the breed.
>
> *The New Book of the Sealyham* by Captain Jocelyn Lucas MC FZS (Simpkin & Marshall, 1929)

The Sporting Lucas Terrier show at Bramham, 2000.

The show ring Fox Terrier, long-headed and straight-fronted.

To-day it is fashionable to hold classes for working terriers at Dog Shows, and specialize in various breeds or strains, each vying with the other for press-puffs and paragraphs, and capping each other's fairy-tales as to their terrier's exploits; for, tell it not in Gath, this is a profitable game, and as one judge and breeder of the latest candidates for fashion's favour said to me, 'I know they're no use except at home amongst themselves, but what would you do? I can sell them like hot cakes.'

Arthur Blake Heinemann on Hunt Terriers in *The Foxhound*, October 1912

If we always remember that there is a great difference between 'breeding' and 'multiplying' foxhounds, any danger to the future of the foxhound through shows will be greatly reduced. For those Hunts where finance is a problem, it must be a comfort to know that to give up showing is the one economy that can be made without the sport suffering!

Hounds, Hunting and Country by Sir Newton Rycroft (Derrydale Press, 2001)

Judging the Sporting Dog

From their institution at Newcastle in 1858 there has been a growing feeling of dissatisfaction with the awards of the judges. Animals which have been successful under one set of judges in obtaining a first prize, have been altogether overlooked by another, not even obtaining a commendation, though in equally good condition at both places, and often with the same or nearly the same competitors.

No, these words were not written this year by a disappointed exhibitor at Crufts. They were written by the esteemed 'Stonehenge' in 1878. He went on to state that single judging requires 'some length of education' and to recommend a scale of points for each breed being judged.

Judging by Points
In the early part of the last century, the blueprint for each breed of dog or breed standard was accompanied by a scale of points. This allowed physical features to be judged against an allocated number of

Head studies of terriers showing the various styles.

The old-fashioned terrier head – Nobby by F.M. Hollams (1931).

ears 15, neck 5, shoulders and chest 15, back and loin 10, hindquarters 5, stern 5, legs and feet 20, coat 10 and what was termed 'symmetry and character' 15, giving a total of 100. For a working terrier I would prefer 50 for movement, which always indicates soundness, 20 for front assembly including the jaw, 20 for rear assembly and 10 for the weatherproof quality of the coat. Nearly every working terrier expert would, perhaps rightly, disagree, but that isn't really the issue: the important thing is that if you are going to judge precisely, you need a technique, ideally including a set sequence, a regular routine. I use one so that each exhibit gets the same examination. Mine starts with an overall impression of the whole entry, especially on the move, mentally grading them relatively. Then I look at stance, which sadly can relate to ring training, but I do not allow exhibits to be strung up on throat-throttling bootlace leads. Then I go from head shape and strength to jaw construction, eyes and nose, set of ears, head carriage, neck, set of shoulders, depth of chest, body-coupling, topline, stifles and hocks, wear on pads, temperament and coat texture. But how they move decides my winners. I try hard not to judge on faults and to reward merit. I rate the European system of grading, in which each exhibit is allotted a firm grade; but a list of points for each physical feature does encourage thoroughness.

Writing in 1897, Hugh Dalziel recalls being told by S.E. Shirley when president of the Kennel Club that, 'life's too short for the practice of judging by points'. This surprised Dalziel as it came from a man who had 'most precisely laid down the absolute numerical value of each point in the breed of Collie' in an article. Dalziel himself argued that each judge was an instructor, with every award he makes acting as a lesson. I think that that is very apt. He supported judging to a scale of points, describing any other system as 'too loose'. There is probably some truth in that. In his valuable three-volume work *British Dogs* (1888), Dalziel writes, perceptively: 'What should be indelibly fixed on the minds of all concerned is that the judge's influence does not end, but really begins, with the distribution of prizes.' We have all seen the produce of unworthy champions and the long term harm done in breeds by newcomers chasing prize-winning but poor quality stock.

points. For example, the Sealyham and Scottish Terriers could be awarded up to 15 points for the body whilst other points could vary – legs and feet were worth up to 10 points for the Scottie and up to 15 for the Sealyham. Every dog could therefore be rated out of 100 points against the same scale of points as rival entries in that breed. Skye Terriers could not be 'commended' unless the exhibit scored over 60. The Irish Terrier could have points deducted for undesirable features such as white nails, toes and feet (minus 10 points). The English Springer Spaniel could attract up to 95 'negative' points and the Sussex Spaniel 100, so theoretically a Sussex Spaniel could score zero.

In 1896, the wire-haired Fox Terrier was judged to a scale of points with these relative values: head and

The author judging a Sporting Lucas Terrier pup at the Rugby show, 2009.

The author judging Lucas Terriers in 1997 (photo: Sheila Atter, courtesy of Dogs Monthly*).*

Show Ring Criteria versus Terrier Criteria

Earlier I stated that of all the types of dog ruined by the effects of the Kennel Club-approved show rings the terrier group has suffered the most, even though experienced terrier judges say they look for 'working appeal'.

But what should 'working appeal' be based on? The original working Fox Terriers were barrel-chested and had a fairly straight stifle and hock; the longer tibia and well-bent hock of the show ring terrier of today is not much use underground. An even bigger difference lies in the shoulder angulation and depth of chest. Show Fox Terriers, without exception, have upright shoulders and slab-sided but deep chests; neither of these physical attributes help an earth-dog. Nor does the short back of the pedigree Fox Terrier, which reduces flexibility and overall suppleness, while at the same

time giving a more compact-looking, showy type of dog; upright shoulders can give an exhibit more presence in the ring. Straight shoulders cause imbalance between the fore and hindquarters and affect the position of the elbow, leading to weaving, toeing out, tied at elbow, and the opposite, out at elbow. Judges should look out for 'pounding', where the dog's foot meets the ground prematurely.

In *The Science and Techniques of Judging Dogs* (Alpine, 2007), Robert J. Berndt writes (referring to the American standards, but ours are similar):

> Much is said about the terrier front and how it differs from the fronts of many other breeds. The standard for the Smooth Fox Terrier calls for the legs to be 'straight with bone strong right down to the feet,

A working Bedlington comes under the judge's scrutiny.

A Wire-haired Fox Terrier being prepared for the ring at Crufts in 1991.

showing little or no appearance of ankle in front, and being short and straight in pastern'. The Kerry Blue Terrier calls for the pasterns to be 'short, straight and hardly noticeable'. The pasterns of the Welsh Terrier are to be upright and powerful. This condition in these breeds will affect the gait of the dogs as there will be less spring since the stress will be transmitted directly up the leg. The gait of these long-legged Terriers is different from that of dogs in other groups, and is different from some of the short-legged Terriers.

That is a point that seems to escape far too many terrier judges.

The craze for long heads in show terriers, exemplified most clearly in the Smooth Fox Terrier, is rooted in the misguided belief that length gives power. You also hear the expression 'plenty of heart room', which is strange when the heart doesn't actually change size when the dog is exerting itself. Plenty of *lung* room is desirable, especially in terriers which run with the hounds. But it is rib space that gives a dog lung room,

A terrier depicted by W. Huggins, showing the well turned-out feet desired in a small digging breed.

not depth of chest. I have heard terrier show judges fault a very muscular terrier, used to hard exercise, for being 'loaded at the shoulders' when the fortunate dog had developed muscle that projected on the outside of its shoulders. Any individual accepting a judging appointment should question their own capability and 'eye for a dog' before proceeding.

In *Shooting Times*, in December 1981, working terrier expert Dan Russell commented:

> It is probably a very good thing that terrier shows have become so popular and have attracted so many people who keep their dogs solely as pets, but this should not blind us to the fact that the terrier was evolved as a worker and that his conformation should be suitable for his job. If we lose sight of this, Heaven knows what shapes and sizes we may see in the ring in the future.

He would not have admired the entry at today's KC terrier shows or indeed at some working terrier shows. He didn't like bull terrier crosses, bulky black Patterdales or 'daddy-longlegs' only favoured because they were 'spannable'. A flexible spine will always be more valuable to a terrier than a narrow chest.

In his informative volume, *The Book of All Terriers* (Howell Book House, 1971), John Marvin makes a key point for judges when examining the terrier's feet:

> A long-legged Terrier, when digging, throws the earth under his body and through his spread back

Working terrier with turned-out 'digging feet'.

legs. The short-legged breeds are different. Because of their low station, these breeds cannot throw earth under their bodies... Rather, they throw the earth sideways so that the low-slung body may pass through. In order to accomplish this it is necessary that the feet turn out slightly to guide the earth sideways of the body...Actually, feet pointing straight ahead on a short-legged breed are not correct and should be faulted although most judges do not look with disfavor on feet pointing straight ahead.

Terriers, whether short or longer-legged were designed to dig. They must always be judged as terriers.

Over a century ago, the respected writer on terriers, Rawdon Lee, recorded in *A History and Desription of The Fox Terrier* (1890):

> Some judges – men, too, who bear a deservedly high reputation as such, will put a terrier out of the prize list if it be even a trifle crooked on his fore legs or slightly heavy at the shoulders; whilst another dog, narrow behind and weak in loins, to my idea a far more serious failing, is considered pretty well all right so long as its fore legs are set on like rulers. As a fact, there are judges who have recently gone to extremes in awarding honours to these so-called 'narrow-fronted' terriers. Such have been produced at a sacrifice of power and strength. Most of these very narrow-chested dogs move stiffly, are too flat in the ribs, they are deficient in breathing and heart room, and can never be able to do a week's hard work in the country...

Sadly, we still live with these faults today; once a show ring fad becomes popular, it soon becomes acceptable. Soundness gives way to rosette-chasing and working structure gets forgotten. Such terriers cease to be sporting dogs and their owners cease to be custodians of their breed.

Standards of Judging

Dissatisfaction with the ability of dog show judges is not new, as these words illustrate: 'The general public, those who take any interest in dogs, are confident that the actual judging for Best in Show may be a farce. They feel, in the first place, that the person appointed is quite often not qualified to make the decision'. No, these are not the words of an anti-dog show journalist or a bitter exhibitor with an unplaced entry. They are the words of R.H. Smythe, a veterinary surgeon who bred, reared and exhibited dogs of almost every known breed, in his much-respected book *Judging Dogs* (1972). The fact that it was written

in the 1970s ago gives it even more validity, for few would disagree that dog show judges were far better then. It could be argued that this is but one comment on the imprecise art of judging dogs on their appearance, made some time ago, but there have been mixed feelings for years about 'beauty-shows for working

A working terrier being 'spanned'.

A patient Border Terrier comes under scrutiny.

from the wrong angle. What we need I think is not so much fantastic physical beauty, which may or may not have nose and voice, but a certain standard of working conformation *below* which hounds must not fall.' That should be a message for terrier exhibitors too.

Hound judges don't always make sound terrier judges. Writing in *Hounds* magazine some twenty years ago, terrier-man 'Daergi' recorded the view:

> Now we come to our terrier show in the summer season and our huntsman is asked to judge terriers at the neighbouring H.S. Club's show. Not being in the swing of things with regards to terrier shows he is blissfully unaware of the keen rivalry that surrounds these events. He stands in the middle of the ring and tries to judge terriers as he would hounds (which is probably the same as Lester Piggot judging Shetland ponies), not one terrier is spanned ... mouths are not looked at and general conformation which can be hidden by various coats is not discovered... A good judge can make or break a show, please choose yours carefully.

He could have added that hound show judges are not expected to place hands on an exhibit or to examine feet. This was once justified to me by one MFH with the explanation that no hound would ever be entered with unsound feet!

The Price of Victory

Henry Webb, in his quaintly titled *Dogs, Their Points, Whims, Instincts and Peculiarities* (1882), made a key point on judges when he wrote that exhibitors should remember 'that by entering their dogs for competition they tacitly approve the appointment of the judges'. He is right – what really is the point of showing your dog under a judge you don't respect? If he places your dog, do you withdraw? In *Prize Dogs*, over seventy years ago, Theo Marples was writing that, 'the prevailing mistake which exhibitors make is thinking that their geese are swans, or, in other words, thinking their dogs better than they really are.' It is this fundamental flaw which not only brings dogs into the ring that have no right to be there but also leads to the quite shocking unsporting behaviour that we have all witnessed at shows.

Winning at a cost to your precious breed seems irrational; why fancy that breed if you don't respect

dogs'. I understand that in Japan, in order to judge one breed, the Shiba Inu, it is necessary to be a member of the breed chapter for five years, a judge's assistant for at least two years, a judge's trainee for at least three years, to attend the judge's course at least twice and pass an examination. Even then an indefinite further period has to be served as an Associate Judge before fully qualifying. Small wonder that the specimens of this breed that I see at shows seem to be a great credit to their breeders, their breed and to their country of origin.

Hound-show judging at shows such as Peterborough and Honiton is conducted with two judges in the ring, who discuss the entry before them. This must increase competence, reduce corruption and encourage confidence. Conformation is judged, mainly by eye; a hands-on examination is not considered necessary, unlike at KC-licensed shows. Masters of Foxhounds do care what their hounds look like. Newton Rycroft, a greatly respected authority on working scenthounds has written: 'Conformation will always be important, but perhaps we look at this importance its function? That win-at-all costs attitude affects reaction to the judge's rulings too. The standard of sportsmanship at some terrier shows is disappointing; if you enter your terrier under any judge you automatically commit your exhibit to his or her decisions. We should all welcome what the Whig politician Edmund Burke called in 1794, 'the cold neutrality of an impartial judge'. No terrier judge should have to carry out his show ring duties wearing running shoes, with the engine of his car running! Terrier shows are for sportsmen, not aimed at disgruntled grown-up children, and can be a way of identifying future breeding stock, as well as being a great day out. At the end of the day, we all take the best dog home.

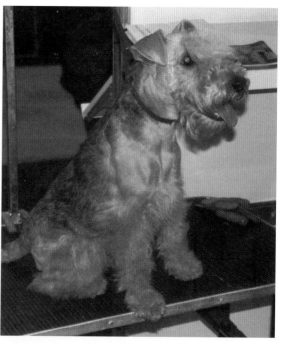

A charming Lakeland Terrier being remarkably patient at Crufts in 2001.

I consider that judges at dog shows have the whole success of a breed in their care. Incompetent, and still worse, prejudiced judging, does incalculable harm. Many a man is afraid of offending his friends, and to such a man I would say, 'Don't risk it; stay outside.' Others desire to please all the exhibitors, and to such a man I would also say, 'Don't risk it; stay outside. You are aiming at the impossible'... Many men, with an excellent knowledge of a dog, have not the 'judging ability', and I see no reason why they should be ashamed of it.

> *The Twentieth Century Dog* by Herbert Compton
> (Grant Richards, 1904)

As I was an exhibitor of Irish Terriers at Ayr yesterday, and as I was very much disappointed with the awards, I feel it is a duty to demand an explanation from you for acting in the manner you did... As for Gifford – had it not been that his chain was in Mr Lumsden's left hand, he would not have been looked at, as no man who knows anything about an Irish Terrier would look at him... Either you know nothing about an Irish Terrier, or, if you do, it was evident that it was the owner and not the dog that got the prize.

> Letter to *The Scottish Fancier and Rural Gazette*,
> May 1887

Who the man with the white waistcoat was who offered a bribe of a fiver to one of the judges at Crufts?

> From 'Things we want to know',
> *The British Fancier*, February 1892

It is only to be expected that some disappointed exhibitors would cavil at the decisions, however the prizes might be awarded; but they should remember that all cannot win, and that by entering their dogs for competition they tacitly approve the appointment of the judges; if they approve not, they should not enter, they are not bound so to do; but having once entered their dogs and submitted them to competition, we think they are duty bound to be satisfied with the decisions, unless any flagrant act of injustice could be proved.

> *Dogs: Their Points, Whims, Instincts and Peculiarities*, edited by Henry Webb (Dean & Son, 1883)

Selecting Breeding Stock

The breed of terrier is not important, and a man can please his fancy – I have used Fox, Wire, Sealyhams, Borders, Lakelands and Jack Russells, and they are all good if bred right – it's the strain that counts.

> *The Terrier's Vocation* by Geoffrey Sparrow
> (Allen & Co., 1976)

The selection of mates will forever be the principal factor in successful livestock breeding. So often, in the working dog world, it's done on a work rating: how good at working are the prospective parents? In the show dog world, however often this is denied, rosette-winning is the biggest single factor, with even unworthy Crufts winners being freely used as breeding stock. This is entirely irrational; it is based on a view that, firstly, Crufts judges are trustworthy in their judgements, secondly that the winning dog is physically and mentally sound, and thirdly, that the chosen mate will actually 'nick' with the other mate. By that, I mean produce the quality offspring the blood behind each mate *should* create. As master-breeder Jocelyn Lucas wrote in *Pedigree Dog Breeding* (Simpkin & Marshall, 1925): 'A stud dog is not good just because he is good looking. He must be bred right and not be "chance got", or his good points will not force themselves on his progeny.'

Charles Castle FZS, in *Scientific Dog Management and Breeding* (Kaye, 1951), wrote:

> Bruce-Lowe traced the pedigree of every racehorse back to the original dam ... he was able to classify these families by their characteristics, such as 'sire-producing families', 'running families', etc ... these families run true to the present day, passing on family characteristics and certain families 'nick in' to each other to produce winners.

There was a serious, enlightened breeder. As vet and exhibitor R.H. Smythe wrote in *The Breeding and Rearing of Dogs* (Popular Dogs, 1969): 'It is true that some kennels contrive to turn out a champion each year, but they are usually those that contain a number of bitches often similarly bred, and their owners have been fortunate enough to discover a sire that "nicks".'

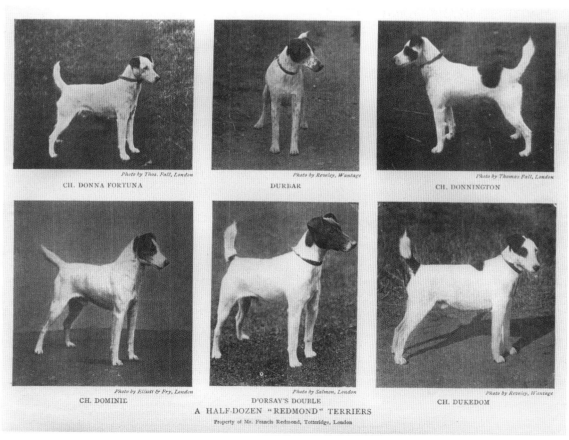

Photo by Thos. Fall, London
CH. DONNA FORTUNA

Photo by Reveley, Wantage
DURBAR

Photo by Thomas Fall, London
CH. DONNINGTON

Photo by Elliott & Fry, London
CH. DOMINIE

Photo by Salmon, London
D'ORSAY'S DOUBLE

Photo by Reveley, Wantage
CH. DUKEDOM

A HALF-DOZEN "REDMOND" TERRIERS
Property of Mr. Francis Redmond, Totteridge, London

Six top-class 'Redmond' Fox Terriers, owned by the great show terrier breeder Francis Redmond of Totteridge, London.

This system has a run-out date as repeat close-breeding can penalize in time.

Breeding or Puppy Producing

I once had a stockman who was astonishingly good at this 'nicking'; he didn't study bloodlines, he wasn't bedazzled by show ring success, he seemed to have a gift at matching sire with dam. I have heard of Irish Greyhound breeders with a similar 'eye'. But my stockman was an older man with decades of experience with livestock; he had learned not from paper but proof in the flesh. He did in fact know a great deal about bloodlines and had shown exhibits for years at agricultural shows. Breeding livestock is very much a science, but he made it into an art. There are show dog breeders with similar insight. It is the blend of phenotypical and genotypical features that produce the offspring; top quality can skip a generation. The concept that a Crufts winner mated to an indifferent bitch can somehow produce top-quality pups is seriously flawed. It is based on wishful thinking, not science. The lazy thinking that leads to a good-quality bitch being mated to the nearest available sire in that breed is mere puppy-producing.

In emergent breeds, stabilizing the gene pool and establishing type is crucial. The creator of the Plummer Terrier, sporting writer/breeder Brian Plummer, at first advocated a back-cross to the 'pit bull type' but later on, as his breed developed, he changed his mind. In a telephone conversation with me, towards the end of his shortened life, he stated very clearly that he no longer favoured that approach. He was wise enough to retain an open mind; kennel or breed blindness can do much harm. Strict conformists can let a breed deteriorate; unskilled non-conformists can wreck a breed. I do hope Brian's impressive breed is in safe hands. When I judged them a few years ago, I saw sufficiently sound, type stock to make a reversion even to founder-blood to my mind quite needless.

Wise Outcrossing

In another emergent breed, the quite admirable Sporting Lucas Terrier, a planned outcross to a Norfolk has restored the red-tan coat colour to the breed.

Breeding back to a Stafford with a Plummer would produce a terrier like this.

An alert Plummer Terrier, a feisty emergent breed.

The author going over a Plummer Terrier.

The Sporting Lucas type of terrier – bright-eyed, alert, showing no exaggeration.

As a breeding advisor to the breed, I am sometimes asked about other possible outcrosses, to farm or working Sealyhams, for example. Without seeing the dogs themselves, not knowing their background, but acknowledging the need to expand a small gene pool, this gives me difficulties. I first judged a Lucas Terrier show over a decade ago and was concerned at the number of 'brown Sealyhams' in the ring. Type in a breed is everything but favouring an undesired physical signature is not breeding for the breed, just using available stock. At country shows, however, I do see throwbacks to the real Sealyham, the type originally used in the hunting field, not over-boned, over-coated or otherwise 'overdone'.

When judging the annual show of the Sporting Lucas Terrier Club (SLTC) at Bramham Moor nearly a decade ago, I commented on the mainly white-jacketed entry, mourning the absence of the fuller range of coat colours sought in the breed and set out in the breed standard, as ratified by the United Kennel Club in America. The committee then undertook the recommended outcross to a top-quality Norfolk Terrier to reintroduce the tan and the black and tan jacketed varieties. When judging the SLTC's 2009 show at Rugby, I was delighted to see some highly promising young pups in black and tan jackets (now known as the 'Hancock' line). The selection of breeding material will forever be the key element in dog breeding and, in this case, the chosen Norfolk Terrier sire used as an outcross has produced a splendid result.

Selecting for Terrier Traits

In selecting breeding material an eye must be kept on the terrier function, the terrier spirit and the spiritual outlet needed by such sporting dogs. Soon, in any number of pedigree terrier breeds, there will be a generation, if there isn't one already, that doesn't know what their breed once looked like. So much for respecting a breed and its functional origin. In *The Principles of Dog-Breeding* (Toogood, 1930), R.E. Nicholas wrote: 'The breeder who returns from each show with a new rather than an improved ideal seldom accomplishes anything worthwhile, for vacillation in [breed] standards is the direct road to confusion of types and to absolute failure. The rolling stone gathers nothing but hard knocks.' Every breed needs breed architects ahead of breed optimists.

When you breed selectively for one feature only, you imperil many other points; ignore working anatomy and go for handsomeness, and you overlook a design for function; forget working ability and you risk losing it. In an article in *Field Sports* in June 1952, working terrier expert R.R. Stopford wrote:

> In the choice of a puppy, one's personal ideas will carry more weight than the show-bench standard, but it is essential that size, shape, and strain are dominant factors in the selection. The dangers of acquiring a youngster, no matter how likeable it may be, from parents of a non-working strain are (a) that it may grow too big, and (b) that it will lack the intelligence or the keenness for the purpose for which it is intended.

We can all get carried away by a charming pup, but breeding working terriers has to be a single-minded, informed and disciplined choice.

My Best in Show winner at the 1997 Lucas Terrier Club show (photo: Sheila Atter).

The Norfolk Terrier – easily confused with its Norwich Terrier sister-breed.

Breeding for the Whole Dog

When you breed selectively for coat, as has happened in the Skye, Sealyham, Scottish and Cesky Terriers and now the Soft-Coated Wheaten Terrier, you can end up with all coat and no dog. When you breed selectively for head shape, you lose genuine type, as in the Bull Terrier and the Bulldog, no matter how widely accepted the new look is. When you breed selectively for 'stance', the longer muzzle and the short back, as in the Fox Terrier, you end up with upright shoulders, an 'ant-eater' head and reduced flexibility in the spine, not exactly earth-dog requirements. Working terriers need suppleness, pliancy – all the flexibility they can get – especially from their spines, and they won't get this from flawed concepts about their anatomy. In the closed gene pool of the pedigree Fox Terrier these needless penalties are built in. Over half a century ago, as a vet's kennel boy, I went with him to Molly Harbut's Airedales, to Manson Baird's Deerhounds, Miss Lipscombe's Bull Terriers and other renowned kennels; it would be good to see such 'type' once more.

When a Sporting Lucas Terrier is outcrossed to a Norfolk Terrier to restore a missing coat colour, unless the breeding stock is wisely selected, you can bring in undesirable traits as well. If you outcross to a working Sealyham, for perfectly sound reasons on paper, you run the same risk again unless the mates are wisely chosen. The resultant progeny may genetically be 50 per cent Sporting Lucas and 50 per cent working Sealyham, but not necessarily phenotypically – that is, in appearance. Genetics isn't a mathematical exercise; it is a battle between dominant and recessive

genes. I have seen a lurcher, claimed to be 25 per cent Whippet, 25 per cent Bedlington Terrier, 25 per cent collie and 25 per cent Greyhound, looking exactly like a purebred Bedlington Terrier. In this mating, the Bedlington blood, despite being only a quarter of the blend, triumphed.

Pursuit of Consistency

All named terrier breeds developed in a planned restricted gene pool; every emergent terrier breed has to face the dilemma of a small gene pool maintaining type or an enlarged one introducing alterations to type. Some Sporting Lucas Terriers are too open-coated, some are too low to the ground, some lack bone and obvious jaw strength. Some Plummer Terriers are too finely boned, some are too thin-coated. Not surprisingly, both these emergent breeds lack consistency of form. Finding the stock that remedies these faults takes breeding skill, patience and single-mindedness. In due course, an outcross may be necessary but only if, firstly, the coefficient of inbreeding reaches worrying levels; and secondly, if inherited defects crop up;

A composed Cesky Terrier, a breed that seems to be bred more for its coat than its many other qualities.

and thirdly, if virility is lost. Both breeds are closely knit, with many breeders knowing each other's stock. Now is the time perhaps for the introduction of an appraisal scheme in which breeding stock, sound enough mentally and physically to justify breeding from, is graded and minor faults acknowledged then bred out under an agreed and accepted breeding plan for every terrier breed. Our irrational, and at times irresponsible, dislike of breeding controls, may prevent this happening, but it will never be enough just to mate dog A to dog B and hope!

Selecting Beyond Appearance

When I was working in Germany nearly half a century ago, I learned of the work, in the German Democratic Republic, of Dr F.K. Dorn, author of *Hund und Umwelt* (*The Dog and his Environment*). Dorn devised a system of four categories: A=Type, B=Appearance, C=Conformation and D=Temperament. Within each category, Dorn devised a numerical scoring system, in which, for example, A1=shelly, A8=too heavy and clumsy; B0=lack of pigmentation, B5=excellent appearance, outline and symmetry; D0=nervous or timid, D3=cautious, not self-assured and D8=unafraid but not aggressive. Such details could then be written on a dog's pedigree for use when breeding plans were being formulated.

This became known as the Merseberg scoring system, after the GSD breed club there. Dorn was seeking to establish a clear picture of the hereditary qualities of the whole bloodline of a dog. Yet now, half a century later, our pedigrees merely list the ancestors for five generations, without any checks on their accuracy or the slightest whiff of real information about the *dog*. Is this progress? Is this in the best interests of good breeding? Prizes for phenotype and beauty are given sole weight and to hell with such basic information as health, intelligence and working ability. In livestock breeding, a stud has no value until the performance of its progeny has been established. But in the pedigree dog world, a stud is valued not on the performance of its offspring but on their successful stance in the ring. Does that produce the best companion animals?

Breeders of working terriers like to maintain breeding records. They rate performance ahead of purity, but all terriers are pets to some degree and temperament in terriers really does matter. The biggest single reason for dogs going into rescue or needing rehoming is behaviour issues relating to failings in temperament. Our terriers deserve to be bred with spirit, it's the basis of their character. But there is a huge difference between a ceaselessly snarling, hyper-aggressive, combat-seeking canine psychopath and a confident, restrained, even-tempered, stable yet still active and courageous little warrior. A badly bred terrier with deep-rooted behavioural problems lets down all terriers. Choosing the right stud dog really does matter. Socializing the young litter is vital too. Breeders are all important. They select the breeding material, they introduce the progeny to the world and they choose their future homes. All these factors contribute to the happy terrier.

If breeders are frightened by their losses this year into putting their bitches to dogs totally unrelated to them, with the idea of getting stamina in their progeny, I am certain they will lose a year's breeding. No doubt the great secret in close in-breeding is never to be tempted into using either a bitch or dog that isn't perfectly sound and healthy. That in-breeding may be carried too far goes without saying, and it requires great care and judgement to know exactly when fresh blood is required, and even greater judgement to know how to introduce it without ruining the strain.

H.J. Ludlow, a distinguished breeder of Scottish Terriers, in *The Kennel Gazette*, January 1892

By far and away the single important factor that can make or mar a terrier is its breeding. You cannot breed a racehorse out of a donkey. So you can't breed an ideal working terrier if it is not from the right stock. Ideally that stock should go back many generations. It will then have the brains to go with the physical conformation to make this the ideal terrier and the envy of everyone.

Tony Kirby, writing in *Hounds* magazine in 1987.

CONSERVING THE TERRIER AS A SPORTING DOG

Decline in Standards

Terrier breeds that emerged in Britain in the nineteenth century, whatever their origin, are, with a few exceptions – like the Border Terrier – markedly different in many respects nowadays from the stock shown at early dog shows. Some of these differences are displayed in even shorter legs, in breeds which already featured short legs, even longer muzzles (and narrower in Fox Terriers) and greater cloddiness, as in the show Sealyham. Even more noticeable are the far heavier coats, in today's Scottish Terrier for example, and, sadly, in so many terrier breeds, upright shoulders and no falling away at the croup.

These two latter features are responsible for the

Spirited Manchester Terriers.

Perseverance! A hundred rats killed in five and a half minutes.

The Borders challenge the Bedlingtons.

Irish Terriers in romping mood.

greatly abbreviated front and rear stride in terrier breeds, resulting in movement falsely described by some as a 'terrier action'. This lack of extension, fore and aft, can never be acceptable in a sporting terrier, especially an earth-dog. Kennel Club recognition has undoubtedly brought uniformity to these breeds and perhaps greater beauty. But in a terrier, beauty at the expense of function is an empty gain. Function dictates form in quadrupeds and form contributes both to health and quality of life. I groan with despair when I hear a TV commentator at Crufts excitedly describing sporting terrier breeds on the move as 'simply flowing over the ground'. Millipedes flow over the ground; dogs, whatever their size, should stride.

The great Fox Terrier authority Rosslyn Bruce warned against a too long-headed dog with a too short back; I see many winning dogs today with exactly these two features. He was very specific on the subject of shoulders, stressing their need to be long and sloping, well laid back. He pointed out that 'where the shoulders are well laid back the dog is at an advantage for work underground'. With most sporting terriers in today's show ring, I find upright shoulders and, increasingly, short upper arms. And so do many judges; it is a far too frequent criticism in their post-show reports. Unless knowledgeable judges penalize this bad fault it will become a breed feature and be bred in for all time. Should we not keep faith with those who developed these splendid breeds for us?

Experience without Knowledge

Regrettably, exaggerations in dogs with a closed gene pool always end up exaggerating themselves still further. Outcrossing to restore true type may be regarded as sacrilege by conformists. But why, once attracted to a breed, not honour its true blueprint? Why betray its original type and true form? Sadly, most show breeders are extraordinarily conformist, even when true breed type in their favoured breed is threatened. Pedigree dog breeders and dog show judges often draw an

Terriers are famous for their determination.

undeserved awe from the general public; some are undeniably gifted, many are very obviously not. An experienced breeder, even to the KC, all too often means someone who has bred a lot of litters, whatever their quality. Judges, similarly, can progress if they have bred prolifically from their stock.

This unsatisfactory situation not only leads to false reputations being gained but far too many puppies being bred. No livestock judge at an agricultural show is ever chosen on the basis of how many calves or lambs he or she has bred. Pony and hound show judges are chosen for their *knowledge* not their production line. The same criterion, if applied in the world of pure-bred dogs, would represent a giant step forward. Far too many dog breeds have been at the mercy of wallet-conscious, power-seeking puppy-

producers posing as experts in their field. No terrier expert would produce a dog with needless working handicaps. Terriers designed originally to work should never feature over-heavy coats, a cloddy build with little flexibility, stiff-limbed movement, anteater heads or limited extension both fore and aft.

Deteriorating Coats

The early Sealyhams were prized for the coconut matting texture of their coats; the current breed standard demands a coat that is long, hard and wiry. The dogs I see in the ring have long, soft and wavy coats. Captain Jocelyn Lucas, who worked the breed, stated, in his *Pedigree Dog Breeding* (1925): 'A hard coat is not only a show point, but also a working one, as soft-coated dogs generally hate brambles.' Today's breed standard of the Wire-Haired Fox Terrier asks for a coat that is dense with a very wiry texture. Just before the Second World War, Rowland Johns wrote, on the wire-haired variety, in *Our Friend the Fox Terrier*, that 'the harder and more wiry the texture of the coat is the better. On no account should the dog look or feel woolly'. In the show ring I see soft woolly coats on many winning dogs.

In his monumental *Dogs of all Nations*, published in 1904, Count Henry van Bylandt describes what we would today call a Schnauzer as a wire-haired German Terrier. The texture of coat is described as '*straff*' or stiff. When you look at Schnauzers of all sizes in contemporary show rings all over Europe their coats

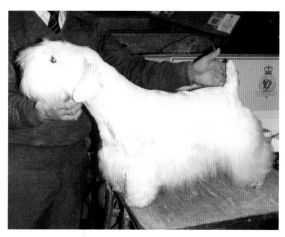

The Sealyham Terrier of today; it must never become 'all coat and no dog'.

Head study of the Border Terrier, a seemingly unchanging breed.

An early Sealyham, shorter-coated and longer-legged, faithfully preserved at the Natural History Museum in Tring.

do not appear to have a stiff texture. Exhibitors emphasize the beard and leggings but not the coat's actual texture.

Today's breed standard for the Scottish Terrier describes the coat as close-lying with a harsh outer coat. In his book on the breed, published over seventy years ago, W.L. McCandlish set out the standard of that time. The coat was described as rather short

Good Friends by G. Paice (1886), showing a Fox Terrier without today's long head and a Schnauzer with a stiff, manageable coat.

(about 2in), intensely hard and wiry in texture; wave in the coat was described as a special fault. The Scottish Terriers that I see winning at shows have an abundance of coat – well over 4in, with waviness, standing off from the body; so much for breed standards! Fox Terrier expert Rosslyn Bruce, in his 1950 book on the breed, wrote: 'The coat, or the outside covering or jacket, is that part of the Terrier which is perhaps the most difficult for the novice to grasp'. He might have included judges in that sentence.

Vision in Breeding

Throughout our social history as a nation, changing attitudes have influenced our use of dogs in the name of sport. Barbaric activities like badger-, bear- and bull-baiting, rat-killing competitions and dog-fighting contests have rightly been outlawed. Nevertheless, we still prize and perpetuate that one-time canine gladiator, the Bull Terrier, even if some legislators retain the view that once a fighter always a fighter. Bull Terrier fanciers need reminding that their dogs were sporting dogs in the field long before they were used in the pits. They should perpetuate their breed as a sporting terrier, not as a role-less gladiator; a working test could so easily be devised to retain their sporting spirit. The spirit behind the trail-hound and Whippet

racing, the Bloodhound packs that hunt a human trail, lure-chasing with Irish Wolfhounds and even nocturnal rat-catching in a maggot-factory, as the late Brian Plummer recommended, provide such encouragement for the future of sporting dogs. Perhaps, sadly, the single-issue lobbyists have them too in their sights. Even well-intentioned people can do great harm.

The early terriers had the weatherproof coat, the extension in their limbs that allowed them to function and the never-say-die attitude that made them invaluable to man in farms and factories alike. I have vivid memories, as a boy, of the wire netting going round

The modern Bull Terrier, with a shape of eye and head quite unlike its ancestors.

The original Bull Terrier head.

The Bull Terrier head of today.

the ricks and the terriers being loosed, to kill over 200 rats per rick despite the odd bite. No machine or chemical could ever do that. Gassing or poisoning is a dreadful way to control rats; terriers are fast and efficient. Anyone with a bored teenager should give them a copy of Brian Plummer's classic *Tales of a Rat-Hunting Man* (1978); it's lively, amusing and uplifting – just like terriers themselves!

In America, Airedales have their own specific hunting trials; can we really not do so here? I live near dog owners who get upset when their terriers are combative and feisty but are unconcerned when their dogs bark all day, every day. Terrier spirit is part of every sporting terrier's make-up – it comes with the dog and is not difficult to redirect.

If sporting breeds are to survive there has to be a planned renaissance, not an abrogation of responsibility for breeds we specifically bred and developed over several centuries to assist us in the sporting field. It would be a major step forward if breed clubs took up this challenge, although I suspect that challenge certificates have more appeal for them. Just as the UKC in the United States fathers a wide range of field activity for dogs, so too could our own KC, extending their field trial and agility interest. Sporting organizations, too, could diversify their sporting agenda, in the interests of the hounds alone, if only to have the canine ingredients of a rebirth one day, should field sports regain legal acceptance. To neglect the best interests of the dogs would be shameful. Positive thinking is called for, not intellectual collapse.

Just over a hundred years ago, the great Bloodhound breeder, Edwin Brough, recorded:

> The greatest benefactor to the ancient race [the Bloodhound] is the man who breeds intelligently, and supports both trials and shows, but there will always be people who are unable to devote time to both, and the trialler should remember that he will always be greatly indebted to the showman, and the showman should bear in mind that he owes the excuse for his existence to the trialler ... their conception of the ideal hound should be the same.

These are wise words from a gifted breeder; without field use many breeds lose the functional anatomy essential to sporting success. As fewer and fewer dog breeders take part in activities involving field sports, the functional aspect of their breed's phenotype can be lost sight of, and that is not good for any breed.

In Rosslyn Bruce's book on the Fox Terrier, one particular statement gladdens my heart: 'I say to the budding enthusiast: the first point to aim at in a terrier is "Character", the second "Character", and yet again the third essential is "Character".' Here is a man steeped in the exhibition world, member of the Kennel Club Committee and founder of the Smooth Fox Terrier Association, having the wit and the perception to see what makes a terrier, in any age. Tenacity, fortitude, fearlessness, dash and perky assertiveness make a terrier what it is, rather than perfection of form. But these qualities alone do not make a successful sporting terrier; such a dog needs the anatomy that allows it to perform its allotted task: the control of vermin above and below ground.

Breeders of show terriers, together with those who judge them, have a duty to respect the remarkable heritage behind their dogs. They may not want their terriers to go to ground but their dogs are not terriers unless they have the mental and physical qualities for such a task. The pioneer breeders handed these precious breeds down to us to safeguard in our lifetime.

It will be sad indeed if future generations inherit terriers with soft wavy coats, a short-stepping gait and a complete absence of adventurous spirit. Such dogs belong in the Toy Group; they are neither sporting dogs nor terriers.

The Pitfalls of Pedigree

No sporting dog can triumph in the field without the physique needed for the sport concerned; as country sports are curtailed the challenge is to retain the working model, not the prettiest one. The best dog show judges retain a concept of a breed's purpose in the ring; their critiques sometimes make disturbing reading. One recent critique from a Lakeland Terrier show made the comment that it should be the fox that runs away from the Lakeland, not the other way round! The Glen of Imaal Terrier judge at Crufts in 2003 found 'quite a few weak jaws and that would never do in my view for what they were originally bred for'. At Crufts in 2001, the Bedlington Terrier judge reported 'some lacked the bone and substance required in a working terrier'. The 2009 Crufts judge

The old-fashioned white Bull Terrier.

remarked on Sealyhams: 'Rear movement was a major concern to say the least,' while the Fox Terrier judge reported: 'I was disappointed to see so many heavy heads… Movement was also bad in a lot of cases.' The Parson Russell judge commented: 'Poor movement is still very much in evidence, with plaiting, paddling and a general lack of co-ordination.' The Irish Terrier judge concluded: 'Movement in general was disappointing, looseness in front and lack of drive behind.' The Cairn Terrier judge was concerned that some males had very poor heads and heavy bone, expressing worry over the lack of good-quality stud dogs. The Border Terrier judge stated: 'Shoulders still need attention with many severely lacking layback, and, of more concern, some foreleg assemblies are placed too far forward, so fore-chests are vanishing. This produces flashiness but it is wrong.' A year earlier, the Fox Terrier judge reported: 'The quality of exhibits in males was disappointing.' It is extremely worrying that our top dog show should reveal such flaws in sporting terriers. Flawed pedigree terriers still cost a great deal to buy and even more to treat.

Dog lovers who pay £500 for a pedigree terrier pup and expect it to hide its sporting instincts and behave like a Toy breed are not engaging their brains. Terriers have an instinct to dig, to explore drains, to hunt small furry creatures and to display a combative nature. If you want a happier terrier, you need to be conscious of their innate yearnings, their inherited longings. Bored, frustrated terriers can end up digging where you just don't want them to, expending pent-up energy by chasing your neighbour's cat and barking, just to relieve tension. Let them hunt a hedgerow, explore a shrubbery, race around the park – be active! You'll have a happier terrier as a direct result – and almost certainly, a happier life. Terriers are essentially sporting dogs; they deserve our empathy.

Britain's Role

For a nation that has given the world a score of distinguished sporting terrier breeds, many of them preferred to the overseas native breeds on sheer merit, we must now work to ensure that all the dedicated work of our forefathers is not thrown away. In this book I have campaigned for terriers that are fit for their time-honoured function; if we do not respect their origins we will destroy many long-established, much-admired terrier breeds, not just by neglect or indifference but from being arrogant enough to attempt their redesign on false criteria. Terriers do not need ground-hugging

Lucas Terrier with Jack Russell friend quietly demonstrating that timeless terrier appeal.

coats, heads like boot boxes or a front assembly that denies them forward reach. Their locomotion should not be so impaired that they end up moving like canine millipedes. They should not 'carry a leg', as so many Jack Russells do, because of knee problems. The Bull Terrier does not deserve to be the only breed of dog with a rugger-ball for a head. This was very much a twentieth-century infliction, never a breed feature before that. The Staffordshire Bull Terrier does not deserve to be proscribed in countries abroad because of confusion between its famed tenacity and the misuse of this by man. The Dandie Dinmont's topknot should not be more valued than a functional anatomy. The Fox Terrier deserves to be put back to work. The terrier breeds are very much Britain's contribution to the canine world and we have much to do to restore most of them to their true form. Here's to a long life for our revered breeds of terrier; they deserve all the affection and care we can muster.

> Perhaps there is no breed of dogs which attach themselves so strongly to man as the terrier. They are his companions in his walks, and their activity and high spirit enable them to keep up with a horse through a long day's journey. Their fidelity to their master is unbounded, and their affection for him unconquerable.
>
> *Anecdotes of Dogs* by Edward Jesse
> (Henry Bohn, 1858)

A Terrier forms the most lively companion one could possibly possess. He is all life, dash, pluck and hunt; and will make more fun for himself and you out of a short country walk than a dog of any other breed would in a week.

'Training Dogs' by 'Bach', *The Stock-Keeper*, 1896

Many a man will tell you that his pipe has solaced many a lonely hour and pulled him through many a rough time. I have known a Terrier act as an anodyne where a boisterously cheerful companion would have been a bore. To bachelors, to sufferers from the 'blues', if they do not smoke, then I recommend a Terrier – both go well together…as a rule they educate themselves in companionable habits…

'Breaking and Training Dogs' by 'Pathfinder'
and Hugh Dalziel, *The Bazaar*, 1906

The Terriers are among the finest of all our dogs. They are strong, alert, inquisitive and courageous, friendly and playful but withal excellent workers. They are endowed with a degree of hardiness seldom encountered in dogs of other kinds, and they have a surprising ability to withstand disease. Asleep or awake, they are alert to unusual sounds and commendably suspicious of strangers. Their inherent curiosity bespeaks their intelligence, and their naturally happy temperament denotes their very joy in living.

The Book of All Terriers by John T. Marvin
(Howell Book House, 1971)

POINTS OF THE DOG

Points of the dog: 1 Nostrils. 2 Nose. 3 Front lips. 4 Cheek. 5 Stop. 6 Orbital arch. 7 Occiput. 8 Face. 9 Lower jaw. 10 Dewlap. 11 Crest or upper line of neck. 12 Withers. 13 Loins. 14 Croup. 15 Stern. 16 Buttock. 17 Gaskin. 18 Point of hock. 19 Front of hock. 20 Pastern. 21 Toes. 22 Seat of the dew-claws. 23 Inner face of thigh. 24 Breast. 25 Point of elbow. 26 Forearm. 27 Point of fetlock. 28 Toes. 29 Brisket. 30 Throat or lower neck. 31 Upper arm. 32 Shoulder. 33 Chest wall. 34 Flank. 35 First thigh. 36 Second thigh. 37 Stifle.

GLOSSARY OF TERMS

Angulation The degree of slope or angle of the shoulder blade in the forequarters and in the sharp angles of the inter-related bones in the hindquarters, thigh, hock and metatarsals

Barrel-hocks Hocks turned outwards, resulting in feet with inward-pointing toes (similar to bandy-legs)

Barrel-ribbed Well-rounded rib cage

Blanket The coat colour on the back from the withers to the rump

Blaze A white patch of hair in the centre of the face, usually between the eyes

Bloom The sheen of a coat in prime condition

Bodied up Well developed in maturity

Breed points Characteristic physical features of a breed, often exaggerated by breed fanciers

Brisket The part of the body in front of the chest

Button ear The ear flap folding forward, usually towards the eye

Cat-foot The rounded, shorter-toed type of foot

Chest From brisket to belly, underneath the dog

Chiselled Clean cut, especially in the head

Chopping Exaggerated forward movement through abbreviated reach

Close-coupled Comparatively short from withers to hip bones

Cobby Short-bodied, compact in torso

Conformation The relationship between the physical appearance of a dog and the imagined perfect mould for that breed or type

Couples Connection of hindquarters to torso

Cow-hocks Hocks turned towards each other (similar to knock-knees)

Dewlaps Loose, pendulous skin under the throat

Drive A solid thrust from the hindquarters, denoting strength of locomotion

Drop ear The end of the ear folded or falling forward

Dudley nose Flesh-coloured or unpigmented nose

Elbows out Elbows positioned away from the body

Even bite Meeting of both sets of front teeth at edges with no overlap

Feathering Distinctly longer hair on rear line of legs, back of ears and along underside of tail

Forearm Part of foreleg extending from elbow to pastern

Furnishings Long hair on ears, trailing edge of legs and under part of tail

Grizzle Bluish-grey or steel-grey in coat colour

Hackney action High-stepping action in the front legs

Hare foot A longer, narrower foot, usually with an elongated third digit

Height Distance or measurement from the withers to ground contact in the standing dog

Hock Joint on the hind leg between the knee and the fetlock – the heel in humans

Hound-marked Coat colouring involving a mixture of classic Foxhound coat colours – white, black and tan – in varying proportions, usually mainly white, especially underneath

Hound tail Tail carried on high, up above the rump

Knee The joint attaching fore-pastern and forearm

Layback The angle of the shoulder compared to the vertical

Lay of shoulder Angled position of the shoulder

Leather The flap of the ear

Level bite (pincer bite) The front teeth of both jaws meeting exactly

Linty A coat with a twisty condition, having plenty of natural spring in it, or a coat colour similar to the cloth lint

Lumber Superfluous flesh and/or cumbersome movement arising from lack of condition or faulty construction

Mask Dark shading on the foreface

MFH Master of Foxhounds

Occiput The peak of the skull

Out at elbow *See* elbows out. A common fault in Bulldogs and in terriers with Bull Terrier blood

Overshot jaw The front upper set of teeth overlapping the lower set

Oversprung ribs Exaggerated curvature of ribcage

Padding A hackney action due to lack of angulation in forequarters

Paddling A heavy, clumsy threshing action in the forelegs with the feet too wide of the body on the move

Pastern Lowest section of the leg, below the knee or hock

Pedigree The dog's record of past breeding; sometimes used as shorthand for pure-breeding

Pile Dense undercoat of softer hair

Pincer bite *See* level bite

Plaiting (or weaving or crossing) The movement of one front leg across the path of the other front leg on the move

Pounding Front action in which the pads meet the ground prematurely, causing a jarring effect; created by faulty shoulder construction

Prick ear Ear carriage in which the ear is erect and usually pointed at tip

Racy Lightly built and leggier than normal in the breed

Ribbed-up Long last rib

Roach- or carp-backed A back arched convexly along the spine, especially in the hindmost section

Root of the tail Where the tail joins the dog's back

Rose ear A small drop ear with the leather folding over and back, often showing the inner ear, as in the Bulldog

Saddle A solid area of colour extending over the shoulders and back

Saddle-backed A sagging back from extreme length or weak musculature

Scissor bite The outer side of the lower incisors touches the inner side of the upper incisors

Second thigh The (calf) muscle between the stifle and the hock in the hindquarters

Self-coloured A solid or single-coloured coat

Set on Where the root of the tail is positioned in the hindquarters

Shelly Weedy and narrow-boned, lacking substance

Short-coupled *See* close-coupled

Shoulder layback *See* layback

Slab-sided Flat ribs, with too little spring from the spinal column

Snipiness Condition in which the muzzle is too pointed, weak and lacking strength right to the nose end

Soundness Correct physical conformation and movement

Spanning Measuring a terrier's chest size by enclosing it in outstretched enclosing hands

Splay feet Flat, open-toed, widely spread feet

Spring of rib The extent to which the ribs are well-rounded

Stance Standing position, usually when formally presented

Standard The written word picture of a breed

Stifle The joint in the hindleg between the upper and lower thigh, equating to the knee in man, sadly weak in some breeds

Stop The depression at the junction of the nasal bone and the skull between the eyes

Straight-hocked Lacking in angulation of the hock joint

Straight-shouldered Straight up and down shoulder blades, lacking angulation or layback

Strain A family line throwing offspring of a set type

Terrier front A narrow-chested, straight-legged forward end to the forequarters, as viewed when dog and observer are head-on to each other

Throatiness An excess of loose skin at the front of the neck

Tied at the elbows When the elbows are set too close under the body, thereby restricting freedom of movement

Topknot A tuft of longer hair on the top of the head at the front

Topline The dog's outline from just behind the withers to the rump

Tuck-up Concave underline of torso, between last rib and hindquarters, lack of discernible belly

Undershot Malformation of the jaw, projecting the lower jaw and incisors beyond the upper (puppies with this condition appear to be grinning)

Well-angulated Well-defined angle in the thigh-hock-metatarsus area

Well-coupled Well made in the area from the withers to the hip bones

Well-knit Neat and compactly constructed and connected

Well-laid Soundly placed and correctly angled

Well-laid back shoulders Oblique shoulders ideally slanting at 45 degrees to the ground

Well let-down Close to the ground, having short hocks

Well ribbed-up Ribs neither too long nor too wide apart; compact

Well-sprung With noticeably rounded ribs

Well tucked-up Absence of visible abdomen, as in Whippets and Greyhounds

Withers The highest point on the body of a standing dog, immediately behind the neck, above the shoulders

Yawing (crabbing) Body moving at an angle to the legs' line of movement

BIBLIOGRAPHY

Armitage, George C., *Thirty Years with Fighting Dogs* (1935)

Badcock, G.H., *The Understanding of a Dog* (1935)

Barton, Frank Townend, *The Kennel Encyclopaedia* (Virtue & Co., 1903)

Beaufort, Duke of, *Hunting* (Badminton Library, Longman, Green & Co., 1894)

Beilby, H.N., *The Staffordshire Bull Terrier* (Blackie & Son, 1943)

Berndt, Robert J., *The Science and Techniques of Judging Dogs* (Alpine, 2007)

Bewick, Thomas, *A General History of Quadrupeds* (1790)

Blaine, Delabere, *An Encyclopaedia of Rural Sports* (Longman, 1870)

Bradley, Cuthbert, *Fox-Hunting from Shire to Shire* (Routledge, 1912)

Brown, Thomas, *Biographical Sketches and Authentic Anecdotes of Dogs* (1829)

Bruce, Rosslyn, *The Popular Fox Terrier* (Popular Dogs Publishing, 1950)

Bylandt, Count Henry van, *Dogs of All Nations* (1904)

Castle, Charles, *Scientific Dog Management and Breeding* (Kaye, 1951)

Chenuz, F., *Sealyhams* (Ernest Benn, 1956)

Clapham, Richard, *Foxes, Foxhounds and Fox-Hunting* (Heath Cranton, 1932)

Colby, Louis B., *Colby's Book of the American Pit Bull Terrier* (1997)

Cole, Robert W., *An Eye for a Dog* (Dogwise Publishing, 2004)

Compton, Herbert (ed.), *The Twentieth Century Dog* (Grant Pritchard, 1904)

Cox, Major Harding, *Dogs and I* (1928)

Cox, Nicholas, *The Gentleman's Recreation* (1667)

Croxton Smith, A. (ed.), *Hounds & Dogs*, The Lonsdale Library Vol. XIII (Seeley, Service & Co., 1932)

Cummins, Bryan, *The Terriers of Scotland & Ireland* (Doral Publishing, 2003)

Dalziel, Hugh, *British Dogs* (1888)

Daniel, William, *Field Sports* (1760)

Drury, W.D., *British Dogs* (Upcott Gill, 1903)

Edward, Duke of York, *The Master of Game* (1909)

Edwards, Sydenham, *Cynographia Britannica* (1800)

Foix, Gaston de, *Livre de Chasse* (1401)

Fouilloux, Jacques du, *La Venerie* (1560)

Fox, Michael W., *Understanding Your Dog* (Blond Briggs, 1972)

Frederick, Sir Charles (ed.), *Fox-Hunting*, Lonsdale Library Vol. VII (Seeley, Service & Co., 1930)

Gardner, Walter J., *About the Border Terrier* (T.C. Farries & Co., 1991)

Hartley, Oliver, *Hunting Dogs* (1909)

Hazlitt, William, *Table Talk* (1821)

Hollender, Major Count V.C., *Staffordshire Bull Terriers* (Carling & Co., 1952)

Horner, Tom, *All About the Bull Terrier* (Pelham Books, 1973)

Hubbard, Clifford L.B., *Dogs in Britain* (Macmillan, 1948)

'Idstone', *The Dog* (1880)

Jackson, Frank, *Dictionary of Canine Terms* (The Crowood Press, 1995)

Jesse, Edward, *Anecdotes of Dogs* (Henry Bohn, 1858)

Kaleski, Robert, *Australian Barkers and Biters* (1914)

Kerr, Eleanor, *Hunting Parson: the Life and Times of the Reverend John Russell* (Herbert Jenkins, 1963)

Lee, Rawdon, *A History and Description of the Fox Terrier* (Horace Cox, 1890)

Lee, Rawdon, *A History and Description of the Modern Dogs of Great Britain and Ireland: The Terriers* (Horace Cox, 1896)

Leighton, Robert, *Dogs and All About them* (Cassell, 1914)

Leighton, Robert, *The Complete Book of the Dog* (Cassell, 1922)

Leslie, John, *The History of Scotland* (1436)

Lucas, Jocelyn, *Pedigree Dog Breeding* (Simpkin & Marshall, 1925)

Lucas, Jocelyn, *The New Book of the Sealyham* (Simpkin & Marshall, 1929)

Lucas, Jocelyn, *Hunt and Working Terriers* (Chapman & Hall, 1931)

McCandlish, W.L., *The Scottish Terrier* (Our Dogs, 1926)

Marples, Theo, *Prize Dogs* (1926)

Marvin, John T., *The Book of All Terriers* (Howell Book House, New York, 1971)

Matheson, Darley, *Terriers* (John Lane, 1922)

Nicholas, R.E., *The Principles of Dog-Breeding* (Toogood, 1930)

Noon, Charles, *Parson Jack Russell, The Hunting Legend 1795–1883* (Halsgrove, 2000)

O'Conor, Pierce, *Sporting Terriers, their History, Training, and Management* (Hutchinson, 1926)

Pfaffenberger, Clarence J., *The New Knowledge of Dog Behavior* (1963)

Plummer, Brian, *Tales of a Rat-Hunting Man* (Boydell, 1978)

Plummer, Brian, *Secrets of Dog Training* (Robinson, 1992)

Plummer, Brian, *The Sporting Terrier* (Boydell, 1992)

Portman-Graham, Captain R., *The Practical Guide to Showing Dogs* (1956)

Redlich, Anna, *The Dogs of Ireland* (Tempest, 1981)

Richardson, H.D., *Dogs, Their Origins and Varieties* (1847)

Robbs, D.H. (ed.), *The Bull Terrier Handbook* (Perry-Vale Press, 1926)

Ross, Florence M., *The Cairn Terrier* (1937)

Russell, Dan, *Working Terriers* (Batchworth Press, 1948)

Russell, Dan, *Jack Russell and his Terriers* (Allen & Co., 1979)

Rycroft, Sir Newton, *Hounds, Hunting and Country* (Derrydale Press, 2001)

Sanderson, G.P., *Thirty Years Among the Wild Beasts of India* (Allen & Co., 1896)

Shaw, Vero, *The Illustrated Book of the Dog* (Cassell, 1881)

Skelton, W.C., *Reminiscences of Joe Bowman and the Ullswater Foxhounds* (Atkinson and Pollitt, 1921)

Smith, Betty, *The Jack Russell Terrier* (Witherby, 1970)

Smythe, R.H., *The Mind of the Dog* (1958)

Smythe, R.H., *The Examination of Animals for Soundness* (Crosby Lockwood, 1959)

Smythe, R.H., *The Breeding and Rearing of Dogs* (Popular Dogs, 1969)

Smythe, R.H., *The Dog – Structure and Movement* (Foulsham, 1970)

Smythe, R.H., *Judging Dogs* (Gifford, 1972)

Sparrow, Geoffrey, *The Terrier's Vocation* (Allen & Co., 1976)

Spira, Harold, *Canine Terminology* (Dogwise Publishing, 2001)

Stevens, Bob, *Dogs of Velvet and Steel* (Walsworth Publishing Co., 1983)

'Stonehenge', *The Dog in Health and Disease* (1867)

'Stonehenge', *Dogs of the British Islands* (*The Field*, 1878)

Stone, Steve and Pounds, Vic, *Celebrating Staffordshire Bull Terriers* (Pynot Publishing, 2007)

Strebel, Richard, *Die Deutschen Hunde* (1903)

Taplin, William, *The Sportsman's Cabinet* (1803)

Thomson Gray, D.J., *The Dogs of Scotland* (Mathew, 1891)

Vesey-Fitzgerald, Brian, *The Domestic Dog* (Routledge and Kegan Paul, 1957)

Watson, James, *The Dog Book* (1906)

Webb, Henry (ed.), *Dogs: Their Points, Whims, Instincts and Peculiarities* (Dean & Son, 1882)

Wentworth Day, James, *The Dog in Sport* (Harrap, 1938)

Whitney, Leon, *The Coon Hunter's Handbook* (1952)

Wimhurst, C.G.E., *The Book of Terriers* (Muller, 1968)

Wood, Carl P., *The Gun Digest Book of Sporting Dogs* (1985)

INDEX

Related Titles From Crowood

Border Terriers
An Owner's Companion

Frank and Jean Jackson

ISBN 978 1 86126 640 8
192pp, 100 illustrations

Rabbiting Terriers
Their Work and Training

David Bezzant with
John Bezzant

ISBN 978 1 86126 882 2
144pp, 110 illustrations

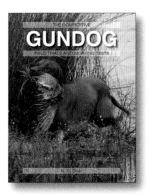

The Competitive Gundog
Field Trials and Working Tests

N.C. Dear

ISBN 978 1 84797 282 8
192pp, 115 illustrations

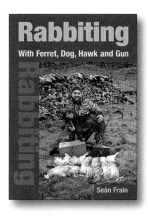

Rabbiting with Ferret, Dog, Hawk and Gun

Seán Frain

ISBN 978 1 86126 802 0
144pp, 110 illustrations

Hunt, Point Retrieve Dogs for Work and Showing

N.C. Dear

ISBN 978 1 84797 082 4
160pp, 80 illustrations

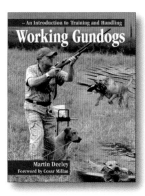

Working Gundogs
An Introduction to Training and Handling

Martin Deeley

ISBN 978 1 84797 099 2
192pp, 150 illustrations

In case of difficulty in ordering, contact the Sales Office:

The Crowood Press Ltd
Ramsbury
Wiltshire
SN8 2HR
UK

Tel: 44 (0) 1672 520320
enquiries@crowood.com
www.crowood.com